Lithic Analysis

MANUALS IN ARCHAEOLOGICAL METHOD, THEORY AND TECHNIQUE

Series Editors:
Charles E. Orser, Jr., *Illinois State University*, Normal, Illinois
Michael, B. Schiffer, *University of Arizona*, Tucson, Arizona

---

ARCHAEOLOGICAL SURVEY
E. B. Banning, *University of Toronto*, Toronto, Ontario, Canada

LITHIC ANALYSIS
George Odell, *University of Tulsa*, Tulsa, Oklahoma

MORTUARY MONUMENTS AND BURIAL GROUNDS OF THE HISTORIC PERIOD
Harold Mytum, *University of York*, York, United Kingdom

LITHIC ANALYSIS

George H. Odell

Department of Anthropology
University of Tulsa
Tulsa, Oklahoma

KLUWER ACADEMIC / PLENUM PUBLISHERS
New York, Boston, Dordrecht, London, Moscow

Library of Congress Cataloging-in-Publication Data

Odell, George H.
    Lithic analysis / George H. Odell.
        p.   cm. – (Manuals in archaeological method, theory, and technique)
    Includes bibliographical references and index.
    ISBN 0-306-48067-0 – ISBN 0-306-48068-9 (pbk.)
    1. Tools, Prehistoric—Analysis.   2. Tools, Prehistoric—Classification.
    3. Stone implements—Analysis.   4. Stone implements—Classification.
    1.Title.   II. Series.

GN799-T6034 2004
930'.1'2–dc22   2003061966

ISBN 0-306-48067-0 (hardbound)
0-306-48068-9 (paperback)

© 2004 Kluwer Academic/Plenum Publishers, New York
233 Spring Street, New York, New York 10013

http://www.wkap.nl

10 9 8 7 6 5 4 3 2 1

Printed in the United States of America.

This book is dedicated to Frieda, who will always be *mijn schatje*.

Preface

Procedures by which archaeological stone tools have been analyzed have traditionally operated on an apprenticeship model, whereby a novice acquires competency at the elbow of a grizzled but revered expert in the field. After shuffling through literally thousands of stones and asking hundreds of questions, the neophite eventually reaches a level at which he or she can fly solo, requiring less and less attention from the Master. While this pedagogical model has been frequently tried and tested, it is not always the most efficient method, it is very labor-intensive, and it requires a resident lithics expert, a situation that often does not exist in reality. Learning the ropes would clearly be more practical if there were a manual to consult, a book that provides information and direction so that the Master might at least be spared the most elemental questions and would not have to be available all the time. For years no such manual existed, but recently the ice has been broken by Bill Andrefsky's *Lithics: Macroscopic Approaches to Analysis*, and Brian Kooyman's *Understanding Stone Tools and Archaeological Sites*. These are good books, and can profitably be employed by fledgling lithic analysts.

My own interest in writing a manual for stone tool analysts derives initially from the way I was trained—literally at the knees of two Masters (in this case, revered but not grizzled): Dr. Raymond R. Newell in typological and technological matters, and Dr. Ruth E. Tringham in functional studies. I was lucky, because these Masters were exceedingly good at their craft, they were available, and they were supplemented along the way by other good people in a variety of disciplines and modes of expertise (e.g., Drs. Hallam Movius, Richard Klein, Andre Leroi-Gourhan, Karl Lamberg-Karlovsky, Stephen Williams, W. W. Howells, George Cowgill, and Rene Desbrosse, to name a few). But I recognized early on that a good how-to book would have offered a varied perspective and would have taken some of the burden off my instructors. I have considered writing such a compendium for many years but, until now, had never reached an appropriate point in my own career or had acquired enough time to pursue such a project. Finally, that time has come.

This volume is intended for aspiring analysts possessing some archaeological background, but not necessarily a lot. It is geared particularly toward people who wish to get up to analytical speed quickly, so that they can understand the issues better or conduct their own analyses. Such people include advanced undergraduates, graduate students, and archaeological contract workers, though the potential audience is surely more extensive than this.

Since this manual has had a long gestation, it is substantially different from the ones Andrefsky and Kooyman have written. For instance, it employs text boxes to make points supplemental or peripheral to the main narrative. It includes a chapter specifically devoted to applications. And it features a major section on functional analysis, which Andrefsky (1998:4) intentionally did not include in his manual.

But most importantly, this book is founded on the maxim that research should be driven by a problem that requires a solution. This principal is not universally adhered to in archaeology and we are all familiar with projects that dictated the accumulation of data with no particular use in mind, but with a general thought that "somebody might need this some day." Indeed, in certain situations this might be the best available alternative—one thinks immediately of the ubiquitous underfunded survey projects that yielded an abundance of sites but neither the time nor money to analyze them properly. So if basic description is all you can do, then record your head off and perhaps someone will use your data some day. But this book is intended for happier moments, i.e., situations involving enough time and money to be able to provide answers to at least some of the questions that require our attention. If you do not have this amount of support or interest, you have my tacit permission to return to wherever you bought this book and try to get your hard-earned money back (and good luck, sucker).

Organizing the volume on the basis of research question rather than general topic avoids certain pitfalls. Emphasis on topics such as "debitage analysis" or "flint knapping" too easily slips into categories accomplished for their own sake, rather than responding to issues generated by archaeological situations. Most sections of this book, therefore, begin by investigating what we wish to know and why we wish to know it. General questions are followed throughout each chapter by more refined or specific questions designed to provide examples of how such types of analyses have been applied to the archaeological record. This manual is designed to be relatively short and cannot be comprehensive of the field, but it is intended to provide a secure grounding and sense of direction for beginning analysts. Specific details can be pursued by consulting sources provided herein.

Acknowledgments

One should never work alone in this business, and I have benefited greatly from the advice and expertise of several of my colleagues. Useful criticism has been offered on Chapter 2 by geologist Brian Tapp; on Chapter 4 by Stan Ahler; on Chapter 5 by Veerle Rots; on Chapter 6 by John Dockall; and on the entire volume by series editor Michael Schiffer. Several of the illustrations were finalized and prettified by Frieda Vereecken-Odell. I appreciate the cooperation of the University of Tulsa, whose Research Office, directed by Al Soltow, has supported my projects throughout the years. Finally, this book is dedicated to Frieda, who has been a lifelong companion and has put up with more of this nonsense than any reasonable person has a right to expect. Thanks to everyone involved, and I'm sorry if I couldn't take all of the good advice that was offered; I will next time.

Contents

Lithic Analysis

Chapter 1

History of Stone Tool Research

Stone tools, which constitute the earliest record of human material culture, have fascinated scholars since archaeology was in its infancy (e.g., Evans 1897; Leakey 1934:3; Roe 1970; Feder 1996:19-21). Early in modern archaeological research, prehistorians were confronted with the difficulty of distinguishing actual prehistorically fashioned stone tools from look-alikes made by natural forces, a situation that spawned a controversy over "eoliths," or "dawn stones," i.e., tools originating at the dawn of humankind (Moir 1912, 1920; Warren 1914, 1923). It was not until several years after the apogee of that discussion that Barnes (1939) formulated criteria for humanly flaked tools that put the matter to rest, though objects of potential archaeological interest are often ambiguous enough that the subject keeps cropping up from time to time (e.g., Peacock 1991).

The recognition of stone objects as of human or natural origin is so elemental that it constitutes a threshold that an analyst must cross before any other type of analysis makes sense. Indeed, the integrity of entire sites and chronological periods has rested on whether or not the purported lithic artifacts from those sites were made by humans. A case in point is Calico Hills, California, a supposedly early occupation based on its lithic assemblage but which spawned a gigantic controversy over the "humanness" of those stones (Fagan 1987:64-66; Kehoe 1992:3-5).

Thus knowledge of human modification of lithic material is integral to the entire study of modern archaeology. Of course, not every archaeologist is able to distinguish the nuances that indicate the human origin of a particular stone tool assemblage, but the lithic medium is so common that most archaeologists need more than a passing familiarity with it. That is what this manual is all about: to outline the fundamentals of lithic research and bring you to a point at which you can strike out on your own; or, for analysts with some experience, to affirm the fundamental principles with which you are already familiar and add a few techniques and ideas to your repertoire.

This chapter is designed to put the rest of the book in perspective by introducing the principal areas of lithic analysis and the rationale for studying them. For each major area a short history of research will be presented to examine the context in which it has been studied. The comments provided in this chapter will serve as takeoff points for more detailed explanations in subsequent chapters.

1

PROCUREMENT

The initial act in the creation of a stone tool is the acquisition of raw material from which the tool is to be made. In areas of lithic abundance, material can frequently be procured simply by picking up nodules or chunks from the surface. In dissected regions with usable stone-bearing deposits, watercourses erode the stone from its beds and carry it downstream. The trick in collecting material from these watercourses is knowledge of the existence of the appropriate deposits and of the erosional properties of the stream system. In the Lower Illinois Valley, where such opportunities existed in prehistoric times, several studies have detailed the processes that collectors would have had to go through in procuring usable toolstone (Meyers 1970; Odell 1984). This type of procurement can be somewhat haphazard and difficult for modern researchers to document, so systematic research into it has not been conducted until relatively recently.

Of greater antiquity is research into lithic quarries and mines, which are considerably easier for an archaeologist to recognize. In Europe the Neolithic was the time of peak exploitation of flint through deep mining at such locales as Grimes Graves (England), Krzemionki (Poland), Spiennes (Belgium), Jablines (France), and Rijckhold-St. Geertruid (Netherlands) (Shepherd 1980; Felder 1981; Bostyn and Lanchon 1992; Migal 1997). Research on flint mining in Europe has been conducted since the latter nineteenth and early twentieth centuries (Andree 1922; Clark and Piggott 1933; Sieveking et al. 1972; Smolla 1987). Siliceous stones in North America were seldom deep-mined, but were often quarried from near-surface deposits. A few specific studies of toolstone exploitation have been conducted since the latter part of the nineteenth century, notably by W. H. Holmes (1894a) at the Peoria flint quarries in Indian Territory, now Oklahoma.

Mines and quarries are specific locations on a landscape at which a resource was extracted, and usually there is little ambiguity about what was happening there. However, most archaeological sites do not occur on top of a lithic resource. At non-quarry locales it can legitimately be asked where the lithic materials present in a given assemblage originated and how they were procured. Knowledge of these parameters can suggest which regions a hunting-gathering group traversed on its seasonal rounds. For more sedentary groups, it can inform on the types of extraction forays conducted or trade engaged in.

Researchers have speculated about the sources of archaeological lithic materials for years, but they could usually do no better than eyeball a piece of stone and guess its origin from memory or by comparison with their own collections. This method can be quite accurate when the factors involved are relatively unambiguous. Alas, this happy situation is frequently not the case because of the large variability in the genesis of popularly exploited rocks like chert, obsidian, basalt and sandstone, the variability in appearance of many stone types even within the same formation, the existence of look-alikes, and so forth.

Only recently have techniques been developed that can securely provide an accurate source determination for a lithic material. Geochemical techniques such as neutron activation analysis, X-ray fluorescence spectroscopy, and atomic absorption spectrophotometry have different laboratory requirements and protocols, but it is safe to say that equipment appropriate for any of these techniques is not contained in the normal archaeological lab. An archaeologist interested in this type of question is usually obliged to send material to a lab specifically established for that purpose and this service does not necessarily come cheap. On the other hand, geochemical analyses are capable of providing definitive answers to specific questions—a powerful claim that can be employed to bolster otherwise uncertain arguments. These techniques, and the types of questions for which they are appropriate, will be described in greater detail in Chapter 2.

TOOL MANUFACTURE

Once a source of toolstone is discovered and exploited, the process of tool manufacture can begin—usually either at the source or back at a living site. By "tool" I am referring to a piece of stone to be used by the tool maker, whether or not it receives additional modification or looks like a tool in the conventional sense. This and other terms employed in this chapter are defined in Text Box 1.1.

Formal characteristics of tools are dependent on the trajectories of manufacture that brought them into being, and archaeologically minded people have long been interested in understanding how tools were made. An early pioneer in this effort, as with quarrying, was William H. Holmes (1891, 1894b, 1919), who laid the groundwork, in America at least, for the systematic assessment of tool manufacture. He developed the concept that the manufacture of bifacial tools proceeded in stages and that crudely shaped bifaces might be products of tools that were terminated at an early stage of manufacture.

As archaeologists, the basis for our interpretations of stone tool manufacture tends to be rather restricted, because we were not present when the tools themselves were made and used. As a society, we have lost the thread of legend and lore that could give meaning to our ancestors' heirlooms; thus we may never be able to recreate entire modes of prehistoric manufacture and use (S. Binford 1968; Freeman 1968). Our ability to provide meaningful interpretations of archaeological remains has therefore been grounded in observations of modern-day societies at stages of technological development similar to the cultures whose artifacts we dig up. This reliance on ethnography and ethnoarchaeology contains the pitfall of imposing possibly irrelevant models of behavior onto ancient peoples (Wobst 1978; Binford 2001), but if cautiously applied, it can be useful in developing hypotheses about the past.

Box 1.1. Definitions

Throughout this manual are terms that lithic analysts usually take for granted because they are used so frequently. This is a dangerous tendency, as these terms are often used in different ways by different researchers, and occasionally in an inconsistent manner by the same researcher. The following is a list of some general definitions of terms employed in this book; additional terms are defined in subsequent chapters.

Artifact: a portable object made or shaped by human beings. It includes all pottery and shaped lithic pieces, as well as the flakes and cores produced in the manufacture process and awls, spatulae, and other intentionally modified bone and antler instruments. It does not include fire-cracked rocks, which may be manuports but exhibit no evidence of having been manufactured into anything; or ecofacts such as unmodified animal bone that constituted the remains of prehistoric meals.

Assemblage: a set of artifacts contextually associated with one another, i.e., in close enough spatial proximity and with close enough stratigraphic relationship that one could argue that they were used or discarded at about the same time by the same group of people. An assemblage is usually distinguished by material class (e.g., lithic assemblage) and may be divided into *sub-assemblages* of items that exhibit even greater spatial association (e.g., specific parts of a settlement).

Industry: the results of a specific manufacture technique. In archaeology, it means a group of artifacts that share both material type (e.g., lithic) and general technological process (e.g., chipped stone).

Lithic: pertaining to stone in some sense.

Tool (stone): as currently employed by lithic analysts, it can mean either 1) an object utilized by prehistoric people (i.e., possessing evidence of use modification); 2) an object secondarily modified through retouch or grinding or one that has been manufactured through a specialized technique (e.g., blade); or 3) a secondarily modified object whose technology and shape are consistent with a typology of stone types for that region. This term can be very confusing if care is not taken to avoid ambiguity. In this book the first definition will be employed unless stated otherwise.

Regrettably, most contacts between aboriginal cultural groups and technologically advanced people who would have been able to record the activities of these groups have been uninformative to the archaeological profession. Either the potential recorders were illiterate or insensitive to cultural differences, or the cultures themselves changed more rapidly than the observers' ability to comment on them. One situation from which archaeologists and the public did profit involved the appearance of Ishi, the last of the Yahi tribe in California (Kroeber 1961). Befriended by Al Kroeber and brought to live out his remaining years at the Anthropological Museum in San Francisco, Ishi willingly narrated his life's tale and helped archaeologists understand his technologies (Nelson 1916; Pope 1917). Important ethnoarchaeological studies involving the manufacture of stone tools are still being conducted among a few indigenous people, such as the Lacandon Maya (Nations and Clark 1983; Nations 1989; Clark 1991a,b). Until a few years ago a small demand for gunflints from Brandon, England, and threshing sledge flints in the Mediterranean (Whallon 1978; Benito del Rey and Benito Alvarez 1994; Whittaker 1996) existed, but these industries, too, have essentially disappeared.

Another method that informs technological analyses is experimentation, which often takes the form of replicating particular artifact types. Although a few individuals in the nineteenth and early twentieth century were engaged in this endeavor (e.g., Skertchly 1879), in the developed world lithic experimentation subsequently waned in popularity. About the middle of the twentieth century a revival occurred, heralded by a meeting at Les Eyzies, France, among flintknappers Francois Bordes, Jacques Tixier, and Don Crabtree (Jelinek 1965). These craftsmen demonstrated their techniques to one another and to other prehistorians, sharing knowledge that spurred interest in experimental flintknapping throughout the archaeological community. From this event, flintknapping took off in both professional and vocational circles, a process that has been chronicled by Johnson (1978). Interest has reached the point that there is now some concern about the future availability of suitable flint, the "making" of archaeological sites through modern flintknapping activities, and the effect of all this on the antiquities market and on archaeological research in general (Dickson 1996; Preston 1999; Whittaker and Stafford 1999).

Experimentation has taken a number of forms, of which I will discuss but one, i.e., the replication of a specific artifact type in order to better understand the techniques that are possible given certain conditions and the constraints that materials place on the reduction process. Of the many types that have been experimented with in the New World, the most effort has probably been expended in replicating the Folsom point (Crabtree 1966; Rovner and Agogino 1967; Flenniken 1978; Boldurian et al. 1985; Sollberger 1985; Gryba 1988). Reasons for this include the complex nature of the projected flaking processes, the potentially large number of steps involved, and the presence of fluting, for which specially fabricated devices may or may not have been productively employed.

The study of artifact manufacture has also benefited from detailed archaeological analyses, often involving specialized techniques and approaches. A technique that has aided the reconstruction of prehistoric manufacturing processes is conjoining analysis (Czeisla et al. 1990; Hofman and Enloe 1992; Morrow 1996b). By refitting flakes onto other flakes and onto their parent cores, archaeologists have been able to reconstruct exact sequences of reduction, thereby ascertaining exactly what tool makers *did*, rather than what they *may have done*. This technique is practical only in situations of primary context, and it is no surprise that much of this type of work has been accomplished only recently and at intensively excavated encampments such as Pincevent, France (Baffier et al. 1991; Bodu 1991; Julien et al. 1992). It is an undeniably time-consuming practice, but its precision and the level of assurance it provides make it a powerful tool for understanding technical processes.

Two parallel approaches have arisen for reconstructing the history of artifact types, from the initial procurement of raw material through discard of the tool and its incorporation into the archaeological record. The first of these, which emphasizes natural and cultural transformational processes, is called *Behavioral Archaeology* (Schiffer 1976; Skibo et al. 1995). Subsequent to the articulation of this development, a European variant known by its French name, *chaine operatoire*, extended its purview from manufacturing techniques to a more holistic view of tool history (Sellet 1993; Graves 1994; Geneste and Maury 1997; DeBie 1998; for a critique, see Shott 2003). In documenting the specific processes that a toolmaker went through and that produced the objects we find archaeologically, both approaches draw heavily on replication and experimentation. Both models have elucidated the natural and cultural forces that influenced the life histories of individual tools, and have clarified salient constraints on tool production and use. These techniques and others will be examined more fully in Chapter 3.

ASSEMBLAGE VARIABILITY

Archaeological stone tools may be found in isolation, as with the hunter's arrowhead that hit a tree and remained in the forest. But more often an artifact is discovered with other ones in at least a loose association that is called an *assemblage* (see Box 1.1). Each assemblage possesses traits that characterize it—traits that, taken together, comprise its *assemblage variability*. Since assemblage-level characteristics run the gamut from raw material type through microscopic use-wear, variables suitable for characterizing an assemblage can be any of these. In practice, however, most of the variables that have been employed for this purpose are morphological in nature, i.e., they describe the macroscopic form or appearance of tools. This statement is not universally true, as certain assemblages are so difficult to distinguish from others on formal grounds that some prehistorians have employed edge damage characteristics for this purpose (e.g., White 1969; Read and Russell 1996). Nevertheless, the use of formal and technological characteristics in describing archaeological assemblages is so dominant that techniques for analyzing assemblage variability are presented in Chapter 4, directly following considerations of fracture mechanics and tool manufacture.

The subject of assemblage variability has spawned debates that have influenced the shape of archaeological thought. The most famous of these involved Francois Bordes and Lewis Binford, arguably the most influential European and American archaeologists of their day. Bordes had devoted a substantial portion of his illustrious career to devising ways to characterize assemblages and comparing them to one another through holistic techniques such as cumulative graphs (Bordes 1961; Bordes and de Sonneville-Bordes 1970; see Bierwirth 1996). To him, assemblage differences were attributable to differences in the ethnic composition of the people who made the tools. Lewis Binford, an American who had already changed the way archaeologists thought about archaeological materials (Binford 1962, 1964), argued that assemblage differences were caused by differences in the way prehistoric people utilized the implements in their tool kits (Binford and Binford 1966; Binford 1973). The arena for this debate, which rages at a lower intensity even to this day, involved Mousterian tools, which are formally and functionally ambiguous enough that either position is tenable. A point that is often lost in the controversy is that other possible explanations for Mousterian assemblage variability also exist, notably environmental and chronological influences (Mellars 1970, 1989). In any case, the discussion is far from over, as archaeologists struggle with the complex meanings behind the variability witnessed in the prehistoric record.

Since formal attributes of stone tools are the most obvious and easy to grasp, they have been employed most often to characterize assemblages. Tools possessing similar attributes have been lumped together into *types*, which have then been compared with similarly derived types from other assemblages (Rouse 1939, 1960; Brew 1946). Such compendia of types, or typologies, have formed the basis for assemblage comparisons for more than a century.

The meaning of types has provided a sparring ground for issues of assemblage variability every bit as fertile, and ambiguous, as the issues on which the Bordes-Binford debate was fought. In America the most well known of these exchanges was between Albert Spaulding and James Ford, coming to a head in the early 1950s. Spaulding (1953, 1954) felt that types were inherent in prehistorically made objects, that objects were manufactured to certain standards, and that their classification would necessarily follow the distinctions that the makers had intended. Ford (1954a,b), on the other hand, believed that types were not inherent in artifacts, but were constructs of the archaeologist. They existed to answer specific questions about the prehistoric record, and there could be as many typologies as there were archaeologists to conceive of them.

The debate also revolved around the kinds of variables that were employed to characterize archaeological assemblages. If Spaulding was right and types were inherent in artifacts, then variables should be separable into discrete classes and able to be compared with other such classes. But if types were not inherent in artifacts, then variables should be more or less continuous, to be divided arbitrarily, if at all. It is no wonder, then, that Spaulding favored chi-square statistics to establish his arguments, while Ford preferred continuum-based statistics described by mean and standard deviation (see Odell 1981b; Bierwirth 1996:62). Although, like the Bordes-Binford debate, these typological issues have never been completely resolved, my sense is that modern archaeologists favor Ford's perception of types more than Spaulding's.

TOOL USE

From questions of manufacture and classification of stone tools, it is only a short step to inquiring about their prehistoric utilization. This concern has been paramount among archaeologists for a long time but, until recently, they have not possessed methods appropriate for dealing with the issue. Thus the early days of functional research were dominated by almost total speculation, though tempered by some knowledge of how certain tool forms were utilized among ethnographically studied peoples such as the Inuit, Bushmen, and Australian Aborigines.

Scientifically oriented functional research can be said to have started when archaeologists began to treat seriously their observations of the tools themselves, recording aspects of those tools that had been modified through processes of utilization. One of the first to do this systematically was Cecil Curwen (1930, 1935), who observed the glossy finish of certain blades and flakes from the Near East. He correctly surmised that this gloss was produced by contact of the implement with silica particles in plants when employing the flints as sickle blades. John Witthoft (1967) took these ideas further, and proposed a theory for explaining the genesis of this type of polish.

Without a doubt, the most influential work in the history of lithic functional analysis was Sergei Semenov's *Prehistoric Technology*, which was first published in Russian in 1957, then translated into English in 1964. Using models derived from metal tools, Semenov derived regularities that could be applied to stone. As metal tools wear, Semenov argued, so do stone tools, and he based his system on features that he observed in, among other places, machine shops. Characteristics of utilization were dominated by surficial scratches, or striations, which Semenov was able to recognize on several prehistoric artifacts from the Soviet Union. Since he was able to document a relatively comprehensive array of wear features corresponding to a wide variety of tool uses, his system gained immediate popularity in a market yearning for such information. So influential was his book that archaeologists felt compelled to acknowledge his system even though they did not use it; in at least one journal (*American Antiquity*), *Prehistoric Technology* became the most frequently cited work of all for at least a decade after its publication (Sterud 1978).

Semenov's ideas were seminal to the field of use-wear studies but they were not very practical, as striations either do not form on a majority of stone tools, or they are not detectable. Therefore, the 1970s saw the inception of three programs of research on three different continents, all intended to develop Semenov's ideas to the point that they could profitably be applied to a wide range of archaeological situations: Johan Kamminga's (1982) at the University of Sydney, George Odell's (1977) at Harvard, and Larry Keeley's (1980) at Oxford. The first two employed a stereoscopic, reflective-light, dissecting microscope, whereas the latter used a binocular, incident-light, metallurgical microscope. These techniques were first discussed by a large body of practitioners in 1977 at the First Use-Wear Conference, held in Vancouver, B. C. The resulting volume (Hayden 1979) stimulated substantial interest in the topic and a rapid development of technique, most significantly within Keeley's high-magnification approach. The scanning electron microscope continues to be considered useful for recording topographic features and investigating topics such as the genesis of polish, but is seldom employed for entire assemblages.

Differences in optical equipment spawned a decade-long debate over the most appropriate use-wear technique to employ, a topic that will be more fully discussed in Chapter 5. Suffice it to say that the answer is consistent with the underlying theme of this book, i.e., appropriateness of technique depends on the questions being asked. In other words, both of the principal use-wear techniques work well for certain questions or programs of research, not so well for others.

Meanwhile, residue studies have been added to the archaeologist's arsenal to complement, or in some cases to replace, use-wear analysis. Residues on stone tools have only been systematically recognized in the past few years, as the archaeologist's resolution has narrowed to ever smaller pieces of evidence. Little work in this field had been accomplished before Briuer (1976) and Shafer and Holloway (1979) isolated tiny rodent hairs and vegetal particles adhering to the surfaces of lithic implements. Meanwhile, Tom Loy (1983) discovered that animal blood can survive diagenesis and taphonomic processes in certain cases and can be detected on the surfaces of stone tools, a finding that spawned considerable interest in this technique. In Australia, where plants were a paramount prehistoric food source, some work has now been done in identifying starch grains on stone tools; and the study of plant phytoliths associated with utilized tool edges has now been initiated. All of these techniques are controversial to some degree, but are currently being developed and hold considerable promise for the future.

BEHAVIORAL QUESTIONS

Given the ubiquity of stone artifacts in the prehistoric record of all continents and all but the most recent periods, this medium serves as a vital element in our understanding of the archaeology of these periods. For many sites, stone tools constitute our only source of information. Thus there is always a need to understand the basic principles of tool manufacture and use, and to record this information.

But this is not enough. Stone artifacts have the potential to answer questions well beyond just manufacture technique or simple subsistence practices; they can also be employed to grapple with issues of behavior, lifestyle, social and economic structures, and organizational principles. Because the resolution of these currently identified problems will be of paramount importance in developing analytical techniques during the next few years, an entire chapter of this book (Chapter 6) has been devoted to clarifying the issues for which lithic analysis has profitably been enlisted and describing specific techniques that have proven useful in their resolution.

For example, recent work on hunter-gatherer lithic technologies has concentrated on the organization of either technology or mobility, or both. These subjects are often intertwined, as the ways by which one of them articulates with other elements of society often affect the other, and vice versa. For instance, Lewis Binford's ethnographic studies of the Nunamiut Eskimo are well known for their ideas about how societies organize their mobility (Binford 1980). On the basis of these studies, archaeologists now regularly refer to *collectors* and *foragers*, or *residential* and *logistical* mobility. But along with these concepts about how groups of people move, Binford (1977, 1979) also proposed structures for how people prepare their clothing, transportation and gear to accommodate the kinds of moves they must make. A person embarking with a friend on a 2-day foray to hunt seal will necessarily carry kinds of gear that are different from a person traveling longer distances with a larger group to hunt caribou, and these differences are reflected not only in the technology of the gear itself, but in the kinds of preparation necessary for the journeys. The differences may be demonstrable on archaeological sites through workshop debris, specific activity areas, or other structures.

A major problem with our database is that an individual lithic artifact frequently does not represent the entire prehistoric tool, but one or more parts of a larger compound object. Without detailed analysis of the implement itself, it is usually impossible to tell exactly what the object represented to the prehistoric tool user. This issue was investigated by Wendell Oswalt (1976), who analyzed technologies with respect to their complexity, measured by the number of parts an implement possessed. This is one way to consider the organization of technology, a subject that has continued to attract attention by lithic analysts through the latter part of the twentieth century.

The issue of mobility organization, spurred initially by Binford, was pursued by Bob Kelly (1983), who established general parameters for foraging populations using data generated through the Human Relations Area Files. His ideas were complemented by Mike Shott (1986), who demonstrated the differing effects of mobility frequency and distance of move on the overall adaptation of a foraging group. These and other studies have affected the field of lithic analysis by providing a basis for postulating likely correlates within stone tool assemblages for different types of mobility organization (Lurie 1989; McDonald 1991; Bousman 1993; Young 1994; Amick and Carr 1996; Odell 1996).

For years lithic analysis seems to have been relegated exclusively to archaeologists interested in hunter-gatherer societies. But recently archaeologists have begun to appreciate that the use of stone tools continued past the onset of social complexity, even well into the age of metals. Analyses of lithic assemblages from complex societies are now relatively common. Examples include studies of Dynastic Mesopotamian tools (Pope 1994; Pope and Pollock 1995), of stone tools used in North or Central American prehistoric rituals (Sievert 1992, 1994), and of lithic implements that survived into the Chalcolithic and Bronze Ages of the Levant (Rosen 1996, 1997b). These situations have induced lithic analysts to pay close attention to the contexts in which these tools are associated, and to the specific roles they played in their society.

PERSPECTIVES

At its foundations archaeology is a science, and science is about answering questions concerning the world around us. The nature of those questions is determined by the perspective from which they are asked. With respect to archaeological stone tools, three perspectives are relevant: 1) that of the people who made and used the tool; 2) that of the tool itself; and 3) that of the archaeologist who discovers and analyzes the tool. These relationships may be visualized in Figure 1.1.

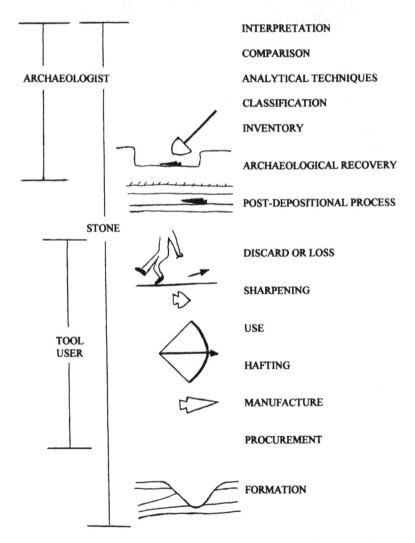

Figure 1.1.   Three perspectives by which an archaeological stone artifact may be viewed.

The stone itself has the longest perspective, as it begins with the formation of the rock from which the tool eventually is made, proceeds through manufacture, use and discard, and ends up in the hands of the archaeologist. From a holistic viewpoint, this is the most comprehensive way to view the object. The tool user's perspective is greatly reduced from this, as it only begins when the appropriate piece of stone is discovered. From there it proceeds through the various phases of manufacture and use, as well as possible hafting and sharpening. In this view, the object's discard or loss is its last relevant stage. Once the tool is discovered several years later, it enters the realm of the archaeologist and may become a victim of any number of indignities, surely far beyond the vision of the people who originally procured the stone. These include many of the processes that are discussed in this book.

It is useful to keep these perspectives in mind during a stone tool analysis. The archaeologist must classify, analyze and compare, but should not remain in that realm forever. Interpretation requires entering the domain of the tool user for a fleeting instant, and sourcing requires considering the genesis of the rock itself. A comprehensive lithic analysis will employ all of these perspectives at one time or another.

Chapter 2

Procurement

Let us suppose that, for one reason or another, you have accepted the task of analyzing and interpreting lithic artifacts from a specific region. You know something about the archaeology of the region, and your principal job at this point is to figure out what to do with those accursed stones that keep appearing at archaeological sites. This is an alarmingly common situation, whether you are a graduate student just starting out, a newly minted PhD with your first job in a Cultural Resource Management (CRM) firm, a pottery expert who is forced to consider lithic artifacts for the first time, an amateur who has taken on the task of doing local prehistory, or a host of other scenarios.

A good place to begin is by ascertaining the places of origin of the stone artifacts in the collection, a process known as "sourcing." This is an advantageous initial strategy, because it may be possible to derive a large amount of usable information for a reasonable expenditure of effort. In addition, the subject itself will force you to become intimately acquainted with your region, from which you will reap inestimable benefits down the line.

This chapter will discuss the most commonly practiced sourcing methods and provide enough written sources to enable you to investigate further those techniques that may be helpful in your specific circumstances. In sourcing raw materials it is advantageous to follow a sequence of research, as more refined knowledge builds on general foundations. Throughout this chapter I will suggest a sequence of research, which is abbreviated graphically in Figure 2.1. This is only slightly different from suggestions offered by Barbara Luedtke (1992:117-119).

This sequence recognizes the breadth of knowledge that archaeologists must have, for it deals with certain background issues before it comes to the human dimension, which is at the heart of what most archaeologists are interested in. We must first have a working knowledge of the material itself. That is, in order to answer the question, "where does this rock come from?" we must first inquire, "what is a rock? What types of rocks exist? And what is the range of materials to be dealt with?" From a tool user's point of view, of course, these questions are irrelevant. It matters not what a tool is made of, as long as it works. Distinctions among materials become important only to analysts, whose job it is to figure out what their ancestors were doing—presumably, the ancestors themselves already knew.

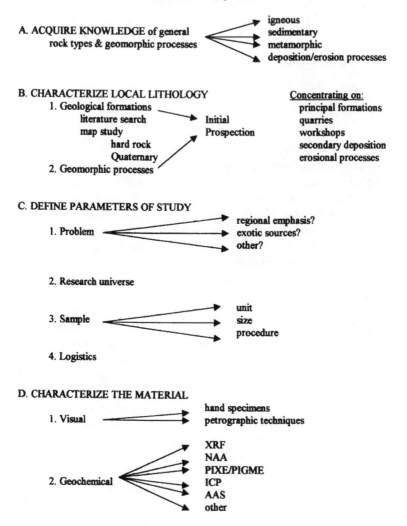

SOURCING SEQUENCE

A. ACQUIRE KNOWLEDGE of general
   rock types & geomorphic processes
   - igneous
   - sedimentary
   - metamorphic
   - deposition/erosion processes

B. CHARACTERIZE LOCAL LITHOLOGY
   1. Geological formations
         literature search → Initial
         map study   Prospection
               hard rock
               Quaternary
   2. Geomorphic processes

   Concentrating on:
         principal formations
         quarries
         workshops
         secondary deposition
         erosional processes

C. DEFINE PARAMETERS OF STUDY
   1. Problem
      - regional emphasis?
      - exotic sources?
      - other?

   2. Research universe

   3. Sample
      - unit
      - size
      - procedure

   4. Logistics

D. CHARACTERIZE THE MATERIAL
   1. Visual
      - hand specimens
      - petrographic techniques

   2. Geochemical
      - XRF
      - NAA
      - PIXE/PIGME
      - ICP
      - AAS
      - other

E. PRESENT RESULTS

Figure 2.1. A proposed sequence for conducting research into lithic raw material procurement and sourcing.

   Throughout this discussion it will be assumed that the general knowledge of rock types and geomorphic processes outlined here is always preceded by an in-depth review of the geological literature in the scholar's chosen region. This review should include not only the literature, but also maps of both bedrock and

Quaternary distributions, which frequently cover the bedrock. As Tim Church (1994:78) put it, "Any project that does not include a thorough, if not exhaustive, review of the pertinent geological literature for the area should be viewed with suspicion." Two initial queries are:

Q1: What is a rock?

Q2: What types of rock exist?

I will start by providing a basic outline of the geological parameters of greatest interest to an archaeologist, but this section is brief and is not intended to be an in-depth synopsis of these processes. For more detail, consult the geological texts cited here and Kooyman (2000:chap. 3), a recent synopsis geared to an archaeological audience. I will then discuss the principal types of sourcing analyses and their respective advantages and disadvantages. Near the end of the chapter I will provide applications that suggest the range of archaeological questions that can be resolved through this type of study.

FORMATION OF ROCK

Geologists have divided lithic materials into minerals and rocks. "Minerals" are inorganic substances of characteristic and homogeneous chemical composition and usually a definite crystalline form. Although a few are elements, most are compounds. Minerals combine with one another under specific circumstances to form "rocks," which are usually heterogeneous in composition. The terms employed here, as well as others in common usage, are defined in Box 2.1.

Lithic analysts need to pay attention to all varieties of rocks and minerals because, although certain lithic properties were favored for specific tasks, the prehistoric record has revealed a large variety of such tasks, and accordingly, a large variety of utilized rock types. In addition, substances optimal for any specific activity were distributed around the landscape and were not necessarily available when needed, necessitating the use of suboptimal materials.

Igneous Rocks

The genesis of rock is best understood with reference to the forces that act on geological materials. The earth is constructed with an outer crust and generally plastic or viscous interior. The crust is divided into approximately a dozen different plates (Wilson 1989:4), which provide conduits for transference of substances from

---

Box 2.1. Geological Terms

Included here are definitions for a few of the terms commonly used when referring to the formation and characteristics of lithic material.

Clastic: mechanical and/or chemical breakdown of a lithic structure with resulting compaction and cementation.

Diagenesis: changes in sediment through biological, chemical, or mechanical action after deposition of the material but before metamorphosis.

Element: chemical structure that cannot be separated into different substances by ordinary chemical means.

Fracture Characteristics:

   conchoidal: having a planar surface similar to a bivalve shell, i.e., flat with rounded edges.

   cryptocrystalline: possessing a very small, or "hidden" crystal structure.

   isotropic: a propensity to fracture with equal intensity and similar characteristics in all directions.

   homogeneous: possessing the same properties throughout the material.

Hydrothermal: pertaining to hot water.

Igneous Rock Crystal Structure:

   aphanitic: containing predominantly small crystals; includes basalt, rhyolite, and andesite.

   phaneritic: containing predominantly large crystals; includes granite, gabbro, and diorite.

   porphyritic: containing large crystals, or phenocrysts, within a fine matrix.

Lithification: compaction and cementation of sediment, which cannot be easily disintegrated.

Mineral: material made of combinations of elements or compounds and possessing a characteristic chemical composition and crystal structure.

Precipitate: dissolution and redeposition of minerals in solution.

Rock: an inorganic material that is heterogeneous in composition, being a combination of two or more minerals.

Rough Stone: an archaeological term often applied to artifacts made from non-vitreous materials such as granite, quartzite, and other granular rock types.

Sediment: small, inorganic particles that accumulate through processes of chemical or mechanical weathering of parent rock.

---

the interior to the crust. Material extruded through this process is magma, which crystallizes at depth but is molten near the surface and may be spewed out in the form of lava. The specific rocks and minerals created by this process depend primarily on the concentration of elements at any one location and the rate of cooling, which occurs more quickly out in the air than embedded within the crust. If, at a particular locality, the cooling substance contains very homogeneous chemical composition and properties and a regular arrangement of atoms, the results are likely to be minerals. If its composition and properties are more heterogeneous, the results are combinations of minerals, or igneous rock. Crystalline rock, in one form or another, constitutes 95% of the earth's crust (Blatt et al. 1980:280).

The rate at which magma cools affects the texture of rock, a quality that is vital to tool-using hominids. Slow cooling allows time for crystals to form, a situation that predominates among intrusive rocks, i.e., rocks formed from magma that cools without ever reaching the earth's surface. Igneous rocks have been classified into general types according to crystal size (see Box 2.1).

The color of igneous rock is a clue to its chemical composition. Light-colored rocks composed of minerals such as quartz and feldspar contain large amounts of silica and aluminum and are termed "felsic." Dark-colored rocks composed of minerals such as amphibole, pyroxene and olivine contain large quantities of iron, calcium and magnesium and are termed "mafic" (McBirney 1993:24). Although color affords an indication of the basic nature of the rock, hydrothermal alteration and weathering cause so many exceptions that this is only a first step in identification (Hibbard 1995:144).

The classification of igneous rocks considers characteristics of texture, or grain size, and elemental composition, but the fundamental distinguishing characteristics have been mineralogical (Carmichael et al. 1974:27-28; Ehlers and Blatt 1982:100-101; Hibbard 1995:144). Textures of igneous rocks vary from coarse granites and diorites to finer rhyolites and andesites, ultimately to glassy structures like obsidian. With respect to composition, classifications have been based on the kinds of feldspars and ferromagnesian minerals included and the presence or amount of quartz.

Igneous rocks have provided a large percentage of the materials used prehistorically for stone tools. Finer-grained stones such as obsidian, andesite, and certain basalts have been valued the world over for their capacity to produce and hold sharp edges. Coarser-grained materials such as granite are durable and useful as hammers, mauls and other percussive implements.

Sedimentary Rocks

Once deposited in the earth's crust, rocks undergo chemical and mechanical weathering that breaks the solid mass into smaller particles, which accumulate to produce "sediment." Sediment undergoes an additional dynamic process known as "diagenesis," i.e., "all the physical, chemical, and biological changes that a sediment is subjected to after the grains are deposited but before they are metamorphosed" (Ehlers and Blatt 1982:386). One of the major changes is compaction, which laboratory studies have shown to reduce pore space of freshly deposited quartz sand from about 45% to around 30%. Processes of lithification are also promoted by the presence of ductile fragments that increase grain-against-grain indentation, as well as by the introduction of chemical precipitates, or cements (Ehlers and Blatt 1982:388-391). Thus under appropriate conditions, sediments are being either transformed into rock through compaction and cementation, or broken down through chemical and mechanical erosion.

Sedimentary rocks cover 66% of the earth's land mass and much of the ocean floor, a result of the normal chemical instability of igneous and metamorphic rocks under atmospheric conditions. More than 95% of all sedimentary rocks are sandstones, mudrocks, or carbonate rocks such as limestone (Ehlers and Blatt 1982:249). In the field, identification of a sedimentary environment begins with the recognition of small-scale structures such as cross-bedding, animal burrows, or slumping, and progresses to the identification of facies and larger stratigraphic units. These structures relate to their formation, whether by waves, flowing water, duning, scouring, aeolian deposition, or some other natural agent (Blatt et al. 1980:chap. 5; Selley 1988:chaps. 5-6; Tucker 1991:2).

Sedimentary rocks are classified according to grain size and composition—the first providing the most meaningful distinction between, for example, sandstones and mudrocks, the second being particularly useful in discriminating the carbonate rocks from the rest and the limestones from the dolomites. Systems of classification differ, but one representative scheme divides sediments into the following classes: 1) siliciclastic (sandstones, mudrocks, conglomerates, breccias); 2) biogenic, biochemical and organic (limestones, cherts, phosphates, coal and oil shale); 3) chemical (evaporites, ironstones); and 4) volcaniclastic (e.g., ignimbrites, tuffs and hyaloclastites) (Tucker 1991:1-2). From an archaeological perspective, the most important types of sedimentary rocks are clastic rocks and cherts. Clastic refers to the process of breakdown of parent structure, compaction and cementation, and resulting relithification; cherts are biogenic silicates with specific properties favorable to stone tool production.

Clastic Rocks

Qualities of rock important to chipped stone toolmakers are brittleness, fine granularity, and isotropism. As we will see in later chapters, the toolmaker wants to be able to fashion the end product to certain desired specifications. He or she therefore wants the stone to be brittle enough to break easily (though not so brittle that it will not hold an edge), and have grain size fine enough that the edge resulting from this fracture is sharp and straight rather than jagged, as happens when forces break around large individual grains. Control of the final product also requires that percussive forces from manufacture follow laws of fracture mechanics, rather than be influenced by unique properties of the stone itself, such as crystal structure or internal fracture planes. In other words, properties of the stone affecting fracture must be equal in all directions, or "isotropic." If all of these conditions obtain, the resulting fracture will be "conchoidal," i.e., it will have curved, planar properties like a seashell.

For sedimentary rocks to be useful for tool manufacture, then, they must be well cemented by quartz (silicon dioxide), which should fill intercellular voids completely so that forces of fracture can proceed equally through both the grains and the surrounding cement. The difference that complete silicification makes in the path of compressive force—from skirting around each individual grain to passing directly through it—is illustrated in Figure 2.2.

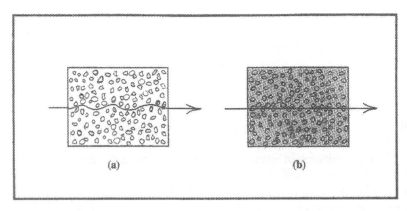

Figure 2.2. Percussive force passing through a non- or incompletely silicified stone (a), compared with a well silicified one (b).

Depending on their degree of silicification, sedimentary stones used pre-historically as tools potentially involve a large range of rock types, including sandstones (in cemented form known as orthoquartzites), siltstones, mudstones, and greywackes (argillaceous sandstone with high feldspar content). However, in most instances silicification of the sediment is not sufficient to enable conchoidal fracture; therefore, prehistorically usable clastic sedimentary stones are relatively rare. Shales, or bedded sedimentary rocks formed from clay, even when moder-ately silicified, are not optimal for tool production because their internal bedding planes tend to influence the direction of fracture.

Cherts

More suitable for tool production than the clastic rocks, in most instances, are the cherts. These rocks are very fine-grained; archaeologists like to call them "cryp-tocrystalline," or "hidden-grained," though most geologists call them "microcrys-talline." Barring impurities, vugs and internal weathering flaws within individual pieces, they are uniformly isotropic and produce firm, thin margins, making them ideal as sharp-edged tools. Although geologists often distinguish among chert, flint, chalcedony, agate, and jasper, these types are compositionally identical and their subtypes grade into each other on other characteristics. Therefore, it does not seem practical to distinguish them in most cases, and Luedtke (1992:5) has subsumed all of the individual subtypes under the rubric "chert." Differences in color and, in some cases, texture are caused by impurities in the matrix.

Chert is composed primarily of quartz, a silicate mineral. Most of this quartz is microcrystalline in structure, though the fibrous form is dominant in chal-cedonies. Vacuoles filled with water are common within the crystalline structure, and the grains themselves are randomly oriented. Cherts occur as nodular and as interbedded inclusions within limestone and sandstone deposits. Nodular cherts are formed by replacing limestone through diagenetic processes of removing calcium carbonate and infilling with silica. Tabular, or bedded, cherts are primarily accumulations that, in many cases, originate with excess alkalinity in the sediments (Blatt et al. 1980:575-577; Selley 1988:394-396; Tucker 1991:212-216). The frequently visible shells of diatoms, radiolaria, and sponge spicules indicate that chert has formed from the crystallization of chemically unstable amorphous silica (Blatt et al. 1980:572).

The precipitation of silica and the genesis of bedded cherts can occur under a variety of conditions. Amorphous silica, or Opal-A, is produced by several plants and animals, particularly as phytoliths and in diatoms. Upon the death of the organism, the silica in these structures is freed to combine with other silica molecules. This first diagenetic stage results in the development of opal-CT, also known as lussatite or cristobalite, which replaces the skeletons of diatoms, radiolaria, and other structures. Because opal-CT is not totally stable (metastable, in the vernacular), continued diagenesis transforms opal-CT into the quartz compound we know as chert (Tucker 1991:215; Luedtke 1992:23-24). The rate of transformation is a function of time, temperature, depth of burial, and composition of associated sedimentary phases. This scenario is probably the most common but not the only one, as bedded cherts are sometimes associated with volcanic rocks and may form from volcanic sediments in very alkaline lakes (Williams et al. 1982:401; Tucker 1991:216).

Metamorphic Rocks

Metamorphism refers to changes in rock that occur "at pressures and temperatures above those of diagenesis and below those of melting" (Ehlers and Blatt 1982:511). They include granulation, recrystallization, fracturing, and plastic flow. Metamorphism typically involves the redistribution of chemical components, often in the presence of aqueous fluids, and may even be overprinted by hydrothermal phenomena (Hibbard 1995:276). A significant amount of metamorphic change occurs in ocean bottoms in the presence of hydrothermic features and circulation (Wilson 1989:122-124). The classification of metamorphic rocks is multifaceted, being based primarily on structural, textural and compositional differences and utilizing concepts unique to metamorphism such as foliation, cleavage and lineation. Naming conventions often involve appending a characteristic structure or compositional feature to the basic rock name, as in granite gneiss (Ehlers and Blatt 1982:512-515).

Metamorphic changes can be either advantageous or disadvantageous to users of stone tools. On the one hand, metamorphosis of shale results in a recrystallized product called "slate" which, with its brittleness and platy structure, is difficult to make into a sharp-edged tool or to use as a percussive one. On the other hand, the recrystallization of sandstone produces a granoblastic metamorphic rock known as quartzite, which sometimes possesses qualities of isotropism and conchoidal fracture favorable for tool production (Ehlers and Blatt 1982:512-516). Other metamorphic rocks that are good for tool production are argillite and hornfels, which are both fine-grained, metamorphic rocks. In both cases the metamorphic process fuses the internal granular structure without the addition of cement (Andrefsky 1998:56).

Summary

It pays to have a good grasp of the qualities of lithic materials available to prehistoric users of stone tools, as this knowledge is crucial for evaluating the original provenance of the rocks and their potential uses. Clearly, not all kinds of rocks were of equal utility to tool users. For edge implements, the most useful were those that were easy to shape and held a sharp edge—substances characterized by relative brittleness, homogeneity, isotropism, and conchoidal fracture. The most frequently utilized throughout prehistory were microcrystalline silicates like flint and chert, and glassy or fine-grained volcanics like obsidian and andesite. Other material types, such as orthoquartzites, fine-grained quartzites, argillites, and mudstones could fit this description, but only if they had been submitted to intense silicification or metamorphic bonding.

The qualities mentioned above do not apply to implements manufactured for percussive activities, such as axes, adzes, hammers, and mauls. These tools did not require sharpness and ease of manufacture; brittleness and conchoidal fracture were actually detrimental. Desirable attributes were durability and the capacity for holding an edge through incessant pounding, qualities that were met by coarse, heavy rocks such as granite, gabbro and diorite. It is important to note that either edge or percussive tools could be produced in a variety of ways in the natural environment, but they often required special, and sometimes rare, conditions of genesis.

GEOMORPHIC PROCESSES

Knowing the genesis of rock types is important, but is not all we need to know about raw material. Additionally, it is necessary to have a working knowledge of the processes by which stones reached their current location on the landscape, because these parameters often dictated how the resource was acquired (Holliday 1992; Waters 1992; Stein and Ferrand 2001). For example, deeply buried nodular cherts probably had to be deep-mined or extracted from cave walls, whereas bedded cherts in geologically dissected environments could be most easily procured in stream beds. Knowing these relationships makes it easier to interpret the human procurement of these materials. Comprehension of geomorphic processes such as deposition and erosion can also improve our ability to interpret the human impact on source areas (see Shackley 1998:263). These considerations highlight the importance of the following research question:

Q3: Which geomorphological processes have dominated the region?

To examine this concept, let us consider Figure 2.3, which illustrates three different occurrences of chert within the same upland sedimentary landform. At the surface is a glacial till deposit containing chert cobbles. Some distance below that is a stratum gravel conglomerate and some chert cobbles deposited in the Pliocene. And below that is a tightly consolidated stratum of tabular chert formed within two limestone layers deposited in the Cretaceous.

To a prehistoric occupant of the region looking for chert, these three situations would have presented very different potentials for exploitation. The till deposit on top (A) may have been the most readily accessible, though this would have depended on ground cover, vegetation, and tendency for erosion on this upland landform. The unconsolidated nature of the deposit would lend itself to human exploitation, since desired fragments would not have to be pried from bedrock. The middle deposit (B) is also unconsolidated, but it occurs considerably further from the surface and is not accessible over such a large expanse as the deposit at A. It would be available only at the valley wall or in some other erosional exposure, and would therefore probably not be as frequently encountered as the till. Because of its different genesis, the compositional and weathering characteristics of its cobble

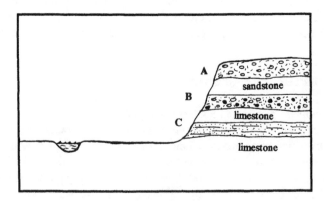

Figure 2.3. Example of chert that ended up in the same sedimentary landform but through different mechanisms: A) unconsolidated glacial till deposit; B) stratum consisting of gravel conglomerate, and some chert, deposited in the Pliocene; C) tabular chert deposit within limestone beds.

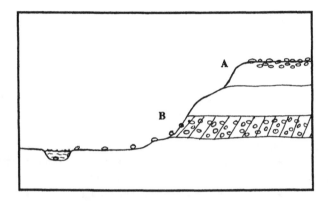

Figure 2.4.   Secondary deposition of chert into other contexts: A) lag deposit of chert from which matrix has eroded away. It currently exists in a formation different from that of its origin; B) nodular chert within limestone formation, eroding downslope to stream bed.

inclusions may have been very different from those of the till. The lowermost stratum (C) would have been inaccessible except where exposed by the valley wall. Deriving from a primary deposit in which angular chunks ultimately break off from a consolidated stratum laid down in tabular form, available chert from stratum C should appear very different from chert in either A or B, at least in its initial, unmodified form. That is, it should occur in more angular chunks than the chert that was deposited either by glaciers or alluviation.

Local erosional processes are very important to a potential exploiter of raw materials, a point illustrated by two situations depicted in Figure 2.4. The deposit at A consists of chert nodules occurring on and immediately under an upland surface. They were originally formed in calcareous beds that eroded away, leaving the more durable flint inclusions resting near the surface in an unconsolidated deposit. The consolidated deposit at B consists of a limestone matrix from which chert nodules are shown migrating out of the formation and into the river bed.

These two sources of chert would have provided very different contexts for exploitation. If ground cover was not too extensive, it may have been possible to gather chert A over a large surface area and pry it from its current matrix rather easily. The nodular chert formed within the limestone formation of the earlier deposit B, on the other hand, is exposed only at the valley wall. There it may have been able to be pried from its hard limestone matrix *in situ*, but would have been most accessible as a secondary deposit in the streambed.

The occurrence of lithic sources on the landscape is not uniform. On the one hand, a source can be restricted to a limited area, as was the case with the Michigan sources that Barbara Luedtke (1976) researched for her dissertation. On the other hand, a source can have a very wide distribution and exhibit as much internal as between-source variability. This is the case with Burlington chert, which covers large parts of three states and, to my knowledge, has still not been adequately characterized with respect to its internal variability (Meyers 1970; Ives 1984; Luedtke and Meyers 1984). These situations, and all those in between, must be taken into account in any sourcing analysis, because they present different problems of sampling and characterization.

The examples cited here have employed chert as the principal material exploited because of the ubiquity of this substance on archaeological sites, but these examples could apply to any lithic material that prehistoric people had to procure. Before attempting any regional project, knowledge of the nature and occurrence of the local resources is crucial. This entails familiarity with local geological literature and distribution maps, and an understanding of geomorphological processes (see Butzer 1982; Holliday 1991, 1996). This knowledge facilitates understanding of the specific behavior in which people were engaged and the problems they encountered when procuring raw material for their tools.

DEFINING THE PROBLEM

A crucial moment in any research program comes in defining the exact goals and parameters of the study. In my experience, the nature of the questions asked in lithic sourcing revolve around two basic issues:

Q4: Is this material local? and

Q5: What is the true source of this material?

In either case, solving the problem involves effective sampling and understanding the nature of the populations being considered.

Is This Material Local?

A typical site-based archaeological problem is this: a site has been excavated and one wishes to know which raw materials are available locally and which come from further away. It is important at the start to define what is meant by "local"— whether it means the area immediately around the site, the entire region, or some other spatial entity. Defining "local" delimits the research universe and places boundaries on the parameters of the study. It is the job of the researcher to make sure that these limits are realistic within the temporal and budgetary constraints that necessarily bound every project.

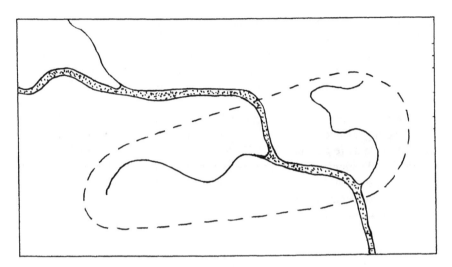

Figure 2.5.   Delineating research boundaries for a hypothetical local regional project.

Once spatial limits have been imposed, one needs to address the nature of the sampling unit, and this is where a lot of issues come crashing down at once. That is, in order to determine the appropriate sampling unit, you need to have some idea of the personnel that will be involved in the project, the availability of transport and logistical support, and the analytical methods that will ultimately be employed. The first two of these are project-specific, while the latter will be addressed later in this chapter.

Let us explore these issues by posing a concrete problem. Suppose you are interested in knowing whether or not a rare gemstone, say lapis lazuli, is locally available in your region of Iran. You define your region narrowly so that it includes only two small stream valleys, part of a river valley, and adjacent upland areas, as depicted in Figure 2.5. Since you have sufficient funding and labor and the material is rare, the most efficient way to sample the landscape might be to have a crew walk the entire region and record every piece of lapis they see. In this case, the sampling unit would be the piece.

Let us now consider a different problem: this time you are interested in a particular type of hornstone found in Zimbabwe (remember, you Zimbabweans, this is hypothetical). The particular type of material in which you are interested is similar to hornstone that occurs locally, but to find out if this particular type is local, and where it is found locally, you need to take samples. In addition, your region is much broader in extent than in the previous example. In such a situation, you cannot define your sampling unit as the individual piece, because there are too many such pieces throughout the region and much would depend on which pieces you chose. You would also probably never have enough time or money to be able to cover every square meter of your region. Since total coverage is out of the question, you need to arrange your sampling strategy to provide the most representative possible characterization of the region for your purposes. A practical solution would be to define the sample unit as a spatial locality from which samples would be drawn.

At this point we are becoming deeply mired in sampling theory and this is not a sampling textbook. Discussions of this aspect of the problem can be found in statistical texts (e.g., Blalock 1972:chap. 21; Drennan 1996: Part II) and in statistical applications to archaeological issues (e.g., Mueller 1974, 1975; Nance 1981; Nance and Ball 1981). For solutions to lithic sourcing problems, consult the case study boxes scattered through this chapter, as well as Shackley (1998) and Church (1994:chap. 3).

What Is the Source of the Material?

The second common type of sourcing problem can be characterized as follows: you know that a particular raw material has entered the region from somewhere, but its origin remains a mystery. This question has arisen frequently in regions in which obsidian or exotic chert shows up on sites, but no known local source of these materials exists. In this situation it is worth investigating all potential local sources, but success may not be forthcoming.

If this substance really originated from outside the region, it must have been worth bringing in, suggesting that it is likely to be associated with a known, frequently exploited quarry or source area. Descriptions of raw materials from such areas exist in the archaeological literature and can be compared with the archaeological material of interest. Such approximations are often accurate in cases in which a wide variety of visual characteristics exists within a material type, as with many types of chert and "rough stone"—a term sometimes applied to non-vitreous or non-cherty materials, including a large suite of sedimentary, igneous and metamorphic rocks utilized by our ancestors. In such cases, it may be possible to determine a specific source area on visual criteria alone, or at least to limit the problem to manageable proportions. Some substances, like obsidian, tend to show little inter-source variation, so visual techniques can seldom be employed for discriminating between source areas. On the other hand, obsidian types are linked to specific lava flows that are known, well localized, and relatively few in number.

In any case, the problem involves determining possible sources for the material in question, then comparing material from each of these to the archaeological specimens of interest. The fact that the research universe now includes not only the local region but the source area(s) does not mean that the source areas do not need

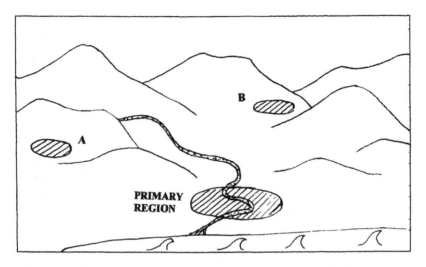

Figure 2.6.   Hypothetical source areas A and B in relation to the region of primary interest.

to be carefully defined; they do. As explained previously, source areas are really rock formations or facies that contain variability throughout their spatial extent. It is important to characterize this variability, because a particular specimen could come from any part of its range. If you are familiar with one part of that range but not all of it, the characteristics of a specific specimen may fall outside known parameters documented for the formation, yet still be part of it. Thus, if you are planning to sample a source area at some distance from your primary region of interest, you must still acquire a working knowledge of that area so that your samples will reflect the variability within the source. Such a situation is depicted visually in Figure 2.6, which illustrates the region of principal archaeological interest and two external areas that served as sources of the lithic material found on archaeological sites in that region.

Investigating exotic source areas may ultimately involve traveling to and sampling each possible source. The concept of sampling is important, as the attributes of the material from each source will exhibit a range of variability. It is crucial to be able to accurately characterize this variability, particularly if it is not being compared to very many archaeological specimens. So once again, the researcher must decide such questions as appropriate sample unit, size, and procedure. To facilitate comparison, these parameters should be uniform from one source area to another.

Let us reiterate the research process to this point. First, delineate the boundaries of the region of interest. Second, do background research on all relevant rock types and geological formations, as well as the dominant depositional and erosional processes, within that region. Third, articulate realistic and solvable research questions based on information acquired through background investigation. Fourth, determine appropriate sampling units and analytical methodology. Fifth, carry out fieldwork. And sixth, characterize and compare the material collected during this process. The following sections are designed to assist you in this characterization—i.e., in figuring out what kinds of specimens you have acquired.

VISUAL CHARACTERIZATION

To source a lithic material, it is necessary to characterize its properties. The more tightly defined these properties are and the more precisely their variability is known, the more successful the sourcing exercise will be. Many methods exist for characterizing raw materials, but for our purposes it is useful to divide them into two basic types: 1) those involving visible characteristics, whether macro- or microscopic; and 2) those involving the elemental composition of the raw material, a process that usually requires some rather complicated instruments. For obvious reasons, visual characterization is the simpler and more common of the two, so let us begin with that.

Hand Specimens

The term "hand specimen" refers to a piece whose assessment of characteristics and origin is conducted by regarding it visually or under low magnification. The most useful properties for this type of determination are color, texture and density. Color can be assessed with the aid of a Munsell color or Rock Color chart. Texture is a relative surface roughness quality that can be judged using templates for comparison to archaeological situations. Density can be measured by water immersion and other methods, though Church (1994:47) has experienced problems achieving suitable precision using this method. Since the technique assumes that the researcher has knowledge of a reasonably wide range of material types, the availability of an extensive comparative collection of rock types is imperative.

Because of its simplicity, the visual assessment of hand specimens is the most common sourcing technique and, when dealing with distinctive raw materials, can be quite accurate. In fact, using visual observation techniques analyzed through discriminant function statistics, Ferguson and Warren (1992) developed an identification key for northern Illinois cherts that has achieved an accuracy rate of greater than 90%. Box 2.2 presents a distributional study of various chert types within a region using simple visual identification techniques.

Many raw materials are not as distinctive as the Illinois varieties; and some seem distinctive until additional fieldwork reveals similar rock types that originate outside the supposed source of the "distinctive" material. A case in point involves Alibates agatized dolomite, a highly vitreous substance favored by people

Box 2.2. Sampling to Determine What is Local

Highway construction disturbs a lot of earth, including archaeological sites, and so it was in the early 1970s when the state of Illinois decided to extend the Central Illinois Expressway 116 km from Springfield to Quincy. The Foundation for Illinois Archeology (subsequently called the Center for American Archeology, or CAA) was awarded the contract by the Illinois Department of Transportation. The CAA conducted an archaeological survey that located 150 sites, of which 92 would be negatively impacted by highway construction (Farnsworth and Walthall 1983).

At the beginning of the project research possibilities seemed limitless, and the eventual form that research would take was uncertain. In this context the organization established a Lithic Analysis Laboratory, and George Odell was hired as its Director. At the time Odell came on board, the initial archaeological survey had been completed and sites were being tested for significance. The site testing operation had its own structure, crew, and budget, as did several important locales that had been slated for intensive excavation. Although these segments of the project were relatively independent of one another and in the beginning nobody knew exactly what kinds of data might be required, it was certain that lithic artifacts would be recovered from all sites, often in prodigious quantities.

Ultimately somebody was bound to ask the questions, "were prehistoric tool users in this region procuring their raw materials locally or from some distance away?" And "what was the nature of their procurement system?" Fortunately, a few years earlier some information on these questions had been gathered on chert in the region by Tom Meyers (1970), though the area he had studied was several kilometers south of the highway transect. An important conclusion of Meyers' analysis was that prehistoric procurement probably concentrated on secondarily deposited chert in streambeds, rather than from less easily accessible bedrock sources. Indeed, at the time he conducted his analysis, no prehistoric chert quarries were known to exist in the region.

Before the individual projects began to produce huge quantities of archaeological material begging for analysis, there was a need to determine the nature of the local resource. That way, regional researchers interested in prehistoric procurement practices would have some basis for comparison with their archaeological artifacts. It was decided to conduct an initial sourcing study directed exclusively toward chert resources, and branch out later to other materials. In defining what was "local" for sites on a linear highway transect, it seemed like a good idea to simply widen the transect to the highway corridor plus territory 8 km (5 miles) on each side of it. Although this area could have been sampled randomly, such a tactic would have been arduous and time-consuming, as most potential sampling locales would have been relatively inaccessible.

Thus it was decided that, in this case, thorough geographic coverage was a more desirable quality than randomness. Sampling locales were therefore spread all over the research transect and located most frequently where a road crossed a streambed. Bedrock samples were also taken from the Illinois Valley bluff face and from a recently discovered prehistoric quarry located in the uplands. Upon return to the lab, samples were graded according to knapping quality and texture, and drainages or locales were compared with one another.

Even though sampling was non-random and relatively loosely structured, the results appear surprisingly robust and conform to knowledge of the region gained through other research. This study revealed several interesting insights: 1) Burlington chert was not the only silicate rock available in large enough nodules for tool use. Silicates from glacial till were available in the western portion of the transect, and Cretaceous siliceous cobbles had been secondarily deposited in a formation in the center of the transect; 2) the territory east of the Illinois River possessed no chert of usable size; 3) chert availability was highly variable throughout the transect, i.e., some locales were better sources than others; and 4) five "hot spots," where chert resources

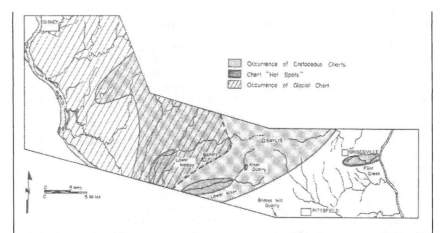

Figure 2.7.   Graphic results of the Illinois chert transect study (taken from Odell 1984: Figure 3.6).

were particularly abundant, were identified (Odell 1984). The principal results of the transect study, including the locations of the "hot spots," are illustrated in Figure2.7. These assessments of the local resource base were immensely helpful in interpreting regional prehistoric procurement patterns.

throughout the Southern Plains and traditionally sourced to quarries near Amarillo, Texas. But through recent fieldwork in northwestern Oklahoma and southwestern Kansas, Berkly Bailey (2000) has determined that a resource known as Day Creek chert possesses visual characteristics that overlap those of Alibates. This discovery calls into question many previous studies, which assumed that specific artifacts that looked like they were made of Alibates actually were. And it only gets worse from there, because entire models of resource procurement and social dynamics have been predicated on the accurate sourcing of specific artifacts to the Alibates quarry.

Two recent studies of Central American obsidian underscore the extent of the inaccuracy problem. Commenting on prehistoric obsidian blade production on the Pacific Guatemalan coast, Jackson and Love (1991) submitted several of these blades to X-ray fluorescence (XRF) analysis. Their study determined that the frequency of use of three obsidian source areas in the region changed through time. Had the authors relied solely on visual assessments for sourcing the blades, their conclusions would have been different, as the XRF analysis did not confirm visual assessments in several instances. In a similar study, Moholy-Nagy and Nelson (1990) submitted 29 obsidian artifacts and 1 unworked nodule from the Mayan city of Tikal to both visual and XRF analysis. Their initial impression that the substantial within-source variability of this gray obsidian would make visual sourcing unreliable was substantiated when they found that the two techniques differed on 14 of the 30 pieces.

Various attempts have been made to improve visual sourcing techniques using hand specimens. One of these involves the use of scanning electron microscopy (SEM), which allows very detailed artifact observations and provides lovely photographs (Church 1994:49). However, improvements in observation have not been accompanied by improvements in sourcing accuracy using the SEM.

Other advances have been made by submitting specimens to different sources of light. The most popular of these is subjection to ultraviolet (UV) light, a technique that Hofman et al. (1991) used to differentiate Central Texas Edwards chert from look-alikes. The technique appears to be unaffected by subjecting the chert to heat for improving the knappability of the material: experiments by Shockey (1994) have established that properties of chert under UV light are not affected by temperatures as high as 800°C. Although the UV technique appears to work well in certain circumstances, problems include a lack of standardization in reporting results, difficulty in describing the effects, and variation caused by the use of different UV lights (Church 1994:47).

Finally, using polarized light on chert, Shockey (1995) achieved some discrimination, though not between types of chert. He found that UV light directed through a polarizer had different effects depending on whether the stone had originated in primary context or had come from a secondary source with attendant weathering. Quarry area (primary) specimens showed an anisotropic (polarized) character, whereas stream-rolled (secondary depositional) stones were predominantly isotropic (depolarized). These findings are interesting but, to my knowledge, have not yet been applied to any other regions or types of chert.

The past few years have also seen the emergence of another simple technique that is employable with chert sources that exhibit variable visual characteristics. Known as "Minimum Analytical Nodule (MAN) Analysis," it was developed by Robert Kelly, Mary Lou Larson and Eric Ingbar (Kelly 1985; Ingbar et al. 1989; Larson and Ingbar 1992; Larson 1994; Larson and Kornfeld 1997). MAN analysis separates lithic objects into groups that probably came from the same nodule. It provides information on the proportion of material from each source and quantifies the material brought to the site and reduced there, data that are useful in studies of on-site technology, procurement, and mobility organization. In the right situation, its low cost makes it a viable alternative to more technologically advanced methods. This type of analysis has been employed effectively in the foothills of the Bighorn Mountains of Wyoming, where the local Madison and Phosphoria cherts show extreme variation within even a limited portion of their ranges, making the determination of exact origin of any specific piece very difficult.

Petrographic Techniques

Sedimentary petrography refers to the analysis of both depositional and diagenetic fabrics from thin sections (Harwood 1988:108). In sedimentology such studies can inform on the sequence of diagenetic events, the genesis of the sediment, and the mineral composition of the material. It is this latter quality that is especially useful when applied to the sourcing of precipitates or other highly siliceous stones. An excellent discussion of sedimentary petrographic analysis is provided by Harwood (1988; also Church 1994:48-49), while standard laboratory techniques for preparing samples, using microscopes, etc., are discussed by Lewis and McConchie (1994).

A technique similar to petrography in that it uses thin sections is cathodoluminescence. This technique involves light emission by compounds in response to the excitation of atoms from their bombardment by electrons. Cathodoluminescence can inform on details of rock structure otherwise unobservable, but it has not been employed extensively for sourcing studies (Miller 1988; Church 1994:50; Lewis and McConchie 1994:133).

Petrographic sourcing studies have been popular for several years in Europe and Great Britain, where its popularity continues to the present day. It has been particularly useful in stone axe studies—employed, for example, in the Irish Stone Axe Project for narrowing the prehistoric exploitation of porcellanite to a few centers (Cooney and Mandal 1995); and, combined with geochemical techniques, in southern England for correlating archaeological axes with sources of glacial erratics. Combined with inductively coupled plasma-atomic emission spectroscopy (known as ICP), it is also proving useful in discriminating flint from mines in the southern Netherlands and northern Belgium used for the production of axes in the Neolithic (McDonnell et al. 1997).

In North America petrographic techniques are only beginning to be effectively employed for sourcing lithic materials. A few recent studies involve chert (e.g., Lavin and Prothero 1992); others include rhyolite sources from North Carolina (Daniel and Butler 1996) and, combined with ICP analysis, volcanics from Washington (Bakewell 1996). Although petrographic studies are well established in geology, they remain underutilized in archaeology because they are not easily accomplished if the researcher has neither available equipment nor the expertise necessary for preparing thin sections. As multidisciplinary approaches become more widespread and the advantages of petrographic techniques become more widely known, this sort of analysis should gain in popularity.

GEOCHEMICAL TECHNIQUES

It should by now be apparent that visual techniques for sourcing lithic artifacts have some utility but also serious deficiencies. Assessing hand specimens in the traditional way is fraught with error. It has potential for inaccuracy because rocks from some formations look like rocks from other formations, many analysts do not possess adequate raw material comparative collections, and some observers are simply not very good at their craft. Petrographic techniques are more accurate, but they require expertise in geology and technical skill in making thin sections, neither of which has had a very high priority in archaeological training.

The problems of inaccuracy and lack of scientific method that have plagued traditional sourcing analyses have opened the door for a suite of new technologies. These are considerably more expensive than traditional techniques and often require equipment that is available in only a few specialized centers. They share a common attribute in concentrating on the composition of the stone being tested, favoring this quality over alternatives such as texture, density, and color. Parenthetically, Shackley (1998:261) has observed that geochemical techniques never truly "source" anything in that their purpose is to provide a compositional profile of a material, which is matched to the profile of the source area. Sourcing makes the assumption that both the archaeological and source samples are truly representative of their populations, but since we can never be sure of either, the result must be expressed with a level of uncertainty.

The following sections will briefly outline the principal geochemical techniques employed to characterize the composition of rocks. The selection of an appropriate technique depends not only on factors discussed here, but also on project- or researcher-specific imponderables such as budget or a friend in a lab somewhere. Applications of these techniques will not be discussed here in depth, but a few will be included in Boxes 2.3 and 2.4.

Neutron Activation Analysis

Let us begin with neutron activation analysis, or NAA, a technique that its proponents claim is "the technique of choice for chemistry-based provenance research" (Neff and Glascock 1995: 280; see also Shackley 1998:266). The technique involves irradiating a sample with a beam of electrons in a nuclear reactor. Resulting radionuclides decay into gamma-rays, which are used to identify the elements present (Parkes 1986:154). Although Purdy (1981:121) and Church (1994:51) call the technique "non-destructive," this is not exactly true, as the material is usually broken into small pieces and it may remain radioactive for a long time (Shackley 1998:266-267).

The principal advantages of neutron activation analysis are its precision, the large quantity of elements that can be detected, the minimal amount of sample preparation required, and the large database built up over the past 25 years (Neff and Glascock 1995:280). NAA can detect a wide range of elements in small concentrations, making it useful for analyzing trace elements, though it cannot detect elements with nuclides possessing half-lives that are either excessively long or short (Parkes 1986:154). It has also been used effectively to discriminate individual areas within a source (Braswell and Glascock 1998). Disadvantages of NAA are its cost, the limited availability of nuclear reactor centers conducting this sort of research, and the irradiation of the sample, which may render it radioactive for a considerable length of time. It is less accurate than other methods for analyzing Ba and Sr, both potentially important discriminating elements (Shackley 1998:267).

The high cost of NAA may be alleviated by combining visual sourcing techniques with limited NAA, which employs short irradiation procedures in searching for only a few elements. This strategy was employed on a sample of 600 obsidian artifacts dating from 200 BC to AD 950 from Quelepa, El Salvador (Braswell et al. 1994). The authors claimed a high rate of accuracy, suggesting that there may be room in the future for creative combinations of established techniques.

X-Ray Fluorescence Analysis

X-ray fluorescence (XRF) spectroscopy can be pursued in an energy-dispersive or wavelength-dispersive mode. Accounts differ as to which of these methods is the more widely used (Church 1994:50; Lewis and McConchie 1994:173), though Church may be limiting his comments to only archaeological applications, in which he believes the energy-dispersive mode is more common. XRF can be truly non-destructive, as only the surface of an artifact is affected by X-ray bombardment.

The sample is irradiated by a beam of X-rays, which excites certain electrons into higher energy levels. These drop back into their original levels, but with the addition of secondary rays, which are fluorescent. The only wavelength reflected is that conforming to a mathematical condition known as Bragg's formula. The energy levels of these fluorescent rays are distinctive of the element whence they derived; therefore, the concentration of specific elements in the sample can be determined by measuring the intensities of X-rays at different wavelengths. In most cases, the excitation of atoms is conducted in a tungsten-target X-ray tube and analyzed by an X-ray spectrograph.

The technique is capable of analyzing most elements of archaeological interest to acceptable limits of detection, and sample preparation is easy. Computation of count rates is a highly involved procedure and must be accomplished with a computer, as correction factors must be added to account for the influence of the concentration of every other element present (Lewis and McConchie 1994:174). Nevertheless, accuracy of the technique for the elements for which it is appropriate appears to be quite high (Goffer 1980:45-47; Parkes 1986:151-153; Church 1994:50).

A couple of traditional disadvantages of XRF have recently been resolved through technological development. The necessity of bringing samples back to a permanent installation for analysis has been alleviated by a field-portable instrument with mercury iodide detector (Williams-Thorpe et al. 1999). Using this equipment, a sample of igneous rocks compared well with wavelength-dispersive

XRF results on fresh surfaces but showed major differences on weathered surfaces, particularly for K, Ca, Ti, and Fe. Another traditional difficulty is that surface irregularities on a sample may render it difficult to calibrate intensity measures for X-rays of different wavelengths (Parkes 1986:153). However, Latham et al. (1992) have developed a technique for analyzing rough surfaces, applying it to basaltic rocks from California.

XRF analysis retains drawbacks that have not yet been resolved. As suggested above, not all elements can be detected by the equipment. Elements with atomic numbers less than titanium (22), which includes common ones such as aluminum, sodium and potassium, are absorbed by air before they can reach the detector. This problem may be alleviated by placing the sample in a vacuum, but this restriction may preclude physically large samples from being tested. And since X-ray fluorescent radiation is largely absorbed by solids, this technique is used for the surface of materials, not their interior. This means that, if the surface to be analyzed is weathered or otherwise modified, it might not provide a representative impression of the composition of the material as a whole. So despite the fact that the technique can be non-destructive, in practice it may be necessary to remove an outside weathering rind or patina in order to derive an accurate reading from the sample. These disadvantages aside, XRF analysis is highly appropriate for most elements, it is conducted in more centers around the world than NAA, and it has achieved acceptable levels of accuracy for the most important elements studied.

PIXE and Similar Techniques

Proton- (or particle-) induced X-ray emission (PIXE) analysis is similar to XRF in that a beam of high-energy particles bombards the surface of a stone, exciting electrons into higher energy levels. As in XRF, these electrons emit X-rays and return to their original K or L inner shells. The X-rays produce a spectrum that is representative of the different elements in the sample. The principle difference between the two techniques is that, in XRF, the entire surface of the object is bombarded, whereas in PIXE, the particle beam is focused narrowly onto a very small area of the sample. This enables different portions of the surface to be compared with one another.

The PIXE technique is considered an advance over traditional XRF analyses in that it uses more sensitive X-ray detectors. This and the large number of X-rays produced by bombardment combine to enable a much shorter analysis time for each sample than is possible for XRF. In addition, the spectrum of elements generated through this analytical mode shows all computed trace elements at the same time, i.e., their generation does not require separate analyses. Operationally, success in detecting trace elements improves with preconcentration of the components of interest (Annegarn and Bauman 1990).

Box 2.3. One Source or Many?

Two thousand years ago, Hopewell people of the North American midcontinent engaged in a trade/distribution network known as the Hopewell Interaction Sphere. Items from faraway places made their way into this network, raising questions about how these materials were obtained and what the process of distribution was. One of the most visible of these exotic products was obsidian, whose center of distribution was in southern Ohio, particularly at the Hopewell site.

Yet for all the attention given to obsidian, most of these sites do not contain very much of it. The largest single deposit by far is the cache discovered in Mound 11 of the Hopewell site, estimated to weigh 136 kg. Most Ohio sites contain a fraction of this, and Illinois Valley sites contain even less. One large, enigmatic chunk of obsidian was discovered several years ago in the northern part of the Lower Illinois Valley and now resides in the Gilcrease Museum in Tulsa, Oklahoma. But this is by far the largest chunk ever discovered in this region. Of all Hopewell sites excavated in the Lower Illinois Valley through the 1980s, Napoleon Hollow contained the most obsidian artifacts, and you can hold all of these artifacts in the palms of your two hands. Early neutron activation analysis of several samples of Hopewell obsidian indicated that they all came from Obsidian Cliff in Yellowstone Park and from one other unidentified source (Griffin et al. 1969; Gordus et al. 1971). This situation induced Jimmie Griffin (1965) to speculate that perhaps all of the obsidian on Hopewell sites was gathered on one collecting trip.

Testing Griffin's hypothesis required establishing two parameters; first, that the obsidian came from one source, though if it came from two nearby sources, a one-trip hypothesis would not be out of the question. More than two nearby sources would render the hypothesis highly unlikely. And second, obsidian-bearing archaeological deposits should all be datable to a very tight temporal range. In a multi-faceted study, Hatch et al. (1990) took on both of these questions. The authors conducted NAA and AAS analyses of obsidian samples from Hopewell, Seip and Mound City in Ohio, plus one flake from the Naples site in Illinois. Using Na/Mn ratios for comparison with earlier results, they confirmed the Obsidian Cliff source and supported the Camas-Dry Creek (or Bear Gulch) locality in Idaho for the previously unidentified source. Other specimens tested differently enough from these two that the authors proposed that at least one other obsidian source had been exploited.

Turning to the chronological question, Hatch and his colleagues procured hydration dates for most of the obsidian that was sourced. Their results showed a fairly wide temporal range, indicating that the obsidian had been accumulated over several generations. Thus obsidian on Hopewell sites appeared to be not the product of one collecting trip, but of several visits to the source and the subsequent enrichment of the Hopewell Interaction Sphere.

The story does not end here, however, because Richard Hughes (1992) criticized Hatch et al.'s study on a number of fronts. With respect to their sourcing analyses, Hughes noted that Hatch and his colleagues insisted on using the old Na/Mn ratios in preference to geochemical profiling of elements, which is more common these days and which would have enabled the researchers to identify a geological source for each specimen. Stevenson et al. (1992) replied that this was not their intention, that they meant only to demonstrate heterogeneity. Hughes also observed that a study of trace elements would have allowed finer discrimination of sources than the major element ratios that were used.

Criticisms of the hydration dating methods employed included contradictory results obtained by some of the authors in an earlier study of Hopewell Mound 11, and the questionable validity of hydration rates derived at high temperatures in deionized water. Most significantly, Hughes recalibrated the hydration rates with standard deviations to a tenth, rather than a hundredth, of a micron as had originally been done. Recalculating the t-ratios suggested that all samples were drawn from the same population—supporting the notion that, chronologically speaking, the obsidian could have come from one collecting trip after all. This recalibration was refuted by Stevenson et al. (1992), who asserted that reporting measurements to the hundredth of a micron is conventional for image-splitting devices.

So where does this leave us? It is evident that more research is needed on several fronts. Elemental profiles of obsidian sources in the West have been added to the literature since these studies were completed, and these should be used for comparison with Hopewell artifacts. This would enable us to achieve a more realistic impression of the total number of sources involved and their distance from each other. The dating of these objects is currently not as tight as it needs to be, either. The different results obtained from the various ways of processing the material and handling the statistics have produced a troubling situation that will probably only be resolved through the application of more controlled samples and alternative dating techniques.

Many of the disadvantages of XRF also apply to PIXE, occasionally to an even greater extent. For example, sample preparation can be a problem with PIXE, as the parts to be bombarded must be very smooth, which often necessitates polishing them. Non-metallic samples must be metal- or carbon-coated to avoid particle buildup on the surface. And, because of the greater sensitivity of the equipment and resulting speed of analysis, cost is greater than for XRF (Purdy 1981:116; Parkes 1986:153-154; Church 1994:51). PIXE analysis is particularly adept at analyzing obsidian, which has a naturally smooth surface (e.g., Seelenfreund et al. 1996). However, it has also proven adaptable to rougher materials, such as red ochre from the western United States (Erlandson et al. 1999).

Other techniques are theoretically similar to PIXE. Proton-induced gamma-ray emission (PIGME) analysis operates under similar principles and is often conducted in conjunction with PIXE analyses. A similar technique involves use of the electron microprobe, which is essentially a combination of an electron microscope and X-ray fluorescence spectrometer. As in XRF analysis, fluorescent X-rays can be detected either by wavelength or energy dispersion. And as in PIXE analysis, only a small area of the sample is excited and is emitting X-rays at any one time. This can be a disadvantage, as the technique can assess only a small spot, thus frequently making the analysis of an entire rock sample a difficult enterprise (Lewis and McConchie 1994:174-175). Despite this drawback, the technique has proven informative in many projects, including the analysis of several hundred obsidian artifacts from the Mediterranean (Tykot and Ammerman 1997:1003).

Other Instrumental Types of Analysis

The three analytical types just described—NAA, XRF, and PIXE/PIGME—dominate the field of archaeological sourcing analysis (Shackley 1998:266). However, alternative techniques also exist, and these may have advantages that render them appropriate for a specific application. I will briefly describe here a few additional types of geochemical assay; if any seem appropriate, it might be worth checking out the relevant literature, then investigating the techniques themselves.

X-Ray Diffraction

Like the last two techniques described, X-ray diffraction (XRD) analysis employs X-ray spectra, but in other respects this technique is substantially different from the others. XRD is used for the identification of minerals, particularly those the size of clay minerals. It works on the principle that X-rays are diffracted by atomic layers in crystals. Rays provide information on these atomic layers and on the spacings between layers, which are different in different crystalline minerals. The technique is capable of identifying not only the types of certain minerals present, but also their crystalline size, degree of disorder, and other properties. Most samples are ground into a fine, homogeneous powder, which is mixed with alcohol as a smear on a glass slide or packed as powder into a small well that fits into the machine. The technique provides ample information on certain minerals, sample preparation is relatively simple, and the machines are easy to operate and maintain.

Unfortunately, these machines cost a lot of money (though each assay is relatively inexpensive) and grinding the sample into powder effectively annihilates part of an archaeological artifact. Also, XRD is useful only for crystalline structures, and gives no information on non-crystalline opals or allophanes (Lewis and McConchie 1994:144-147). Although XRD is employed frequently in archaeological pottery studies, it has seen little use in lithic sourcing. This may be an oversight, as the technique is suitable for certain applications; most recently it was used in an analysis of catlinite from Wisconsin (Penman and Gunderson 1999).

Atomic Absorption Spectroscopy

Atomic absorption spectroscopy (AAS) analysis is destructive in that part of an object is dissolved in acid, but a plug can be taken from the artifact and the hole filled with another substance. Part of the resulting solution is vaporized and passed through a flame, through which light from a hollow tube source lamp also passes. A monochromator or prism/detector device is used to isolate light of a specific wavelength that can be absorbed by the element of interest. Each element absorbs light of a characteristic wavelength, and the concentration of that element can be determined by comparing the intensity of the light beam before and during the injection of the sample into the flame. This means that each element must be assayed independently. This method detects only metallic elements, but does include those of low atomic number (e.g., sodium), which are difficult to detect through X-ray analysis.

AAS is quite accurate and can work with relatively low concentrations of the substance being tested, though a larger sample is required when looking for trace elements. Necessary equipment is cheap and widely available, and operation takes minimal training. Disadvantages of the technique include the destruction of part or all of the sample, the detection of only metallic elements, and the ability to run only one element at a time. In addition, since the operator must choose the elements of interest, surprise elements that may provide good discrimination among samples may be omitted entirely from the analysis (Goffer 1980:51-52; Parkes 1986:151; Lewis and McConchie 1994:175-176).

My own experience with this technique is limited to pottery, for which it provided clear separation among sampled areas (Shingleton et al. 1994). Applications to lithic materials have included English polished flint axes (Craddock et al. 1983), and basalt artifacts from two sites in the Levant (Weinstein-Evron et al. 1995). AAS has also been combined with NAA for analyzing obsidian samples from Ohio Hopewell sites (Hatch et al. 1990).

Box 2.4. Exploring Environmental and Social Factors

Obsidian is a beautiful substance, and may have been valued for qualities other than simply utilitarian ones. Questions of prehistoric exploitation, including the role of both environmental and social factors influencing the acquisition of material, were investigated by Torrence et al. (1996) for obsidian from New Britain in Melanesia. The authors limited the scope of their study to the central and western parts of the island, particularly the regions of Mopir and the Willaumez Peninsula/ Garua Island. Although the existence of several lava flows throughout the region complicates the picture, the authors were able to isolate the Mopir and Willaumez regional groups and four subgroups, probably related to specific lava flows, within the latter. Exploitation of obsidian on archaeological sites was partitioned into four periods: 20,000-10,000 BP, 10,000-3500 BP, 3500-1500 BP, and 1500-present. The study draws on the geochemical characterization, by PIXE-PIGME techniques, of a substantial quantity of source samples and of artifacts from well-dated archaeological sites.

Results of the analysis differ according to the scale of the populations being compared. On a regional scale, differences in prehistoric exploitation depended primarily on environmental factors. That is, during the period 20,000-10,000 BP, Mopir obsidian dominated the region because access to Willaumez Peninsula obsidian was restricted by factors related to the lower sea level at that time. Conversely, during the period 3500-1500 BP, the eruption of Mt. Witori transformed the local coastline and effectively cut off all northern access by water to the Mopir source. With its availability restricted, this source was drastically underrepresented on regional archaeological sites. During the other two periods, both sources were available for exploitation and distance from source is an accurate predictor of the origin of obsidian at a given site.

When one switches to a smaller scale of inquiry, the factors influencing obsidian exploitation change drastically. In Torrence et al.'s analysis, scale was reduced by comparing the four subgroups of the Willaumez Peninsula regional source. At this level, the occurrence of obsidian from a specific source could not be explained by environmental factors, distance from source falloff curves, or relative quality of material. As a case in point, in two of the periods the Gulu and Baki subgroups were exploited locally but not exported, whereas obsidian from the Kutau/Bao subgroup was exported. Even on Garua Island, where the Baki source resided and was utilized extensively on a local level in other periods, it was not employed there during the period of Lapita pottery (3500-1500 BP). The locals were passing up a perfectly fine source of obsidian (Baki), one that had been used there before and would be used again, to import obsidian from the larger island. This imported obsidian was utilized very casually, even wastefully with no intention to conserve it. This phenomenon was also observed among imported obsidian tools from archaeological sites in the southeastern Solomon Islands.

Like the American importation of Argentinian beef when American ranchers could easily supply local requirements, influences other than simple economics or subsistence must have been operating here. The most likely explanation for these trends is social: inhabitants with their own local obsidian sources were importing obsidian in order to foster trade in other items, probably to maintain social relationships. Studies such as Torrence et al.'s demonstrate that materials such as obsidian could be used by prehistoric people for social purposes. Only further research into these issues will reveal what those purposes might have been.

Inductively-Coupled Plasma Analysis

A recently developed technique that has seen some archaeological use is inductively-coupled plasma (ICP) analysis which, like AAS studies, attempts to identify specific elements by placing samples in solution. The solution is heated by jetting it through radio-frequency coils in an argon stream at a temperature in excess of 6000°C to form plasma. At this juncture, the technique branches into two modes. In optical emission spectroscopy (ICP-AES), the high-energy elements in the plasma emit wavelengths that are split up and detected in a photomultiplier tube, and analyzed by computer. In the mass spectrometry (ICP-MS) mode, ions in the plasma are submitted to a quadrupole mass spectrometer, which separates the sample into constituent elements (Parkes 1986:166-167; Lewis and McConchie 1994:177-178).

Because the technique is relatively new, there has been a need to establish standards and rates of accuracy which, if high enough, would promote the technique as a viable alternative to more firmly established competitors. Using ICP-AES techniques on rock powders, Norman et al. (1989) tested its results against results from XRF, NAA and isotope dilution mass spectrometry (ID), the latter being a highly accurate but expensive technique. The authors concluded that "the comparisons of major and trace element analyses of silicate rocks described here display excellent agreement among the four labs utilizing different analytical methods and widely differing sample preparation methods" (Norman et al. 1989:289). They noted that among the advantages of ICP are a capacity to process more samples at a faster rate and for a more diverse group of major and trace elements than other techniques. However, they noted difficulties of sensitivity or spectral interferences for several important trace elements.

The positive results of these tests and the wide applicability of the technique should increase the popularity of ICP among geologists. The technique will be slower to catch on among archaeologists, but it has already seen some applications, particularly to volcanic materials. For example, Bakewell (1996) combined it with standard petrographic methods to characterize major elements, trace elements, and rare earths of volcanic rocks from the British Camp midden on San Juan Island off the coast of Washington. And Stevenson and McCurry (1990) employed it to discriminate among obsidian sources in New Mexico.

Remnant Magnetism

It has been suggested that differences in remnant magnetism could be employed to source obsidian artifacts (McDougall et al. 1983; Church 1994:48). If true, this could provide another potentially useful technique for some materials, as the equipment is not difficult to use and the technique is relatively inexpensive. Testing of remnant magnetism on American Southwest obsidians by Church and Caraveo (1996) showed some degree of discrimination between sources, but the technique was evaluated as not robust enough to be used alone to source obsidian artifacts.

GENERAL REMARKS

Effective sourcing of lithic materials requires a general knowledge of rock types and a detailed familiarity with the particular geological characteristics of the targeted region. This latter point cannot be made too strongly, as knowledge of local bedrock types and dominant geomorphological processes facilitate interpretations of the human use of the region. As a case in point, consider Shackley's (1992) study of obsidian sources in the Upper Gila River basin in the southwestern United States. Had he been content with locating only bedrock sources, he would never have thought to look in the alluvium or the Quaternary gravels of streambeds. In this context he located two major sources, the variability of which he tested with the aid of energy-dispersive XRF techniques. Prehistoric tool users would have gathered their material from a number of different contexts, depending on availability, quality of material, and ease of access, and it pays to be aware of as many of these conditions as possible.

When it comes to conducting the actual sourcing analyses, many techniques are available and it is generally a good idea to use more than one method (Parkes 1986:161). Visual sourcing of hand specimens will probably never go out of favor, because it is so quick and easy. Given this fact, analysts would benefit by accumulating as comprehensive a lithic comparative collection as possible. Collection from source areas, whether for curation or for geochemical analyses, should be accomplished in a rigorous manner (Church 1994:76), so that the exact source of each sample is known. If sourcing does not constitute an important component of your overall lithic analysis, the monetary commitment that these new technologies require will probably not be worth the effort. But if the provenance of your artifacts provides a crucial cornerstone on which your interpretational edifice is grounded, then the increase in accuracy that these techniques provide may be well worth the expenditure.

The recent proliferation of sourcing studies in the archaeological literature (Odell 2000:270-281) attests to the usefulness of these techniques for answering questions of interest to archaeologists. The principal strengths and weaknesses of the most popular of these have been outlined in this chapter, but this is only a brief introduction and should be used as a launching pad for investigating further those techniques of especial interest. In Shackley's (1998:263) opinion, many geochemical analyses are now being performed by archaeologists rather than by physical scientists. This is a gratifying development, but it means that archaeologists who wish to pursue this kind of research may be faced with the responsibility of learning appropriate geochemical techniques.

This chapter has offered technical advice on sourcing *per se*, but has not attempted to venture into the realm of interpretation. It is, of course, the nuances of interpretation that interest us in conducting sourcing analyses in the first place. Once a raw material is determined to be exotic to the region in which it was found, for example, the question becomes, what mechanism was responsible for bringing that material into the region: mobility, trade, or some other mechanism (Church 1994:79-80)? Questions like this only begin with sourcing analyses; they will be pursued in greater detail in a later chapter. For now, let us be content to consider the case studies included in this chapter, which provide a small taste of the diversity of questions that can be addressed through sourcing studies.

Chapter 3

Tool Manufacture

We study the manufacture of prehistoric stone tools for at least two reasons: 1) different peoples often made their tools differently and knowledge of this variation can help us discriminate among cultural groups in time and in space; and 2) studying tool manufacture provides a measure of a people's level of cognitive advancement. These are compelling reasons for concern, and they help to explain why probably more archaeological effort has been expended in trying to figure out how tools were made than in any other aspect of lithic analysis.

Chapter 2 has summarized the principal raw materials utilized by our prehistoric ancestors and has suggested some techniques for analyzing them. Some of these substances were appropriate for making chipped stone tools, others for making rough or ground stone tools. Since the dominant technology on most prehistoric settlements was chipped stone, most of this chapter will be concerned with that. Grinding techniques will be considered at the end of the chapter.

As mentioned in Chapter 2, the manufacture of lithic implements demands certain characteristics of raw material, though a toolmaker may have had to settle for lesser quality if these characteristics were not found among local rock types or could not be easily traded for. A workable stone for this technology must possess relatively small internal grain size and/or thoroughly cemented matrix, as large, incompletely cemented grains naturally impede fracture (see Figure 2.2a). The material must be brittle, i.e., non-elastic, in order to break easily. And it must be isotropic, meaning that it has uniform susceptibility to fracture in all directions. Part of being isotropic is relative homogeneity, i.e., not containing vugs, impurities, weathering planes, or other anomalies that would either block fracture or induce fracture along a path different from the natural path developed from the initial force. Materials that best fit these requirements are obsidian and crypto-crystalline silicates such as chert, flint, and chalcedony, but other homogeneous and highly silicified or indurated materials may also be suitable.

Prehistoric tool technology is a potentially complex subject, one that requires learning certain fundamental principles. The primary goal of this chapter is to facilitate that process. Most of the research questions that involve applying technological knowledge to archaeological situations—the kinds of questions we came to this field in the first place to answer—will be discussed in a subsequent chapter.

The first order of business in understanding chipped stone technology is to understand the forces that govern the fracture of brittle solids. To facilitate ingesting the concepts described in this chapter, common terms and frequently distinguished elements of the reduction process are described in Box 3.1. This section may not be of especial interest to flintknappers, as they normally develop an intuitive knowledge of these relationships through practice. But it is crucial for analysts, because they must be able to work with attributes that are relevant to fracture, interpret different fracture types, and explain these relationships to others. Knowledge of this aspect is an imperative without which effective lithic analysis cannot proceed, so we will begin with this general question:

Q6: How do rocks break?

Box 3.1. Some Terminological Distinctions

APPLICATION OF FORCE ON MATERIAL:

stress: force per unit area of surface in a solid substance.

compression: squeezing molecules together, which results in tension with contiguous molecules that are not compressed.

tension: pulling molecules apart from each other.

tensile strength: the stress under which a material will break under tension.

DEFORMATION TYPES:

plastic: material deforms permanently upon application of force.

elastic: material does not deform permanently upon application of force, but reverts to its original form.

FLAKE ORIENTATION:

ventral surface: inside surface of flake, i.e., surface from which the flake broke off from its parent core.

dorsal surface: outside surface of flake; surface opposite the break surface.

proximal end: end including, or closest to, the striking platform and application of force.

distal end: end furthest away from applied force.

lateral edges: side edges of flake, or margins between proximal and distal ends.

FRACTURE SEQUENCE:

initiation: application of force to a solid and beginning of rupture.

propagation: progression of fracture in tension subsequent to the application of force and initial rupture.

termination: end of the flake, or place where force exits the core.

KNAPPING EQUIPMENT:

hammerstone: stone percussor employed to knap other lithic material; can be hard (e.g., granite) or soft (e.g., limestone).

billet: percussive implement used to knap stone, but made of organic material such as bone, antler or hard wood.

pressure flaker: blunt pointed tool such as an antler tine used to apply pressure to the edges of a stone for the removal of flakes.

---

abrader: coarse material such as sandstone used in knapping to knock off thin parts of edges in an effort to "strengthen" the edge for flake removal.

LITHIC FORMS:

nodule: often considered to be any piece of usable stone from which no flakes have been removed; some scholars limit its meaning to individually formed pieces within the parent bedrock (e.g., limestone) to distinguish this type of formation from that of layered, or tabular, raw material.

core: a stone from which one or more flakes have been intentionally removed.

flake: piece removed from a core; to be recognized as such, a flake must possess certain characteristics such as a striking platform or ventral surface features such as lances or undulations.

blade: long, thin, flake; a common definition requires a length at least 2X width and roughly parallel sides; a more stringent definition requires evidence for the use of a blade technique involving true blade cores.

blocky fragment: a piece of stone that does not exhibit recognizable flake features; can be produced in the flaking process or by excessive heating or frost.

REMOVAL TYPES:

direct percussion: act of striking a blow on a solid material with a soft or hard indenter.

indirect percussion: use of punch as intermediary between percussor and core.

pressure flaking: removal of flakes not by striking, but by applying pressure directly to the edge of a piece.

RETOUCH TYPES:

unifacial: retouch on only one surface of an implement.

bifacial: retouch on opposing surfaces of an implement.

marginal: retouch scar negatives that are restricted to an area not more than about 5 mm from the edge from which they were removed.

invasive: retouch scars that extend past the immediate area of the edge into the interior of the piece.

STAGE DESIGNATIONS:

blank: unmodified stone in the form of a blocky fragment, flake or blade from which a tool could be fashioned; also used for a biface, if it was turned into another tool, e.g., a burin on a biface break surface.

preform: blank that has been partly, but not completely, shaped into a finished tool.

FRACTURE MECHANICS

General Principles

Rock can fracture in a number of ways—including internally, as with freeze-thaw conditions in temperate climates—but most of these are not the kinds of forces that are immediately relevant to tool manufacture. In this chapter we will be concerned with forces external to the object of fracture. For all practical purposes, this means that breakage requires an objective stone (i.e., one whose fracture is desired—let's call it A) and another relatively hard object for inducing fracture (B). The forces on A may be exerted by B, as with a hammerstone, or by A itself when B becomes an anvil, but the result is the same. For ease of comprehension, let us assume, unless indicated otherwise, that A is a core on which an outside force (B) is exerted, as in hand-held, direct percussion.

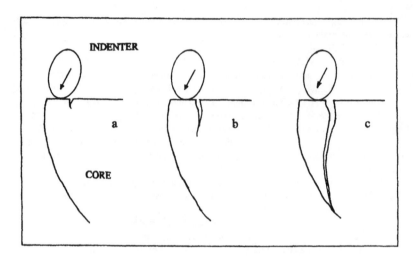

Figure 3.1.   Three stages of flake fracture: a) initiation; b) propagation; and c) termination.

Forces can be *static*, as when steady pressure is applied to an edge, or *dynamic*, as when a stone is hit by a billet. Both static and dynamic forces may be operative in the manufacture of a particular tool but, since dynamic forces related to stone tool making are more widely employed and variable than static ones, most of this section will be concerned with percussion flaking.

The object applying force to a stone, illustrated in Figure 3.1, is the *indenter*. Indenters can be blunt or sharp, depending upon the specific characteristics of the contact point. Most indenters used to break rocks, including hammers, billets, even pressure flakers, are considered blunt, and a blunt indenter will be assumed here unless indicated otherwise. Sharp indenters induce a special type of fracture, but one that is analogous to a type involving blunt indenters that will be explained below. In understanding fracture it is useful to divide the process into three stages: *initiation*, *propagation*, and *termination*.

Force exerted on a point creates *stress*, a measure of force per unit area. Stress is multidimensional, but can be expressed as vectors on any chosen plane. A stress vector may be broken down into components of normal and sheer stress. *Normal stress* is perpendicular to the chosen plane, and can be either compressive or tensile. *Shear stress* is parallel to the surface of the plane and may assume any direction through a full arc. For analysis it is usually divided into two components: orthogonal to the normal stress and to each other (Faulkner 1972:23-27). A representation of these forces is illustrated in Figure 3.2, which shows the shear stress, T, broken into orthogonal components T_{yx} and T_{yz}, both at right angles to the normal stress of σ_{ny}. Although the dominant stress may be compressive, stresses ahead of a propagating crack are always tensile (Cotterell and Kamminga 1987:678).

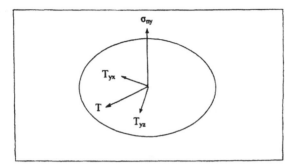

Figure 3.2. Components of stress on a selected plane, expressed in rectangular coordinates. Taken from Faulkner (1972: Fig. 3.3).

It is important to keep in mind that brittle solids like obsidian and chert are *elastic* rather than *plastic*. That is, they do not permanently deform upon application of force; they either return to their original structure upon removal of force, or they break. The amount of stress necessary for fracture has been calculated in the engineering literature for various kinds of materials. It turns out that the theoretical strength of solids is considerably higher than their actual strength. Theoretical strength is calculated on the basis of the energy it would take to separate two atoms on the surface of the material, which are already in a higher energy state than atoms inside the material. The energy required to break these surface atoms is therefore quite high, but this is based on the assumption that the degree of bonding is equally high over the entire surface of the material. Griffith (1920, 1921) showed that this assumption was probably incorrect, and that fracture most likely initiated from tiny surficial cracks or flaws.

From the point of fracture initiation several attributes, such as stress intensity, material hardness, and fracture toughness, govern the eventual form of the resulting breakage. The engineering principles behind these relationships have been elucidated for an archaeological audience by Cotterell and Kamminga (1987, 1990), and will not be reiterated here.

Types of Fracture

Bending

Fracture to brittle solids has been classified into three categories: bending, wedging, and Herzian (Figure 3.3). Bending fractures can be caused by all kinds of percussers and pressure flakers. As in relatively thin metal objects, the thinner the edge of the stone being impacted, the more likely that forces to that edge will produce bending stresses (Tsirk 1979:85). Bending initiations usually occur

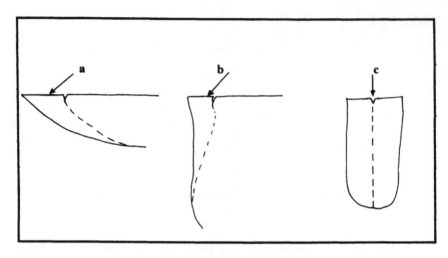

Figure 3.3.   Types of fracture: a) bending; b) Herzian; and c) wedging.

relatively far from the indenter, as compression immediately under the indenter causes tensile stresses at some distance from it (Figure 3.4). Tsirk (1979) has proposed a two-dimensional model for the development of these kinds of fracture.

Bending initiations do not produce a bulb of percussion as on Herzian initiations, but frequently leave a small lip, or overhang, near the point of impact. They also typically lack secondary flakes of the type that are often produced in a Herzian mode (Cotterrell and Kamminga 1990:142), because the impact of the blow, being at some distance from the resulting initiation, does not crush the striking platform.

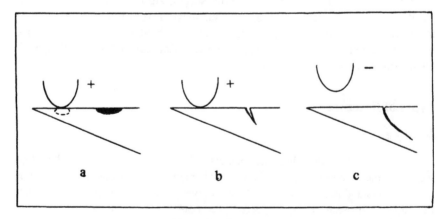

Figure 3.4.   Postulated sequence of loading (+) and unloading (−) for a bending fracture. Illustration at (a) indicates compressive (area in dotted outline) and tensile (black area) stresses.

Wedging

Wedging initiations (Figure 3.3c) can occur if a blow is struck relatively far from an edge of a core or if the angle of the nearest edge is more than 90°; such a flake is controlled by compression (Cotterell and Kamminga 1987:685, 1990:141). This initiation type is dominant in bipolar flaking, a technique for splitting nodules or cores in the interest of economizing raw material. The resulting flakes or wedges often show crushing on both proximal and distal ends, as the latter is stabilized on a hard surface.

Bipolar wedging with a blunt indenter is analogous to fracture using a sharp indenter, a mode that will be used here for illustrative purposes. The dominant stresses in this form of initiation are quite different from those of either Herzian or bending initiations (Lawn and Marshall 1979). The principal deformation zone is immediately under the applied force, causing the development of a median crack that expands with continued loading (Figure 3.5a, b). Upon unloading, fracture

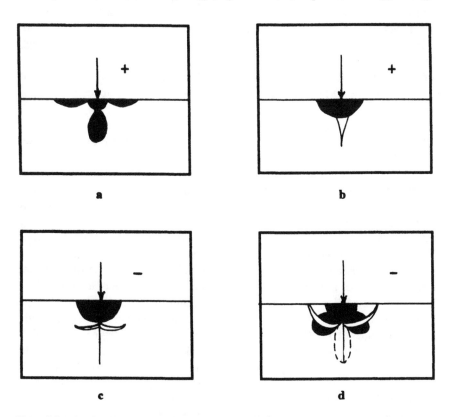

Figure 3.5.   One loading (+) and unloading (−) cycle of fracture with sharp indenter. Dark region is deformation zone. Point-loading and residual stress fields are indicated in (a) and (d) respectively. Taken from Lawn and Marshall (1979: Fig. 8).

debris prevents complete closure of the median crack and lateral cracks open up along highly tensile zones (Figure 3.5c) that may spread and eventually reach the surface (Figure 3.5d). Although to my knowledge the mechanics of bipolar wedging with a blunt indenter have not been studied at a degree of detail comparable to Lawn and Marshall's (1979) work on sharp indenters, the two modes appear to be very similar.

Herzian

Another fracture type that exerts an important influence on the production of usable flakes for tools is the Herzian cone. In this type, fracture initiation is not usually very far from the edge, as it is in wedging. Neither does it normally involve very thin edges, as in bending, because edges that are too thin are crushed and splintered. The process of flake removal can be described as follows. As an indenter contacts the surface of a brittle solid, it creates a zone of compression immediately below the indenter (Figure 3.6a). Deformation in this region creates a spherical zone of tension around the contact area. If tensile stresses are sufficient to break molecular surface bonding, fracture results as a ring crack (Figure 3.6b), the diameter of which is slightly larger than the diameter of the contact (Faulkner 1972:126-127; Texier 1984:142). The crack, originally oriented orthogonal to the surface, soon slants outward at an angle of about 136° in the form of a cone.

Fracture propagation is not controlled by compression, as in wedging initiations, but by material stiffness, defined as a flake's resistance to deformation (Cotterell and Kamminga 1987:676, 1990:142). Thin flakes develop under both bending and compressive forces. With cores possessing edge angles of more than 45°, the most important factor for flake propagation is the force angle, defined as the angle between the flaking force and the side of the core; this is not the same as flaking angle (motion of indenter), but depends on the stiffness of the developing flake. For breakage to occur, the force angle needs to be in the neighborhood of 10° from vertical (Cotterell and Kamminga 1987:676, 692; 1990:142).

If the force angle is different from the flaking angle (angle of percusser motion), then what is the importance of the latter—the only one of these variables that can be controlled by the knapper? According to Cotterell and Kamminga (1987:695), not much. They assert that there is little difference in the force angle for flaking angles of 0°–60°, suggesting that there exists a large degree of variability in the angles at which one can hit a core and knock off a flake. That may be true, but if it is not easier to successfully remove a flake from the edge of a core by inclining the angle of blow somewhat toward the outside, then why do these authors (as well as everybody else) consistently show angles of blow as much as 40° from vertical in their diagrams (e.g., Cotterell and Kamminga 1987: figs. 4, 7, 12, 16; 1990: figs. 6.8, 6.11)? Clearly, maintaining this angle is advantageous, as any teacher

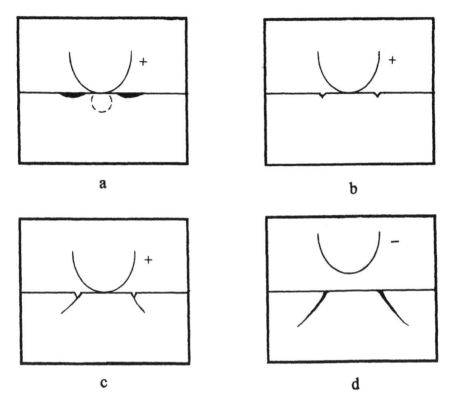

Figure 3.6. Herzian crack pattern during one sequence of loading (+) and unloading (−). (a) shows compressive stress immediately below the percussor and tensile stresses (in black) on either side of it. Taken from Lawn and Marshall (1979: Fig. 2).

knows who has watched a novice turn an angular core of beautiful flint into an amorphous, baseball-shaped blob.

Figure 3.7a illustrates the operation of Herzian fracture on a core with exterior platform angle of about 65°. Striking a blow near the edge of that core results in a vertical crack followed by a change in fracture path in the form of a cone on all sides of the contact area. The outside part of the cone reaches the material boundary quickly and dissipates. Crack propagation on the inside of the cone experiences boundary effects related to an increase in bending of the developing flake. This causes the crack to change direction outward (Cotterell and Kamminga 1987:686-687) and continue propagating roughly parallel to the surface of the core, ultimately terminating, or exiting the material, at some point. The directional change from cone initiation through propagation phase produces the typical bulb of percussion seen on most Herzian flakes, mirrored by the negative bulbs of percussion left on the cores themselves. The direction of such a fracture path near

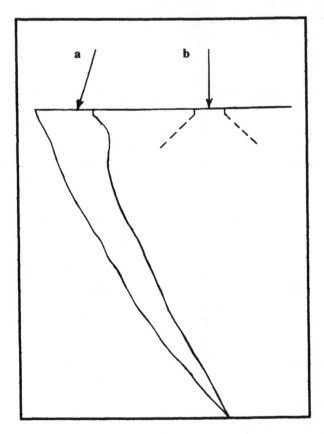

Figure 3.7.   Schematic drawing of flake detached near edge of core through Herzian fracture (a). At (b) a blow is struck far from the edge; unless excessive force is exerted, the cone of force will dissipate without visibly fracturing the rock.

a free boundary is strongly influenced by the geometry of the core. If a dorsal ridge exists, for example, it will concentrate applied stress and induce fracture to occur in a direction parallel to it (Faulkner 1972:132-133). Fracture propagation proceeds according to the following regularities:

> As the flake develops, its bending and compressional stiffness, together with the angle of motion of the flaking tool, determine the flake angle. Long, thin flakes are detached because, over a wide range in direction of the motions of the flaking tool, the actual direction of the flaking force determined by the developing flake's stiffness is almost precisely that required to maintain a mode I crack opening at the top of a crack that is propagating parallel to the side of a nucleus. (Cotterell and Kamminga 1990:144)

In contrast to a blow struck near the edge of a moderate-to-large core, a blow struck further from the edge (Figure 3.7b), if it does not have wedging properties referred to above, requires excessive force for breakage to be successful. The reason for this is that there is no free surface for forces to dissipate, as in Figure 3.7a; fracture must occur along the entire cone until it reaches a free surface. On all but small cores, the amount of material to be fractured by this method usually exceeds the amount of force at the knapper's disposal. Instead of fracturing visibly, the core will most likely exhibit only a ring crack or no visible characteristics at all. For small cores, it is usually more expedient to employ bipolar techniques, resulting in compressive, not Herzian, fracture.

Fracture Features

If you are faced with the prospect of having to interpret what people were doing on a site from the conceptually challenging flakes and cores they left behind, then you will be faced with answering the following question:

Q7: Which flake characteristics can be used to provide behavioral interpretations of an archaeological assemblage?

Several features of individual flakes are indicative of their genesis and development and can contribute to higher-level interpretations. Two sets of flake features are generally more useful than other variables: 1) the interior, or ventral, surface of a flake, because this constituted its original break surface and it may contain information about the nature of the forces that caused breakage to the stone; and 2) flake terminations, which provide information on angle of blow, knapping success, etc.

Ventral Surface Attributes

When force is exerted onto stone, waves are transmitted through the material (Bonnichsen 1977:106-108; Cotterell and Kamminga 1990:151), the most important of which are longitudinal and transverse waves. The amplitude of the longitudinal wave is greatest in a direction perpendicular to the crack plane, although this wave does not tend to promote breakage because it induces particles to move along the plane of fracture rather than at right angles to it. Most rupture is caused by transverse waves (Faulkner 1972:77). Because of impurities in most materials, however, fracture seldom proceeds as it would through a totally homogeneous material. This is a useful fact, since much of a lithic analyst's information about forces that resulted in a specific flake is generated by the reaction of these forces to impurities they encounter.

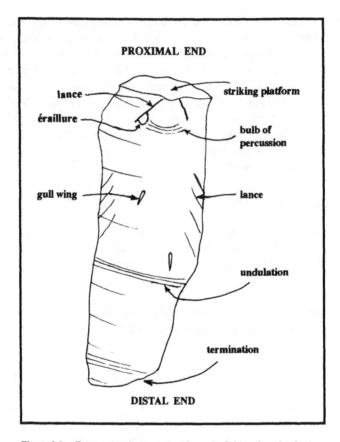

Figure 3.8.   Features on the ventral surface of a flake, referred to in text.

A salient variable governing fracture is the stress-intensity factor (K), which possesses two components: 1) the symmetrical mode I factor (K_I) that causes the two surfaces of an expanding rupture to split perpendicularly from one another; and 2) the asymmetrical mode II factor (K_{II}) that causes slippage over planes other than the one on which the crack is propagating (Lawn and Wilshaw 1975:52; Cotterell and Kamminga 1990:138-139). In the absence of impurities, only the mode I factor operates and the stress field around the furthest extent of the crack is symmetrical. An impurity makes the fracture path deviate in a K_{II} mode. If this deviation is substantial, the fracture path will be unstable and will terminate in a place not predicted by models of brittle fracture. If the deviation is relatively minor, the fracture path will readjust and stabilize in response to the K_I factor. Recognition of these mechanical adjustments can help an analyst establish that a humanly induced blow caused fracture, and it can suggest the nature, origin and direction of that blow. Some of the features left by these adjustments, illustrated in Figure 3.8, can be observed only in obsidian or extremely vitreous flint, but others are more universally recognizable.

The most noticeable result of Herzian fracture is the *bulb of percussion* which, as already discussed, is initially a product of Herzian cone forces followed by a deviation toward the outside of the core caused by stiffness-controlled bending of the incipient flake. The cone of force is usually readily observable as an outward protrusion immediately below the striking platform of the flake and as a negative impression on the core from which the flake derived. This feature is readily recognizable and is indicative of Herzian fracture where it occurs.

Below the striking platform one can frequently observe features referred to as *ripples, undulations,* or *compression rings.* These appear as raised areas on a flake's ventral surface running in a pattern concentric to the point of force, and are useful on flakes lacking striking platforms for indicating where the force blow was delivered (Crabtree 1972:52). They are caused by either an irregularity on the surface of the core or an interface with a shear wave (Cotterell and Kamminga 1990:147).

Shear waves originate when the fracture front reaches a free surface, where they propagate radially at a velocity faster than the fracture front itself. As portrayed in Figure 3.9, a shear wave originating at O will travel obliquely across the fracture plane, intersecting the fracture front AA' at aa', BB' at bb', and so forth. At the free surface C' the wave is deflected again, but in the opposite direction. Thus shear waves pass the fracture front several times during the normal breakage of a brittle solid. When they encounter an impurity in the material at an interface with the fracture front, this encounter results in *Wallner lines.* These are too subtle to be noticed on most substances on which tools were made, but occasionally can be detected on obsidian (Cotterell and Kamminga 1990:150-151).

More frequently observable ventral features are *lances, fissures,* or *radial striations,* which are produced by a rotation of the stress field perpendicular to the fracture front. At some point the fracture front cannot adjust on one plane to this rotation and breaks into multiple fronts, each oriented to a new direction along the path of fracture propagation. These appear as tongues emanating from the fracture front, perhaps resulting from uneven dorsal topography, and they always point back to the origin of force application (Crabtree 1972:64; Faulkner 1972:149-152; Schousboe 1977; Cotterell and Kamminga 1990:149-150). The formation of an *éraillure,* or *bulbar scar,* is closely associated with the formation of lances, particularly those that form on the bulb of percussion through the application of excessive force or irregularities on the dorsal surface. The éraillure scar initiates at a radial striation on the bulb and propagates perpendicular to it, usually ending in a feather or hinge termination (Faulkner 1974).

Another useful ventral feature is frequently referred to as a *gull wing,* but this structure appears to be different from what Faulkner (1972:152-159) referred to by this name. The gull wing described here originates from an impurity around which the fracture front must progress. It does so by deviating around the impurity, then adapting and converging on the other side, producing a ventral structure that

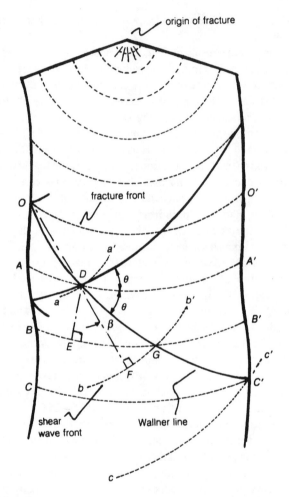

Figure 3.9.   Wallner lines on the ventral surface of a flake. Taken from Cotterell and Kamminga (1990: Fig. 6.17).

looks like a wing. Since the convergence always points away from the direction of applied force, this feature can provide information even in the absence of lances or undulations.

Flake Terminations

The termination of an individual flake shows how force exited a nodule. Termination may be associated with the direction at which force was applied,

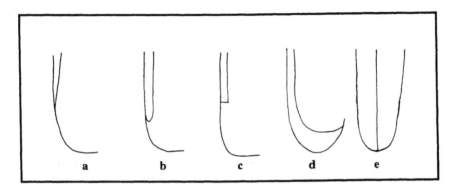

Figure 3.10.   Forms of flake termination: a) feather; b) hinge; c) step; d) outrepassé, or plunging; and e) axial.

qualities of the raw material, topographic irregularities on the outside of the core, and/or internal vugs or fractures. These categories are not mutually exclusive on an individual flake as more than one termination type may occur on an edge, but excessive ambiguity is usually not a problem and information derived from this variable is considerable.

In most cases, the type of outcome desired by a flintknapper is a flake with a *feather termination* in which a fracture propagating roughly parallel to the outside surface of the core gradually comes to meet it. This situation results in a flake possessing a relatively thin edge all around, as illustrated in Figure 3.10a. Any other outcome is usually considered undesirable, unless the knapper is engaged in bipolar reduction or for some reason wishes to remove the bottom of the core. The reason that other kinds of non-feather terminations such as hinge and step are undesirable is that they leave irregular topographic features on the surface of the core which, if not removed, induce subsequent flakes from the same striking platform to also terminate at that location before they can go any further. These subsequent removals increase the core's topographic irregularities to the point that it eventually becomes impossible to remove a long flake.

A *hinge fracture* occurs because the direction of force is deflected suddenly toward the outside of the core. This appears to be caused by an increase in the bending component and may be related to an excessive outward force applied to the stone (Crabtree 1968:466). The change in force direction is immediately preceded by a dramatic decrease in the velocity of crack propagation, which results from a loss of energy (Cotterell and Kamminga 1987:700-701). There is also a tendency for hinge terminations to be more prevalent on flatter surfaces. In this situation the propagating fracture front tends to spread out and increase in width, requiring more energy to sustain fracture. Thus the amount of force that produces a feather termination on a keeled surface might not be enough to produce a similarly feathered termination on a flat surface. As energy dissipates, the force path angles outward, resulting in a flake with a curved-over distal end, as illustrated in Figure 3.10b. This curving over, or retroflexion, is caused by instability in the crack path and is the most common type of finial on hinge-terminated flakes (Cotterell and Kamminga 1986).

Step terminations are flakes that have broken at the distal end (Figure 3.10c). They are caused either by a complete dissipation of energy or by the intersection of the fracture front with an internal crack or impurity. In either case, the energy necessary to drive the fracture forward is lost and bending forces perpendicular to the fracture front complete the removal of the flake. Occasionally, the fracture front will bypass the location at which bending occurs, resulting in an internal fracture in the core that extends past the termination of the departed flake.

Unless the distal end of a core contains a gibbosity or imperfection, a flint-knapper usually wishes to retain it in the interest of conserving useful material. Thus any flake that removes the bottom of a core is probably a mistake; however, such mistakes can provide substantial information on the constraints on technology faced by knappers who produced specific assemblages. A flake that does not exit the core on the near side but curves away to terminate on the opposite face (Figure 3.10d) is called *outrepassé, plunging,* or *reverse hinge* (Tixier 1974:19; Bonnichsen 1977:132). According to Cotterell and Kamminga (1987:701), the greatest influence promoting plunging terminations is the form of the distal end of the core. If the distal end is sharply rectangular, for example, stress at the corner is zero. Since cracks cannot propagate into areas of zero stress, the fracture front will tend to veer away from this zone, terminating on the opposite surface. The likelihood of plunging terminations can be increased by impacting the striking platform further away from the edge of the core.

A final termination type that can be helpful to archaeological interpretation is called *axial* (Figure 3.10e). It is most commonly associated with bipolar technologies and, when recognized in an assemblage, can be diagnostic of them. In this type of flake, fracture proceeds directly through the nodule to its opposite end, and often roughly bisects the nucleus (Cotterell and Kamminga 1987:699-700).

TYPES OF FLAKING AND FLAKERS

Percussion Flaking

To enable the effective analysis of lithic artifact collections, one must have comprehensive knowledge not only of what kinds of flakes were produced, but also of *how* they were produced. Posed as a query,

Q8: What types of stone knapping were practiced in prehistory?

This question is tightly circumscribed, as only a few ways exist to remove flakes from cores. The most energetic, known as *percussion flaking*, contains static and dynamic components, the latter imparting the energy needed to remove the flake. Dynamic force can be delivered in several ways, the most commonly practiced being *freehand percussion*. In this mode the nodule from which flakes are to be removed is held stable in one hand and may be supported on the ground or on one leg. The other hand holds the dynamic element that delivers the blow (Figure 3.11a; also illustrated in Whittaker 1994:94-95; Patten 1999:37).

The active element in percussion flaking may be another stone or a softer substance such as antler or wood. These materials differ from stone in density, resilience, toughness, strength and elasticity, qualities that can have a significant influence on the nature of the resulting flakes, or on whether or not flakes come off at all. Percussor variability is difficult to measure accurately from the resulting flakes, however, and for ease of reporting are often lumped into hard and soft. "Hard" percussors are stone, whereas "soft" percussors are bone, antler or hard wood (e.g., ironwood). Some discrimination between percussor types may be possible, as hard hammers tend to produce flakes with pronounced bulbs of percussion, whereas soft hammers frequently produce flakes with small bulbs or no bulb at all and a *lipping* or protrusion of the edge of the striking platform over its contact with the ventral surface (Crabtree 1970; Newcomer 1970; Henry et al. 1976). However, each percussor type can produce flakes characteristic of the other, and there is so much overlap that definitive statements on individual flakes are notoriously difficult to make (Mewhinney 1964; Hayden and Hutchings 1989).

Another problem resides in a gray area among percussor types. This area includes soft stone such as limestone, which may result in flakes consistent with either or both of those produced by stones such as granite and by antler or wood billets. Exactly how to categorize the products of soft stone percussors remains an issue that has never been adequately resolved.

The use of a freehand technique assumes that the knapper has enough of a core to hold onto. But anyone who has obliterated a thumb while bashing a nearly exhausted core knows that at some point it must be supported on the ground rather than in the hand. This point comes early in the process in regions in which the only available toolstone occurs in the form of small nodules. This point is supported by core studies in one region of the American West, where the average size of bipolar cores is substantially smaller than the average size of freehand cores on all sites on which the two types co-occur (Andrefsky 1994).

In these cases the most practical way to procure sharp-edged tools is through wedging initiations by placing the nodule on a hard surface and splitting it (Figure 3.11b). Kobayashi (1975) and Callahan (1987) have demonstrated

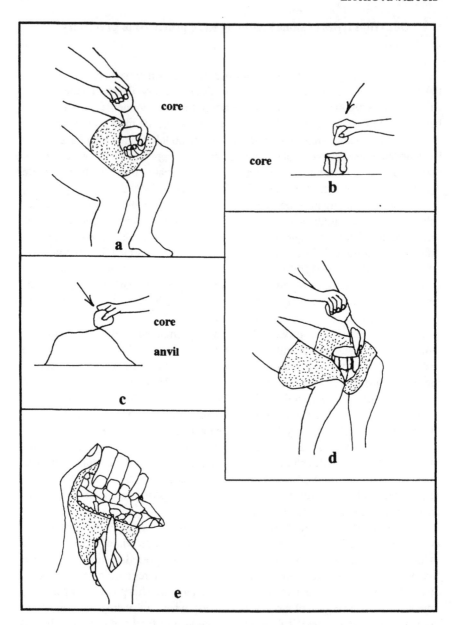

Figure 3.11. Ways by which flakes can be removed from a core: a) free-hand percussion; b) bipolar technique; c) anvil technique; d) punch technique, or indirect percussion; and e) pressure flaking.

effective strategies for reducing nodules by this method, called the *bipolar technique*. Archaeological signatures of the technique include opposing smashed surfaces, diffuse bulbs of percussion, and small-to-nonexistent striking platforms (Kooyman 2000:56). Unfortunately, these indicators are not present on every flake in a bipolar assemblage. So while blind testing of analysts has exhibited a high accuracy rate in discriminating freehand from bipolar industries at the assemblage level, accuracy on individual flakes has proven to be considerably lower (Jeske and Lurie 1993).

The percussion techniques described so far have assumed that the core remains mobile while the hammer or billet provides the dynamic energy, but the elements can also operate in the opposite way. That is, flakes can also be removed by making the core the active member and striking a blow at an appropriate location on a stationary block of stone (Figure 3.11c). Known as the *anvil* or *block-on-block technique* (Crabtree 1972:34-35; Shen and Wang 2000), this method is effective for removing large flakes but it lacks precision, since it is frequently difficult to strike the core at exactly the desired location. This use of the term *anvil technique*, while common, differs from other valid definitions. For example, Bordaz (1970:13-15) and Callahan (1987) envision an anvil as a hard lower support for a core, which is not placed directly under the force of impact in such a way as would induce wedging initiations.

Whereas the previously described techniques involve a direct blow from either the percussor or the core, it is also possible to employ a device intermediate between the two. Usually made of antler, wood or bone and called a *punch*, this device enables the knapper to control the precise spot that is to receive the force, which is transferred from the percussor through the punch into the body of the core (Figure 3.11d). This is a particularly useful technique in the production of prismatic blades, which require regularity and precision in the placement of each blow. Interestingly, there is no evidence for the use of indirect percussion before the Mesolithic (Inizan et al. 1992:61).

Pressure Flaking

The most common method for retouching and trimming flakes and blades is by pressure flaking (Figure 3.11e). In moderate latitudes the preferred pressure flaking tool among Aboriginal peoples was a bone or antler tine, though a copper-tipped dowel serves nicely among contemporary knappers. To remove a flake, the pressure flaker is placed on or just back of the edge, and pressure is applied inward and downward, using primarily the shoulder and upper arm (Whittaker 1994:129-133). This technique can also be employed for removing large flakes such as flutes on Paleoindian points (Boldurian et al. 1985; Sollberger 1985; Gryba 1988), and can be quite effective for producing regular blades (Binder 1984; Pelegrin 1984; Tixier 1984).

To support forces of this nature and produce a flake rather than just anni-
hilating the edge, thinner parts of the margin must be crushed or abraded away.
Results of this process are often still visible on pressure flaked portions of tools
and can provide evidence of the technique. These clues must also be understood
and factored out when observing tools for use-wear.

PRIMARY AND SECONDARY MODIFICATION

The topics discussed above have concentrated on the essential properties
of stone, the kinds of forces that interact to produce rupture, some characteristics of humanly fractured flakes, and the main types of flaking practiced by our
ancestors. The next logical step is to apply these principles to the technological
analysis of an archaeological assemblage. Unfortunately, this is exactly the juncture where the most gut-wrenching decisions are likely to be required, because
you must immediately decide what's in and what's out; that is, which stones are
worth analyzing and which are not even archaeological. Phrased as a research
question,

**Q9: How does one decide which pieces, or which portions of pieces, were
produced intentionally through human agency?**

There are actually two components to this question. The first involves
whether or not an individual piece came into existence as a product of human
manufacture, or whether it is a naturally flaked piece of rock. The second involves
modification of that piece subsequent to its manufacture. Secondary modification
is relevant to the basic question, because naturally flaked blanks may be just as
effective for tools as humanly flaked ones. That is, a natural, frost-fractured chert
blocky fragment whose edges have subsequently been flaked by humans is just as
valid an "artifact" as a prismatic blade that was produced by a human being from
the outset.

Primary Modification

The question of primary agency became an important archaeological issue in
the first two decades of the twentieth century with the "eolith" controversy alluded
to at the start of chapter 1. The issue concerned whether certain lithic assemblages
were comprised of actual artifacts that constituted evidence of early hominid activity in the area, or whether the objects had been made into pseudo-artifacts

through natural forces such as rock falls and solifluction. An uneasy truce was reached as protagonists became aware of the immense complexity of the issue, which depends for its resolution both on qualities of the individual piece and on the context in which the piece was found. By the 1930s, Alfred Barnes (1939) had gathered enough data to be able to propose a few characteristics commonly possessed by humanly struck flakes. Among these are regularity of secondary flaking and generally acute (<90°) edge angles (Barnes 1939). Barnes' research did not solve all the problems that habitually crop up, but it was the best response that could be offered at the time to an ambiguous situation, and by then most scholars were tired of the issue. Only limited work has been done on this issue since that time (see Patterson 1983; Schnurrenberger and Bryan 1985).

The flip side of the issue of discriminating humanly struck flakes, of course, is recognizing the cores from which they were produced. Most cores are chunky and rather thick. Individual removals on their surfaces tend to be large—as should be the case if the removals, rather than the core itself, were the objects of interest. Some cores are bipolar, with striking platforms on opposite ends; others are radial, the striking platforms extending around the core on both sides of a lateral margin much like a biface. Figure 3.12 illustrates three idealized core forms derived from indices of shape and location of striking platforms: *pyramidal, cylindrical,* and *radial.* Cores that do not conform to these or other idealized geometric forms are often termed *amorphous.*

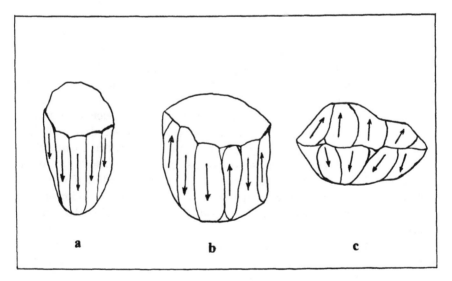

Figure 3.12. Three idealized core forms: a) single-platform pyramidal; b) opposed-platform cylindrical; c) radial.

Secondary Modification

Intentional Retouch

The second component of the human agency question concerns whether or not an individual piece was intentionally modified subsequent to its initial manufacture. *Modification* can be produced in two ways: through chipping, or removal of flakes from the edge(s) of the piece; or through abrasive forces such as grinding or polishing. In this section I will discuss only modification by chipping; abrasive modification will be addressed at the end of the chapter.

Distinguishing intentional modification is important for at least three reasons: 1) its presence on a natural blocky fragment enables the analyst to include the piece with other humanly produced artifacts; 2) the existence of secondary modification may indicate processes such as tool maintenance or recycling, which have important ramifications for the interpretation of the site as a whole; and 3) intentional secondary modification shows that a particular piece received greater attention (or cultural input) than similar non-modified pieces, justifying considering it in a special category. In much of North America, an assemblage of pieces bearing secondary modification have constituted a *type collection*, so called because the items in it are further classified into familiar types such as projectile point, drill, and graver.

Intentional modification by chipping for purposes of blunting, sharpening or shaping is known as *retouch*. Unfortunately, in my opinion, it is common archaeological parlance to include in the definition of this term any form of secondary modification whatsoever. By this latter definition, a piece can also be called retouched if it possesses use-wear or extraneous damage from prehistoric trampling, agricultural machines, excavation equipment, or rough treatment in a lab.

Defining the term so broadly is counterproductive, because it does not enable one to separate lithic artifacts by any criterion that is meaningful in a prehistoric sense. The principal reason for employing a term such as retouch, other than to distinguish curiosities, is to create a class of artifacts with enhanced cultural input, for the purpose of more effectively delineating the elements that connect these artifacts to humanity and that separate one type from another. Such classes constitute our principal database and must be derived from characteristics of prehistoric manufacture, not from damage that the stones received during utilization or from extraneous forces exerted after the piece had lain in the ground for hundreds of years. If the latter types of criteria are allowed to creep into the definition of retouch, then one is never sure what this class of objects represents—was an object an intentionally produced tool, or was it simply included on the basis of bone-chopping wear or the damage it incurred when it got in the way of a plow?

The creation of a category based on criteria of manufacture presupposes that the analyst can distinguish intentional retouch from other forms of damage. This can be difficult, as various studies have established similarities between intentional retouch and trampling by humans and animals, rock fall from cave walls, damage from agricultural equipment, insensitive curational policies, and other phenomena. But copping out by lumping pieces with different kinds of damage together will cause serious interpretive problems down the line. So the only real alternative is to develop your eye to the point that you can distinguish the different kinds of extraneous damage from one another, and especially from intentional modification. There is no better aid to recognition than experimentation—making your own tools, walking on a few of them, using others, putting a few out in a farmer's field (with her permission, of course)—then studying the resulting damage very carefully.

Experience has shown that certain forms of damage can be characterized by specific traits that commonly recur. I will enumerate some of the more useful of these below, but these comments are most effectively employed in concert with your own experimental series. It should also be kept in mind that these characteristics are gross generalizations; exceptions are easy to find. Specific types of tools and retouch will be illustrated with analyzed specimens from three typical sites of varying ages in eastern Oklahoma.

In the term *retouch* I include all forms of intentional secondary modification, from shaping with an antler billet to fine notching or trimming with a pressure flaker. This means that the term can include small, edge-limited fractures known as *marginal retouch*—removed, for example, for purposes of sharpening a blade knife (Figure 3.13b), blunting a scraper edge (Figure 3.13c), or refurbishing a drill (Figure 3.14a). The term also includes large removals employed in shaping a piece of stone, known as a *blank*, into a tool form. This can be done by reducing only one surface of the object, rendering a *unifacial* tool such as a scraper (Figure 3.13a; 3.14d, e) or graver (Figure 3.13g). However, most intensive tool shaping is conducted on opposing surfaces of a piece, resulting in *bifacial* reduction (Figure 3.14b, c; 3.15a). Common bifacial tools include projectile points, drills, axes, adzes, and generic oval, rectangular, or triangular forms called simply "bifaces."

The term "retouch" therefore captures any intentional modification to an artifact, from initial shaping through the maintenance and recycling of one tool form into another. This definition is inclusive for the practical reason that, at this stage, it makes no sense to distinguish different forms of modification from one another, although this will subsequently be necessary when putting the artifacts into type groups.

If retouch was intentional, then it logically follows that: 1) forces applied to the edge were within human capabilities; 2) the modification was inherently purposeful, though the underlying purpose may not be readily apparent; 3) it was probably performed with a relatively blunt instrument no sharper than an antler tine; and 4) basic forces of removal were perpendicular to the margin. The first consideration precludes certain types of extreme damage, particularly to obtuse or otherwise thick edges. Ramifications of underlying purposefulness of intent are

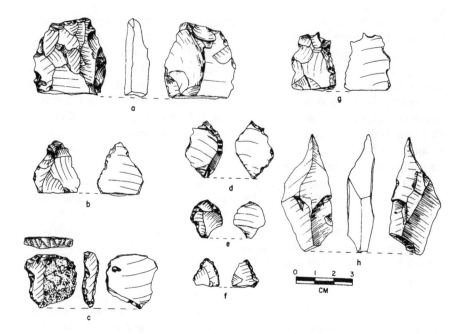

Figure 3.13. Artifacts from the Wilmoth site (34Ad-66), Adair County, OK: a) uniface on blocky fragment; b,d) retouched flakes; c,e,f) flake scrapers; g) graver on flake; h) unretouched blocky fragment. Taken from Odell-Vereecken and Odell (1988: Fig. 10).

that retouching was not conducted randomly but to achieve some purpose, whether that was to blunt, shape, or sharpen the piece. Achievement of any of these goals requires a certain regularization of the modified edge, as flakes are removed next to one another for at least part of that margin. By "regularization" I mean that the removals are usually contiguous and of roughly equal size, though they may be distributed bifacially. Use of a blunt instrument usually precludes ultra-sharp edges or notches, but produces localized crushing from the indenter. And the necessity for humans to create removals through pressures perpendicular to the margin largely disqualifies scars whose orientation is significantly directional toward either end.

Extraneous and Utilization Damage

Let us consider how other forms of damage usually (but not always) differ from intentional retouch. Nash (1993) discussed the effects of spalling from cave walls on artifacts deposited in the underlying sediments. To simulate this situation, he conducted experiments in dropping objects of varying weights and from varying heights onto clasts of jasper and tuff. Although the purpose of his paper

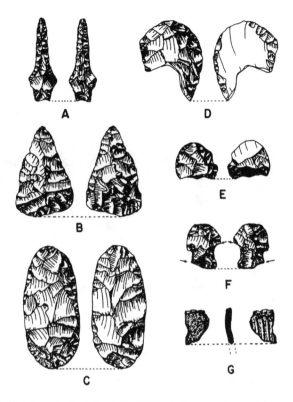

Figure 3.14.   Artifacts from the Duck Creek site (34Dl-52), Delaware County, OK: a) cross-based drill; b) bifacial axe; c) oval bifacial hoe; d) distolateral scraper fragment; e) thumbnail scraper; f) reworked hafted scraper; g) cord-marked potsherd. Taken from Gifford and Odell (1999: Fig. 5).

was to deliver a cautionary note, removals resulting from his experiments, shown here as Figure 3.16 (which supposedly are his best examples of natural forces producing retouch), exhibit patterns that are different from most intentional retouch. Removals are of different sizes; they are usually scattered about the edges rather than purposely placed; and where they are contiguous, they do not cover the entire edge, but leave certain parts unretouched. Excavation and laboratory damage also results in unpatterned and relatively random fractures, though more documentation and analysis of this kind of damage needs to be done (Gero 1978).

Trampling experiments have yielded similar results. The effects of trampling by cows on pieces of glass around a stock tank were recorded by Knudson (1979). A typical assortment of these pieces shows a lot of scarring on the edges, as one might expect with glass. The overall impression is one of random scar distribution and clusters of different-sized removals. The best candidates for intentional retouch are also those edges that logically would have been most affected by

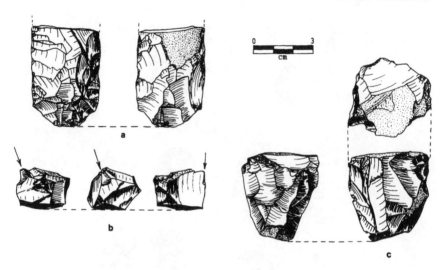

Figure 3.15.   Secondarily modified objects from the Day site (34Wg-171), Wagoner County, OK: a) stage 1 biface; b) burin on blocky fragment; c) pyramidal flake core. Taken from Odell and Vereecken-Odell (1989: Fig. 10).

casual contact such as the downward-curving edge of the piece illustrated in Figure 3.17d.

Trampling by human beings presents a similar range of edge damage. Several recent experimental series agree that human trampling can produce damage that appears very similar to intentional retouch. Important determinants of the amount and distribution of damage are edge angle and the substrate on which the stones lay, pieces on clayey soils being damaged to a greater extent than pieces on sandy soils (Flenniken and Haggerty 1979; Gifford-Gonzalez et al. 1985; Pryor 1988; Nielsen 1991; McBrearty et al. 1998). Contrary to the findings of Tringham et al. (1974), damage does not necessarily occur on surfaces opposite the trample, nor are individual scars necessarily elongated. However, scars do appear to be sparsely distributed along edges in most cases. Nielsen (1991:500) concluded that:

> Most pieces show one to three isolated scars randomly distributed along the edges, regardless of their angle. They originate on either surface and no distinctive shape or size could be identified, except for a trend of larger scars to occur on steeper edges. However, six or seven pieces from the dry-trampled assemblages depart from this general trend. They show rows of continuous parallel scars along one or more edges that could be mistaken easily for intentional retouch.

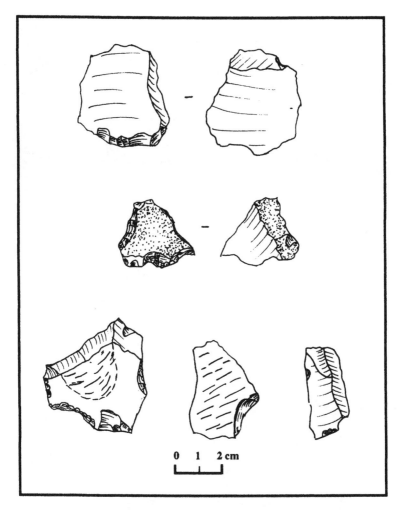

Figure 3.16. "Retouch" produced in spalling experiments. Re-drawn from Nash (1993: Fig. 3).

So it is obvious that an analyst may misinterpret some specimens and must be continually aware of this type of damage. Trampled flakes have been observed to possess "scuff marks" (striations and abrasive tracks), particularly on dorsal ridges and protruding bulbs of percussion, and this evidence may help discriminate particularly difficult cases (Shea and Klenck 1993; McBrearty et al. 1998:124).

Damage from agricultural equipment has been amply recorded by Prost (1988) and Mallouf (1981). The flakes from Mallouf's Brookeen Creek Cache in

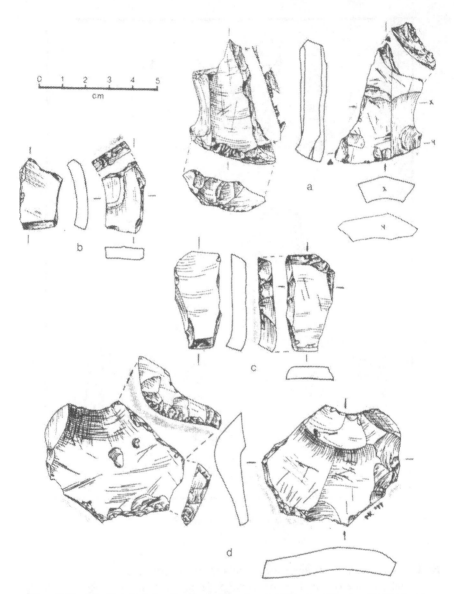

Figure 3.17. "Bovifacts" of glass found around stock tank. Taken from Knudson (1979: Fig. 2).

northeastern Texas were severely damaged by plowing in a dense, clayey substrate. The author identified several damage types from which I will emphasize a few salient characteristics that distinguish plow removals from intentional retouch. One is the general irregularity of the scarring, which does not appear purposeful in most instances. A second is the nature of the frequent notches produced when the steel plow blade penetrated the flint. These notches, as well as other portions of the edge, may retain metal surficial residues, which are inclined to rust to a brown color in the presence of water. Notches tend to be V-shaped, sharp-edged, and occasionally possessing unidirectional scarring. Crushing features that are usually present on retouched margins, caused by blunt indenters such as antler tines, are typically absent. Breakage is frequent in agricultural situations, but breakage types do not tend to be very diagnostic. An experiment that illustrates some of these features with greater specificity is described in Box 3.2.

Box 3.2. Experimenal Plow Damage

Characteristic plow damage features were produced abundantly in a series of experiments that Frank Cowan and I conducted several years ago to investigate the effects of tillage on artifacts in the plow zone (Odell and Cowan 1987). In those experiments, 1000 flakes and retouched tools were painted blue, labeled, planted at regular intervals under the surface of a field, and subjected to 12 episodes of plowing and disking. The blue paint made the pieces easy to recognize in the field and had the added advantage of rendering plow/disk damage unambiguous, because it scraped off the paint.

A continuously recurring feature of this damage is the presence of a sharp notch, shown in Figure 3.18. This notch was produced by the steel blade at its deepest penetration into the interior

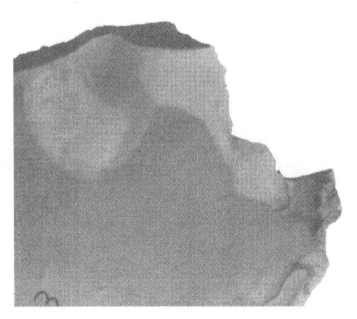

Figure 3.18.   Sharp V-shaped notch and contiguous fractures resulting from plowing and/or disking.

of the flake. At this point the flake probably rotated away from the blade, causing a row of small fractures next to the notch. Not only is the notch itself sharp and V-shaped, but the portions of the edge on either side of the notch, though fractured on one surface, are sharp on the other. The margin shows little of the crushing that one would expect had a blunt indenter such as an antler tine been used intentionally to remove retouch flakes.

Similar phenomena can be recognized on Flake #193, photographed in Figures 3.19 and 3.20. In this case the steel plow blade contacted the flake at the upper left of Figure 3.19, then raked across the edge, removing a contiguous row of fractures in the form of a rounded notch. The movement of the plow blade relative to the piece itself can be deduced from the removals in the right-hand portion of the notch. These terminate at right angles to the edge and show that dominant plow movement occurred from left to right. The scars isolated here could not have been produced by intentional retouching, which would have removed flakes in a direction toward the interior of the piece, resulting in fracture terminations roughly parallel to the edge. Again, the entire margin of this plow-induced notch is sharp, i.e., not blunted or crushed by the intentional removal of individual flakes by a pressure flaker. The sharp edge of the notch can be seen best by inspecting the opposite side (Figure 3.20), though in this case edge sharpness is masked in the photo, because the plow also chipped a little of the paint off the opposite surface.

Figure 3.19.   Shallow notch and directional scarring produced by plowing and/or disking.

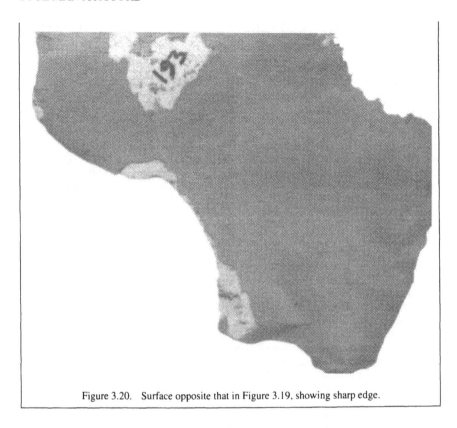

Figure 3.20.   Surface opposite that in Figure 3.19, showing sharp edge.

Diagnostic characteristics described above are generalities and need to be operationalized through experimentation and experience. They also do not work in every case, as ambiguities always exist. Yet it is worth putting some time into your ability to discriminate among these forms of damage, because this is the juncture at which your most basic decisions as a lithic analyst are likely to be made. On these decisions hang the nature of the statistical population that you will be working with and conceivably taking samples from, as well as the basis for whatever typological system you use. Thus being able to discriminate various types of damage is crucial. Variability in retouch types is discussed in Box 3.3.

To sum up, chipped stone tool manufacture is all about force and stress. At this level, the subject is closer to engineering than to archaeology—an aspect that has probably frightened away many an aspiring lithic analyst. This is a pity, but a prospective analyst must make a concerted effort to understand these forces because, unless they are comprehended at the individual level, one will never be able to make sense of them in the aggregate. It helps to anchor the abstractions discussed in this chapter in a sea of practicality by picking up some flint and attempting to recreate the forms one encounters in the archaeological record.

Box 3.3. Retouch Recipes

Shortly after you have made the initial decision that a specific object has been retouched, you will be forced to evaluate what *kind* of retouch it is. Retouch on lithic artifacts can be classified into three basic types. The first is *marginal* or *edge retouch*, in which the margin itself is the focus of the modification. A margin may be blunted for holding in the hand; shaped for hafting or utilization; or sharpened if dull. Such modification is confined to the edge itself, pressure usually having been applied perpendicular to the lateral margin. Removals rarely exceed a length of 5–8mm. Typed objects with this kind of retouch include scrapers, gravers and, for objects without a unique form, generic retouched pieces or retouched flakes. Typical examples from Oklahoma are illustrated in Figure 3.13b–g.

A different type of edge retouch is characterized not by a row of contiguous removals along a lateral margin, but by a minimal number of blows (usually 1–3) delivered to a corner or oriented perpendicular to the plane of the piece itself. The principal objective of this maneuver is to produce a stout but sharp projection capable of inscribing hard materials such as bone, antler, and cave walls. Known predominantly from the European Upper Paleolithic period, this technique is loosely termed *burination* and the resulting tool is called a *burin*. An example of a corner-struck burin from an Archaic context in eastern Oklahoma is presented in Figure 3.15b.

A second type of modification is *invasive retouch*, in which individual removals cover a significant portion, if not all, of the interior of the piece. Removals normally extend to the middle of the artifact, a trait that can occur only if the piece is not "humped" or overly thick. Objects with this kind of retouch tend to be relatively thin, and both unifacial and bifacial examples are common. Many bifacial thinning flakes were utilized as tools by our predecessors, and in some cases were removed for this purpose from the bifaces, which also served as cores in a mobile tool kit (Kelly 1988). Other goals of bifacial reduction were to sharpen dull edges and to modify the form of the tool by recycling it into another activity. Projectile points, drills, axes, hoes, hafted scrapers, and other tool types were created by this technique (see Figures 3.13a; 3.14a–f; 3.15a).

A third type of retouch occurs in the process of *core reduction*. The primary purpose of core reduction is the production of flakes to be used as tools, leaving the parent core unused or utilized expediently subsequent to functioning as a core (see Figure 3.15c). Although most archaeologists would not call these removals "retouch," I mention them here because the flakes removed from the surfaces of cores constitute secondary modification, just as the small flakes taken off the end of a scraper do. To ignore this fact would be illogical and self-deceiving. To avoid terminological confusion, removals from a core should be called "retouch" only if part of that core's periphery is shaped or otherwise modified in a manner inconsistent with its primary function as purveyor of usable flakes.

GROUND STONE

Ground stone tools are distinguished from chipped stone in having been modified through abrasive, as opposed to percussive, forces. Useful manuals for ground stone analysis, which delve into detail not possible in this manual, have been written by Jenny Adams (1997, 2002).

As used in archaeological parlance, the term "ground stone" is confusing, because it refers to two distinctly different processes. On the one hand, it includes specimens that have been shaped to a specific form, like an axe or a pipe bowl. In this case, abrasion was a manufacturing technique for the purpose of producing an object of a specific size and shape. On the other hand, the term also includes specimens that were used to grind other materials, such as maize, wheat or pigment. These specimens, which include manos, metates, mortars and pestles, existed for processing other substances and, in many cases, their specific form was not crucial for performing their primary function. For purposes of this discussion, I will refer to these objects as *manufacture-ground* and *use-ground*. We can pursue this topic as a general research question formulated as follows:

Q10: How can manufacture- and use-ground objects be distinguished and studied?

Manufacture-Ground Specimens

We know from clues on extant ancient artifacts that prehistoric people made a variety of manufacture-ground objects. These ranged from soapstone vessels to pendants, beads and other ornaments, to utilitarian tools such as axes and adzes. The initial shaping of such an object was often accompanied by chipping, especially if the tool was made of flint. Chipped axes and adzes were frequently ground extensively on their bit in order to straighten and strengthen a sinuous chopping edge (see Figure 3.21). Igneous and metamorphic stones were more effectively pecked into shape, then ground. Often such an implement retains evidence of pecking on its butt end, a roughening that undoubtedly rendered the axehead more secure in its hafting device (see Figure 3.22).

Unfortunately, ethnographic accounts of the production of these tools is very difficult to find because, at least for the more utilitarian of them, new technologies quickly drove the old ones to extinction. In the case of soapstone vessels, pottery technology rang a clear death knoll. For example, in New England stone bowl quarries such as Horne Hill, Oaklawn and Bakerville (Fowler 1966, 1967; Neshko 1969–70) appear to have been used most intensively during the Late Archaic period. Radiocarbon dating suggests that the advent of pottery did not suddenly curtail stone bowl manufacture, which continued into the Ceramic Period, but it certainly affected, and ultimately halted altogether, the activity in these quarries. The replacement of ground stone adzes and axes in Oceania by steel was also rapid, because steel axes were considerably more efficient than stone ones (Sillitoe 2000:59).

To understand the essential principles of manufacture grinding, let us refer to one of the rare written accounts of the production of a ground stone axe—a technology practiced by the Héta Indians of Brazil, a cultural entity that no longer

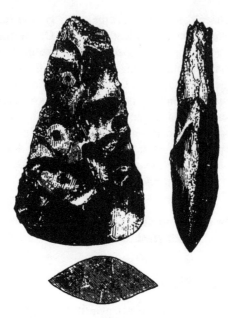

Figure 3.21.   Chipped flint axe with ground bit from Sawdon, North Yorkshire, England. Taken from
Evans (1897: Fig. 33).

exists (Kozák 1972). The Héta traditionally manufactured a long, ovoid axe-head
with a finely ground bit, oval in cross-section, that was forced into a wooden handle
without the addition of mastic. A nomadic, hunting-gathering people, they used
the axe to cut saplings for their houses and for a variety of other tasks. Like similar
peoples throughout the world, the Héta readily embraced metal tools when they
became available, and were somewhat puzzled by ethnographer Vladimir Kozák's
request to produce a stone axe-head several years after these tools had gone out of
use. Their reaction is not difficult to understand since, under favorable conditions
and applying themselves continually to the task, it would take a man 3–5 days to
produce the axe-head alone (the production of Kozák's example was interrupted
and took 7 months).

The first step in the production process was to choose an appropriate stone,
a hard, unflawed river cobble of a size and shape (an elongated ovoid) not much
larger than the intended finished item. Placing the cobble between his feet, the
craftsman proceeded to peck the stone into shape very carefully for fear of breaking
the piece. Kozák (1972:19) noted that, "No chips or flakes came off during the
pecking, only fine granules." Such work continued for days until the axe-head
acquired its determined shape, at which point the craftsman brought in a large
sandstone cobble and a container filled with water and white clay. The worker
would dip the pecked stone into the clay-water solution, then rub it onto the

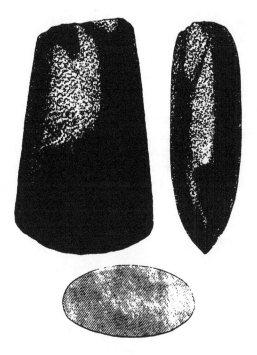

Figure 3.22.   Greenstone axehead from Bridlington, England, that was ground on its bit but retains evidence of manufacture pecking on its butt end. Taken from Evans (1897: Fig. 74).

sandstone abrader. This process allowed the Héta to both grind and polish the axe at the same time. The end product was a symmetrical ungrooved axe-head—a celt, in archaeological parlance—that was ground and polished near the bit. The butt end was left unground for its eventual insertion into the wooden handle, which required an additional half-day to manufacture.

The Héta was one of four tribes in Amazonia found, by the mid-1970s, to have recently employed axes of stone. Not all were hunting-gathering people and, among agriculturalists, these tools acquired considerable importance in the task of clearing garden plots. Felling a tree with one of these tools was arduous; it would take a man 6 hours to fell a tree about 30 cm in diameter (Carneiro 1974). Ethnographic experimentation suggests that it took 7–8 times longer to clear a patch in a forest using a stone axe than using a steel one (Carneiro 1979). This is a substantially greater differential than the steel:stone efficiency ratio of 1.4:1 that Sillitoe (1979) worked out for the Wola, shifting cultivators of the southern Papua New Guinea Highlands. Despite disparities in efficiency differential, however, all relevant comparative studies of Aboriginal axe use have indicted that steel axes are substantially more efficient than stone ones.

The Amazonian example provides a suitable model for our purposes because it is authentic and detailed, and it encompasses many of the processes whose remnants have been encountered among archaeological artifacts. But not all: craftsmen in other parts of the world occasionally roughed out their blanks not by pecking but by chipping, a technique recorded, for example, for the Anga of the eastern fringe of the New Guinea Highlands (Sillitoe 1998:115). Variation can also be noted in the kinds of abrasives employed in grinding and polishing, as well as in the sequence of these activities. I suspect that the same kinds of processes witnessed in the manufacture of ground stone adzes and axes, where some ethnographic evidence exists, also occurred in the manufacture of pipes, ornaments, bowls, and other manufacture-ground objects for which the lack of ethnographic accounts is virtually absolute.

Use-Ground Specimens

Grinding and pounding of most organic or soft inorganic substances can be accomplished with a few simple kinds of tools, and these tend to recur wherever such activities were practiced. Since processing of this nature frequently requires the action of one stone against another, these tools were often used in pairs. One of the most common of these pairs consists of a large, stationary basal stone that sits on the ground or a table and a smaller, active stone held in the hand(s). These have different names depending on their geographic location: the stationary stone is known as a *millstone*, *saddle-quern* or, in many New World locales, a *metate*; the smaller, hand-held counterpart is a *handstone* or *mano* (Figure 3.23). The handstone was drawn over the millstone in either a back-and-forth or rotary motion, and the pair was used for grinding starchy foodstuffs such as maize or

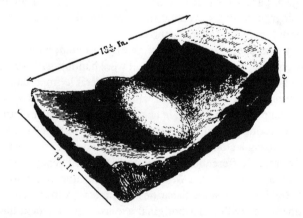

Figure 3.23.   Grinding stones from Holyhead, England. Taken from Evans (1897: Fig. 170).

Figure 3.24.   Quartz pebble from Bridlington, England, used as a grinding stone and in which a deep depression has been pecked. Taken from Evans (1897: Fig. 164).

grain; hides for removal of adhering tissue; inorganic chunks such as stone or old pottery for ceramic tempering material; or minerals for pigment (Nelson and Lippmeier 1993).

Grinding stones and other objects made from igneous and metamorphic substances have been found with depressions pecked into their surfaces, as in Figure 3.24. Artifacts with this type of utilization trace have been recovered from sites representing a large variety of subsistence and economic practices. The most prevalent explanation for their existence is their proposed use for cracking open nuts—hence their name, *nutting stones*. Given the lack of experimental and ethnographic information on this issue, this proposal, though reasonable, remains hypothetical.

Another pair of tools used in the processing of materials was the mortar and pestle. The *mortar* is the concave receptacle that receives the material to be processed, which is usually crushed by the pestle, a cylindrical pounding tool. The distinguishing feature of the mortar is its concavity, which may be shallow or deep. Presumably the concavity of a stone mortar began as a natural depression or was initially pecked into a rock before it was used for processing. The concavity tends to become deeper with use, and some are as deep as a person's arm. The mortar can be a separate, portable substance or can be pecked into the bedrock, in which case it is known as a *bedrock mortar*; or, of course, it can be made of some other substance altogether (e.g., wood).

Schneider (1996) has classified these tools into "bowl-like" and "hopper" mortars, the latter consisting of a shallow depression to which a bottomless basket was attached, the basket acting as the walls of the receptacle. There is a paucity of ethnographic information on the manufacture and use of mortars, a situation that induced Osborne (1998) to replicate a stone mortar experimentally. It took him 8 hours to peck a suitable concavity in a slab of granite—a beginning in the quest for calculating manufacture time, concavity volume, and other parameters.

The *pestle* is the cylindrical pounding tool used to crush the substance contained in the mortar. Like mortars, ethnographic descriptions of the manufacture and use of pestles are few and far between, but Wilke and Quintero (1996) have replicated the manufacture of an andesite pestle by percussion flaking the preform and pecking it into final shape. Their experiment can be used to establish preferred techniques, production times, etc. We should be aware that, although pestles were cylindrical tools, not all cylindrical tools were pestles. Basalt cylindrical tools from the American Southwest were tested by Kamp (1995) in a number of activities, including working wood and removing corn kernels. Her closest fit to the wear on prehistoric specimens was in the smoothing of a clay pot.

There may be a tendency among certain lithic analysts to suffer from a sort of lithic myopia, believing that, since stone tools are so ubiquitous on archaeological sites, they must have been the implement of choice for every need. Yet from time to time experimentation shows stone to be inferior to other media for certain tasks. One such experimental series involved the most effective means for early Neolithic Europeans to have dehusked glume wheats such as einkorn, emmer and spelt. Comparing two viable options—a stone saddle quern and a wooden mortar—Meurers-Balke and Luning (1992) established the clear superiority of the wooden prototype on a number of parameters.

Analyzing Ground Stone Tools

Determining Human Grinding Modification

The first step in analyzing a ground stone tool must be the identification of a ground surface. The salient characteristic of such a surface, whether manufacture- or use-ground, is that it is flattened, i.e., the microtopography is reduced such that the tops of all projecting parts on that surface are on the same plane. In many cases this quality can be ascertained through visual or tactile means, as most ground surfaces feel smoother than areas around them. This is a very inexact measure, as patina, stream rolling, raw material characteristics, and other elements can produce smooth surfaces whose tactile and visual qualities are not noticeably different from those produced by grinding. Shining light at a low angle to the surface can often highlight features, such as striations, produced by grinding. Microscopic techniques should be employed at this stage to search for evidence of modification.

Once the existence of grinding has been affirmed, its origin must be determined. Strict rules cannot be applied here, as both manufacture- and use-grinding can take a myriad of forms, but some directionality to the constituent striae is usually evident. That is, in both manufacture and use contexts, motions tend to be purposeful, whether grinding wheat in a rotary orientation or sharpening an axe blade by abrading its edge uniformly in one direction. Some work has also been accomplished by studying the hammers that rejuvenated these implements and their debris, a subject covered in Box 3.4.

Box 3.4. Milling Stone Rejuvenation

Milling stones are abrasive media, their effectiveness being achieved through topographic differences as the two tool surfaces are rubbed together. With use, the interstices between topographic highs become filled with the material being ground and with portions of the surface itself through attrition. To maintain grinding efficiency, milling stones require frequent rejuvenation to clean out the interstices and re-establish surface relief, a task that is usually accomplished by pecking with a hammer.

Millingstone Horizon sites in California often contain an abundance of hammers, suggesting that at least some of them were milling stone rejuvenators. Pritchard-Parker and Torres (1998) conducted a series of experiments and blind tests to evaluate whether or not an analyst could accurately determine that millingstone rejuvenation had occurred on a site from analysis of the hammers and the larger spalls, or debitage, removed from the hammers through this activity. Their relative success provides a basis for some optimism for future studies of milling stone rejuvenation.

General Classification

From these observations one should be able to categorize a tool into one or a combination of manufacture- or use-ground categories. These categories are not universal, but are regionally specific and should be defined in classificatory systems particular to the locality in which these artifacts occur. If classification systems do not exist for your region or the ground stone types are poorly defined, you will have to fill these gaps yourself.

The purpose of manufacture-grinding is to produce an implement of a particular shape; therefore, morphological indices are most useful in categorizing these tools. Within a type, specific attributes of shape or of manufacture are used to characterize subtypes. For instance, in a typology developed for west-central Illinois (Odell 1996: Appendix A, pp. 385–390), the ground stone axe is defined on its "symmetrically bevelled bit with planar or convex sides." Subtypes include the chisel and expanding-bit axe, defined on the basis of formal attributes; and the three-quarter and fully grooved axe, defined on the basis of its hafting modification.

In contrast, the purpose of use-grinding is not to shape the tool, but to process material extraneous to the piece itself; therefore, tool form is not as important for characterization as features of its grinding surfaces. Type designations for these kinds of tools subsume this functionality and emphasize processing surface over tool shape. Thus a mano is an implement defined on its possession of a processing surface. Subtypes can consist of the possession of one or more than one grinding surface (e.g., a bifacial mano), or specific kinds of use-modification (e.g., pitting or battering). For example, a specific mano might be subtyped as "unifacial, multi-pitted, and edge-battered." In regions where specific forms of use-ground tools were made, these can be useful in constructing a typology.

The Illinois typological system contains 30 or more ground stone types and includes such diverse entities as bannerstones, abraders, beads and gorgets. For most prehistoric assemblages, however, most of these types are never encountered. I invoke the Illinois system because I am used to it and it is typical of ground stone typological systems employed in regions of moderate climatic conditions. It is employed here for illustrative purposes only, since each region should have its own lithic typology.

Description and Analysis

At some point before real analysis begins—ideally before the objects are classified—it is a good idea to make sure that the assemblage contains specimens that are as complete as possible. Although the discovery of large-scale breakage of these generally massive pieces of stone appears somewhat counter-intuitive, some sites provide intriguing possibilities for piece refitting. In fact, there exist settlements on which large ground stone implements were apparently intentionally broken into smaller pieces. Such a situation occurred at the Lasley Vore site, a protohistoric Wichita settlement in Oklahoma that was occupied during at least part of the period between the first European contact in 1719 and the evacuation of the tribe from the region around 1750 (Odell 2002). One pit feature at the site contained metate fragments that were refitted to form all or part of at least three large grinding slabs.

Classification systems such as the one discussed above provide information on the types of ground stone implements present and their frequencies. For some types of analysis, this may be as detailed as the situation warrants, but frequently individual artifacts must be described and/or analyzed for a report. In this case it is informative to provide general characteristics of shape, raw material, and any special features or anomalies the piece may possess. Length, width, and thickness measurements can be taken with calipers or a tape measure. The grinding surface of a metate is usually concave; one can measure the depth of this concavity by extending a straightedge from one side to the other, then lowering a ruler down to the point of greatest concavity. The curvature of manos, abraders, hammerstones, pecked stones, or other rounded or chunky pieces can be measured with the aid of a copy cat or flexible rule (see Schneider 1996 for illustrations).

Further analysis usually requires inspecting the surfaces of the implements for traces of manufacture and/or use. Ground stone that was shaped to a specific form frequently contains evidence of manufacture through pecking or flaking, damage that is usually more robust than any use-wear on the piece. This kind of manufacture evidence is useful for discriminating specific methods, and sometimes stages, of fabrication.

Box 3.5. Grinding Efficiency, Intensity, Use-Life

Use-ground implements acquired consummate importance in Neolithic-type settings in arid lands such as the Levant and the American Southwest. Archaeologists working in these regions have been able to explore a wide range of ground stone types and behavioral concepts. For example, Adams (1993) was concerned with the evolution of grinding efficiency and intensity in relatively sedentary societies of southwestern North America. Testing basin, trough and flat metate/mano sets, she found that efficiency was related to user fatigue and to grinding surface area. Over time, a need for more grinding intensity induced an increase in the employment of the flat metate-mano set, a strategy that reduced user fatigue and increased grinding area.

Grinding area was also studied by Hard et al. (1996), who noticed that the grinding surfaces of manos and metates, which had remained constant in size through thousands of years of foraging, suddenly became dramatically larger with the advent of maize. The authors demonstrated a positive correlation between the overall size of grinding surfaces and maize dependence as exhibited in macrobotanical and coprolite samples and stable carbon isotopes. Although the timing of the transition to maize dependence varied from region to region, the process occurred throughout the American Southwest; for example, there was substantial dependence on maize in southern Arizona by 500 BC. Likewise, Morris (1990) demonstrated a correlation between the replacement of one-hand by two-hand (i.e., larger) manos and an increase in both maize dependency and sedentary lifestyles.

Pre-eminent functional models have also been recently examined and found wanting. Stone (1994), for instance, addressed the conventional wisdom that assemblages dominated by basin metates and small manos were employed in grinding seeds, and those dominated by trough or slab metates and long manos were used for grinding corn. Instead, because of transportation costs, she showed a tendency for manos and metates of nonlocal origin to have been smaller, more heavily used, and more formally shaped. In other words, raw material affects conventional efficiency models to such an extent that such models should all be re-examined in this light.

Rather than concentrating on size, shape or nature of grinding surfaces, Wright (1993) studied working time and loss of tool material caused by the utilization of a replicated trough metate and two-hand mano. From these data she was able to calculate rates of wear, which can ultimately be translated into estimates of tool use-life. These estimates are of considerable importance in evaluating the kind and amount of food processing accomplished in a prehistoric kitchen.

The study of use-modification can sometimes be conducted by low-angled light and hand lens without the aid of a microscope; in fact, it is sometimes necessary to proceed in this manner if a particular piece is too large to fit under the microscope. As mentioned previously, surface scratches are most helpful in determining direction of working motion. Polish indicators may provide some information on the specific material processed, though use-wear analysis of these sorts of tools has not progressed very far (Hamon 2003). Materials from which ground stone tools were made—such as quartzite, granite, and andesite—possess qualities different from chert, and it is a good working assumption that their

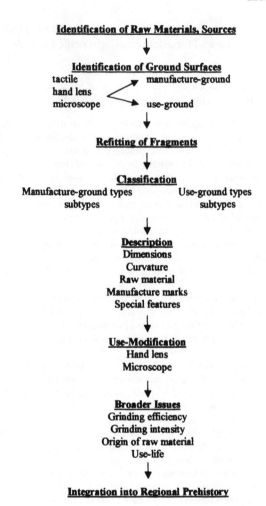

Figure 3.25.   A schematic sequence for analyzing ground stone tools.

use-polish characteristics are also different. Not enough research into this area has yet been accomplished for an analyst to be able to accurately discriminate use-polish on any of these materials. In addition, grinding surfaces are often discontinuous—indeed, they are kept that way by occasionally pecking the grinding surface, a process that makes the surface more abrasive and increases the implement's effectiveness. Whatever use-polish survives the pecking occurs only on the tops of this rugged topography, rendering the polish as discontinuous as the surface itself and therefore difficult to interpret.

   If variables such as those discussed previously have been recorded for a number of archaeological sites in a region, they can be employed to resolve broader issues of human settlement and subsistence. Analyses of ground stone can contribute to our understanding of the technological and cultural processes involved in the activities with which they are associated. As explained in Box 3.5, the grinding of maize using a mano and metate is long, arduous labor. Comprehension of the elements involved in making this process more efficient or in being able to process greater quantities of food are essential for comprehending the impact of the technology on the society in which it was used.

Once these technology-based issues are understood, this knowledge can be integrated into behavioral accounts and reconstructions of culture history. Such reconstructions can contribute to understanding the relations between ground stone technologies and environmental factors such as the availability of resources, a topic probed more deeply in Box 3.6. A suggested sequence of analysis of ground stone, from the identification of ground surfaces through the integration of this knowledge into regional prehistory, is presented in Figure 3.25.

Box 3.6. Ground Stone and Resource Stress

The prehistoric processing of food, hides and inorganic substances is important to record simply for the purpose of understanding the full range of activities in which these groups were engaged. But on a general level, this information may provide clues to some of the conditions faced by the groups that employed these implements. For example, throughout the Natufian culture of the Levant, populations grew, mobility decreased, and exploitative territory was reduced. Under such conditions, Natufian groups undoubtedly experienced stress caused by increased demands on a shrinking resource base. People became broad-based foragers and began to use resources that they had previously avoided or consumed in low quantities. Such a resource was seeds, which were processed with milling equipment. In fact, Wright (1994) recognized an association between the presence of grinding tools and camps where seeds were heavily consumed. In this case, study of the ground stone helped establish a trend toward an intensification of labor in plant processing from the early Natufian onward.

A similar situation occurred in southeastern Australia, where investigators of the Cuddie Springs site have excavated grinding stones going back 30,000 years (Fullagar and Field 1997). Use-wear analysis on these stones documented utilization damage consistent with grinding starchy and siliceous plants or seeds, and studies of phytoliths revealed the presence of grasses. In Australia, seed grinding is associated ethnographically with arid zones. Prehistorically we know that a period of general aridity in this region began around 30,000 years ago. This situation induced human occupants to pursue a broader spectrum diet in which lower-ranked resources such as seeds were utilized increasingly, while the exploitation of higher-ranked megafauna declined. This relationship was shown clearly in the use and relative quantities of stone grinding equipment.

Chapter 4

Assemblage Variability

The purpose of Chapter 3 was to impart a sense of the forces involved in rock fracture, the most elemental event in the production of stone tools, and to isolate certain distinguishing characteristics that result from that event. This subject forms the basis for all of lithic analysis; however, projects and problems are not presented to a lithic analyst as individual entities, but in the aggregate. That is, stones come to archaeologists in bunches of associated objects—this is partly how we recognize that they were humanly produced in the first place. The trick is not in ascertaining what each individual object means, though that would be helpful, but in deriving meaningful relationships among artifacts and in the assemblage as a whole. The purpose of this chapter is to discuss the principal methods used to make sense of lithic aggregates; some common terms are defined in Box 4.1.

Box 4.1. Definitions

Attribute: an observable and definable trait. Although used in a general sense, it is also employed to depict qualities of a larger entity called a "variable." For example, the variable *striking platform modification* can have attributes of *uniplanar, abraded, faceted*, and so forth.

Classification: an ordering of material, usually into a smaller quantity of subsets using specific criteria for inclusion. Although a typology is a system of classification, not all classification systems involve the ordering of objects into types.

Trajectory: specific production system employed by tool makers of a particular cultural group.

Type: a cluster of attributes of an individual piece that occurs together in the same group of artifacts. Types may be defined on morphological, stylistic, technological, functional, or any other consistent set of parameters.

Typology: a regional series of types involving one material class.

Variable: in statistical parlance, a trait that includes a specific subset of attributes, which can be discrete (nominal), ordinal, interval or ratio in form.

It is assumed here that the artifacts that comprise a lithic assemblage to be studied are genuinely associated. That is, issues of context, disturbance, and transformation (see Schiffer 1976) have been resolved before they are considered for analysis. If this is not the case, then you do not have a real assemblage in the traditional sense, and should seriously evaluate the integrity of the collection.

Most lithic assemblages, when randomly spread out on a table, show a be-wildering array of formal variability. Although most of the objects in modern excavated assemblages are usually flakes, shape alone does not impart that in-formation. To figure out what is represented in the collection, each item must be considered individually, or the collection must be selected in such a manner that the sample is representative of the entire assemblage. Most of the objects prob-ably look like "waste" in the pursuit of a loftier goal, and other items appear to have been part of a planned strategy, the culmination of whatever was trying to be achieved. Look at a beautiful North American Archaic dart point or an Upper Paleolithic backed bladelet, and you get the impression that that was the intended end product of the entire lithic industry, the rest of the lowly flakes and shatter being mere byproducts of this process. Disavow yourself immediately of these impulses, because you are probably spectacularly wrong.

DETECTING VECTORS OF INFORMATION

There is no doubt that prehistoric artisans had specific goals, or mental templates, in mind when they manufactured certain tool types—a point made by Spaulding (1953, 1954) in his debate with Ford (1954a, b) about the nature of artifact classifications. But these were not the only goals. Ethnographic studies (White 1967; Gould et al. 1971; Hayden 1977) and lithic use-wear analysis (Wylie 1975; Odell 1981b; Lewenstein 1987; Yerkes 1987:128-129) have demonstrated repeatedly that lithic implements on most habitation sites of less technologically advanced people were employed for a substantial variety of tasks, and that the tools used for those tasks involved a wide range of forms and technologies, including unretouched "waste." So it is a mistake to perceive of a lithic tool assemblage only in terms of the manufacture of a few obvious tool types; the assemblage contains mysteries that can be ferreted out only through appropriate analytical techniques.

Thus all portions of a lithic assemblage contain information and one should not ignore major parts of it. By the same token, some objects or attributes contain more information than others so, at least for the most basic analyses, it makes sense to isolate those portions of a collection that promise to provide the greatest return for the effort. The basic question, at this stage, is:

Q11: Which attributes of stone tools are most useful for providing fundamental information from a lithic assemblage?

The answer to this question lies, at least partly, in what you want to know. Fortunately, at this stage in the analytical process most archaeologists are interested in similar, and basic, questions: e.g., what do the tools look like? How were they

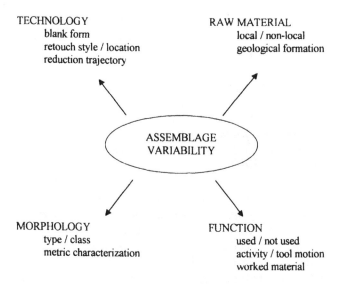

Figure 4.1.   Principal vectors of variability in an assemblage of stone tools.

manufactured? Where did the tool users get their raw material? What did they use the tools for? These questions are quite varied and require different datasets for their resolution.

For ease of comprehension, let us break the basic questions down into four large areas: raw material, technology, shape, and function. Each constituent may be regarded as a vector along which information at varying levels of integration and complexity may be retrieved. Because of the variability inherent in the data and in the questions being asked, one should not expect to be able to ascertain adequate answers by using only one system of analysis—for example, a comprehensive typology (a method of classification to be covered later in this chapter). Instead, one should consider these vectors as separate categories of information that can be related to one another at higher levels of integration. A simple schematic representation of the problem might look like Figure 4.1. In this graph each of the principal vectors is divided into at least two sub-areas that will be discussed presently. Variation in the sub-areas may be continuous or discrete, depending upon the nature of the variables involved and the type of information required.

Raw Material

Raw material is inherent in each artifact and is useful in characterizing the lithic assemblage. Knowledge gained from sourcing lithic artifacts can be employed on several different levels. At the level of local vs. exotic, it can inform on trade or exchange relations or the extent of seasonal nomadism. At a greater level of precision, this information may be employed for recreating prehistoric hunter-gatherer seasonal rounds or the nature of the territories that a group of people inhabited or passed through. Methods of artifact characterization and analysis have been discussed in Chapter 2.

Technology: Basic Partitioning

Technology involves the manufacture of stone tools and follows principles of fracture mechanics described in Chapter 3. The analysis of stone tool manufacture may be pursued on several levels, but the basic question is: in this assemblage, how were stone tools made?

Early in a lithic analysis it is useful to isolate from the rest of the artifacts those elements that represent a greater degree of creative energy or cultural input. For instance, it is readily apparent that considerably more effort went into the manufacture of a finely crafted dart point than in one of the unmodified flakes removed in the production of that point. To consider these two pieces on the same conceptual or behavioral level would be ridiculous.

A simple surrogate for denoting energy or input in a chipped stone assemblage is the presence of secondary modification, or retouch. Criteria for distinguishing intentional retouch were discussed in considerable detail in chapter 3 because, at the stage of assemblage analysis, it is crucial to be able to isolate those pieces that exhibit characteristics of intentional modification. It is important that the criteria used to define "retouch" not extend to similar forms of damage caused by prehistoric use-wear or by extraneous factors such as excavation, laboratory handling, or tillage practices. Though there is some controversy on this issue, I feel strongly that, if an analyst accepts as "retouch" non-intentional or utilization damage and does not differentiate these from other sorts of damage, one runs the risk of not being able to define the basis on which individual pieces were isolated. Giving too much leeway to criteria of inclusion could render the entire construct meaningless.

Ground and rough stone tools are different from chipped stone in that abrasion, rather than fracturing, is the principal form of modification. As we have seen in Chapter 3, abrasion may have been caused by either manufacture or utilization, both of which are generally regarded as sufficient for discriminating these pieces from specimens that lack such modification. Though the inclusion of utilization abrasion adds some inconsistency to a system otherwise based on manufacture criteria, the practice does serve to distinguish behaviorally important pieces right from the outset.

Chipped stone pieces distinguished on the basis of retouch and ground/rough stone specimens distinguished on the basis of use- or manufacture-abrasion form a special subset of the assemblage. Many archaeologists call them "tools," but this term is too functionally laden for my taste, as no assessment of their actually having been utilized has been made at this stage. A less biased term is *type collection*, which refers to the fact that each piece receives a designation in the type-variety system, and does not presuppose utilization. I am not totally enamored of this term either, as the designation "cortication flake," for example, is a technological type, yet the flake itself, being non-modified, is placed outside the type collection. This terminology is a holdover from traditional European Bordesian typologies that did not consider debris categories within the typological system. So be it: since I have not heard a better term than type collection for this concept, I will continue to use it for the moment. Your assignment is to scout out more accurate terminology.

Technology: Distinguishing Trajectories

One of the most basic and useful bits of technological information involves the relationship between the core and the pieces that came off it. The core can exist for the purpose of delivering expedient flakes or can be prepared for yielding specialized flakes, such as Levallois flakes or blades. Or the core itself can be the focus of attention for producing objects of a particular shape, as in a bifacial technique. A specific production system pursued by toolmakers of a particular cultural group is called a *trajectory*. The depiction of technological trajectories is important enough to constitute another research question:

Q12: How does one determine the principal technological trajectories pursued by ancient flintknappers?

One can make some initial headway in ascertaining technological trajectories by recording the *blank form* on which every tool in the type collection was produced—whether on a flake, a blade, a blocky fragment, or a biface. Although not very sophisticated, this type of study provides baseline data that can be supplemented by additional analyses. Let us inspect each of the principal trajectories in turn.

Flake Trajectory

The flake trajectory is relatively simple, unless one is dealing with prepared cores as in the Levallois technique (Bordaz 1970: chapter 4; Boeda 1986; Van Peer 1992). This European Middle Paleolithic procedure for producing a usable flake tool involved trimming the edges of a nodule, shaping the upper surface of the core, creating a striking platform on the end of the core, and removing a Levallois flake whose shape was dictated by the surface topography that had been created (Figure 4.2). When processing certain Middle Paleolithic assemblages, one must be familiar with the range of Levallois cores and flakes and of core preparation flakes.

For less specialized flake assemblages, a useful initial step in determining the nature of flake production is by classifying cores into largely morphological categories such as pyramidal, cylindrical, tabular and discoidal (or radial). One can then study individual cores for further clues to sequences of flake removal, which

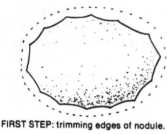

FIRST STEP: trimming edges of nodule.

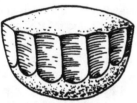

Side view of the edge-trimmed nucleus.

SECOND STEP: top surface is also trimmed.

Side view of the fully-trimmed nucleus.

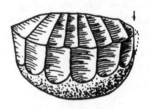

THIRD STEP: striking platform is made.

Top view of nucleus (*platform, right*).

FINAL STEP: flake struck from nucleus.

Top view of nucleus (*flake is removed*).

Figure 4.2.   Illustration of the Levallois technique, employed in the western European Middle Paleolithic period for removing a flake from a specially prepared core (taken from Bordaz 1970: Fig. 12).

provides further technological clarification. Jean-François Pasty (2001) recently
developed a schematic model of the possibilities of flake removal from an undif-
ferentiated rectangular block (Figure 4.3). This he applied to directional evidence
derived from scar negatives on cores from the Middle Paleolithic site of Nassigny,
France (Figure 4.4).

Another way to document the sequence of flake removals is through *piece
refitting*. This involves a painstaking process whereby hundreds—sometimes
thousands—of artifacts are displayed on lab tables for the purpose of conjoining

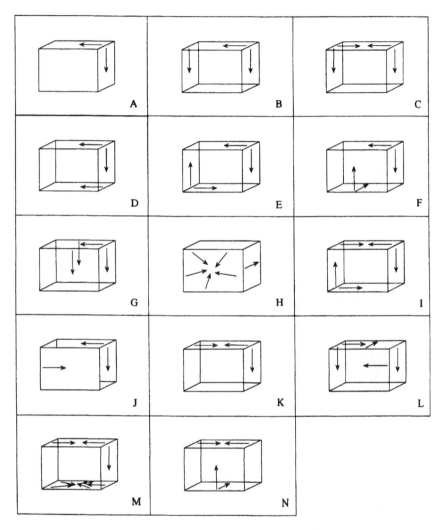

Figure 4.3. Schematic model of possible removals from a rectangular block of stone (taken from Pasty 2001: Fig. 2).

them to one another. If most of the relevant specimens were present on the site and recovered, and if refitting is extensive enough, this procedure can reveal entire flake removal sequences and the exact technological strategies employed (Hofman 1981; Czeisla et al. 1990; Morrow 1996b).

  If refitting is unsuccessful, one might try *Minimum Analytical Nodule (MAN) Analysis*, a useful technique in regions that yield lithic sources of variable appearance. In such cases pieces may not be able to be conjoined, but they can be established with reasonable certainty to have originated from the same nodule

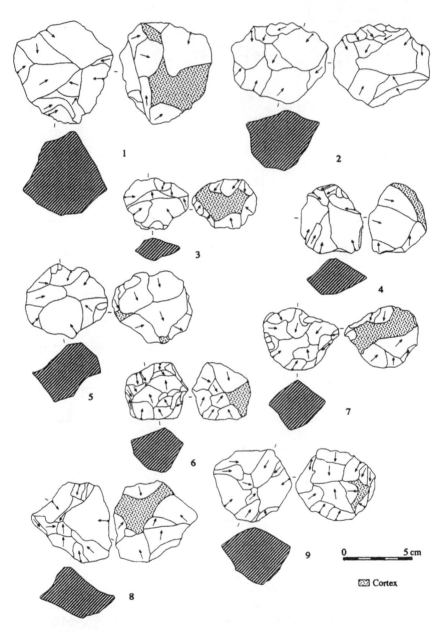

Figure 4.4. Organization of flake removals from discoidal nuclei from the site of Nassigny, France (Pasty 2001: Fig. 5).

(Kelly 1985; Larson 1994; Larson and Kornfeld 1997). This information can be employed for many of the same purposes as piece refitting analysis, including sourcing and limited assessment of production trajectories.

Blade Trajectory

The production of blades is effected through a process different from normal flake reduction and requires knowledge of a different set of production techniques. A blade core fashioned from a flint nodule, for example, requires the creation of a striking platform and a prominent, straight lateral ridge running from the

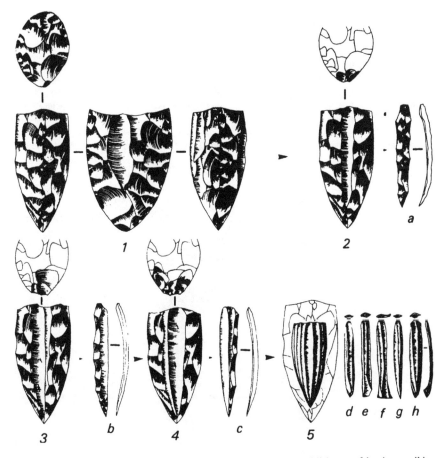

Figure 4.5.   Schematic view of Capsian blade removal technique: 1) establishment of dominant striking platform and lateral ridge; 2) lame à crête removed from lateral ridge; 3–4) initial blades containing evidence of preparation on their dorsal surfaces; 5) later blades and development of core form (taken from Tixier 1984: Fig. 5).

striking platform to the end of the core. The first blade, or *lame à crête*, employs this ridge to control its form and point of termination. Once the first blade is removed, succeeding blades can be taken from either side of the resulting blade scar, continuing radially around the striking platform in regular fashion (Bordaz 1970: chapter 5; Tixier 1984; see Figure 4.5).

This was not the only accepted procedure for producing blades, but was the most common. Contrast this with two techniques for the production of microblades in Paleolithic Japan, described in Box 4.2. Like flakes, blades became blanks for a wide array of tool forms. Any of these elements—the cores, core preparation flakes, blades and blade tools—are indicative of the existence and nature of a blade technology and should be carefully noted at this stage.

Box 4.2. Japanese Microblades

Microblades are small, elongated flakes whose average width is about 5 mm. They are found in assemblages from late Paleolithic and early Holocene occupations of the Japanese archipelago, and are thought to have served as inserts in the edges of composite tools. Their manufacture is of interest here, because it differs from the production of larger blades from conical and cylindrical cores, described in other parts of this chapter.

Studies of cores and by-products of this period allowed Tatsuo Kobayashi (1970) to postulate the existence of two separate techniques for the production of microblades (Figure 4.6). In System

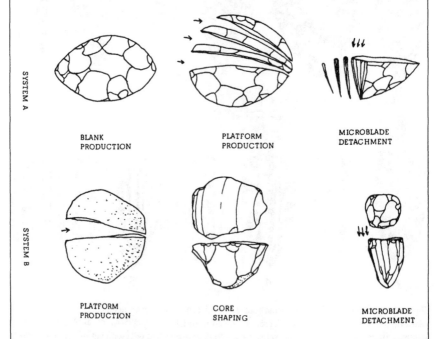

SYSTEM A

BLANK
PRODUCTION

PLATFORM
PRODUCTION

MICROBLADE
DETACHMENT

SYSTEM B

PLATFORM
PRODUCTION

CORE
SHAPING

MICROBLADE
DETACHMENT

Figure 4.6.   Two systems for producing microblades from chert in the late Paleolithic of Japan (taken from Kobayashi 1970: Fig. 2).

A, a nodule was worked bifacially into an oval core blank. From one end, one or more long, narrow "ski spalls" were removed from one side of the core, ultimately resulting in a flat platform from which microblades could be removed from the lateral face. Some of the ski spalls exhibit wear at their extremities reminiscent of graving tools, and may have also been desired end products of this procedure. In System B, a nodule was broken longitudinally in order to expose a flat surface. This surface was shaped to produce a more optimal striking platform; then blades were removed from the side of the core.

Although the microblades that resulted from these two techniques were quite similar, System A blades tended to be slightly smaller and thicker than System B blades. Differences in technology suggest that they had different origins and perhaps different purposes, i.e., their end products served functional niches that were different from one another. If archaeologists had lumped all these technologies into a generalized "microblade technique" without going to the added labor of discriminating at the technological level, we would have lost distinctions that could inform on ethnicity, function, and a host of other problems (also, see Parry 1994:89).

Biface Trajectory

Bifacial tools, i.e., items that show intentional flaking on opposing surfaces, were usually produced along a specific reduction continuum. Some tools made it to the end of the trajectory, but others were aborted at some stage along the way because they broke or were useful for particular tasks at that point. Therefore, it is helpful to gain an intimate familiarity with blank and preform stages for the production of bifacial tools in the assemblage in which you are working. For instance, first-hand knowledge of transitional forms gained through experimenting with the technology enabled Bruce Bradley (1975) to propose technological interpretations of the lithic assemblage of the Gumu-sana Cave in North Africa, a schematic interpretation of which is presented in Figure 4.7.

If a significant ground and rough stone component exists in your assemblage, you will have to determine technological parameters of these objects, as well. It is easiest to divide this component into manufacture- and use-modified specimens. Manufacture-modified artifacts may include a maul shaped entirely by pecking, or an axe that was chipped to approximate shape, then ground and polished to final form. Use-modified specimens may include manos and metates with large ground surfaces; or depressions pecked through use as *nutting stones*; or grooves in sandstone abraders resulting from sharpening bone tools. Some of these tools may also have been intentionally shaped by pecking or grinding.

Reduction Trajectory Modeling

Recognizing the existence of different reduction trajectories and recording the type of blank on which specific tools were made can help characterize a lithic assemblage. Called *Reduction Trajectory Modeling*, a flow chart of the modeling process is depicted in Figure 4.8. This outline includes three chipped stone trajectories: flake, biface, and blocky fragment. In assemblages in which blades are

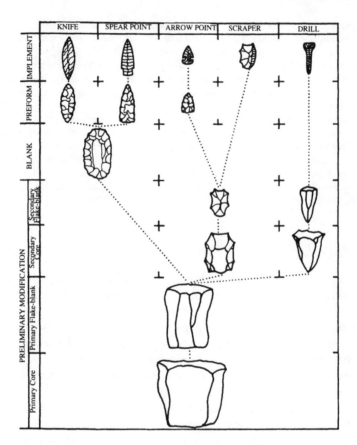

Figure 4.7.   Principal lithic reduction sequences in the northern African Gumu-sana assemblage (taken from Bradley 1975: Fig. 1).

produced, a specific Blade Trajectory should be added. Since its internal categories are almost identical to those of the Flake Trajectory, they have been omitted from this illustration.

Trajectory models follow an individual piece from blank to discard as either a modified or unmodified object. A piece that started out as a flake would be placed in the flake trajectory. It may ultimately have remained an unretouched flake or may have been sharpened (retouched) before being discarded, which would change its type to that of retouched flake or another type pertinent to flake tools. Retouched "non-shaped objects" include not only generic retouched flakes, but also pièces esquillées, wedges, and other minimally modified pieces. "Shaped objects" can be either edge or surface modified and can be classified into one of several types contained in classification systems that will be discussed later in this chapter.

Artifacts belong in the Blocky Fragment Trajectory if the blank from which the piece was made does not exhibit flake characteristics and the object has not

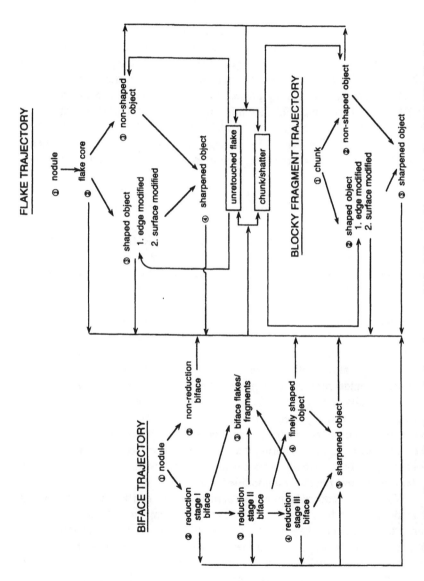

Figure 4.8.   General chipped stone reduction trajectory model for lithic assemblages (taken from Odell 1996: Fig. 3.4).

been reworked to the extent that its original form can no longer be determined. In this case the object starts out as a *chunk*, but the possibilities of its techno-logical development from that stage are similar to those of pieces in the Flake Trajectory.

Pieces in the Biface Trajectory started out as a nodule, flake or blocky frag-ment, but the forms in which we find these specimens do not provide sufficient clues to be able to determine their original blank form. If the piece has been ex-tensively bifacially worked, whether or not we can tell that it started out as a flake or blocky fragment, it is usually placed, for the sake of consistency, in the Bi-face Trajectory. Producing a finished bifacial implement is an involved process, a contention that is documented in the model's three reduction stages. These have been borrowed from Callahan's (1979) stages 2–4 (his stage 1 is procurement). The definitions that follow are taken directly from Callahan, as restated by Odell (1996:380):

Stage 1 = initial edging, in which relatively widely spaced scars produce a sinuous outline in lateral view. Biface itself is relatively thick (width:thickness = 2:1).

Stage 2 = primary thinning, in which major projections and irregularities are eliminated as the edge becomes more centered and less sinuous in lateral section. Blows usually do not travel past the center of the piece, but thinning has restricted edge angles to the $40°$–$60°$ range, and the width:thickness ratio to 3:1 or 4:1.

Stage 3 = secondary thinning, continuing the trends of the previous stage. Manufacture scars are close together, the edge is straight, and the edge angles are consistently in the $25°$–$45°$ range. The piece is characteristically thin, the width:thickness ratio usually exceeding 4:1. Shaping flakes frequently travel past the center and undercut previously produced flake scars from the opposite margin.

Not all bifacially worked pieces were originally intended to progress to a finished product such as projectile point, bifacial knife, or drill. Instead, the initial blank may have been too small or oddly shaped for it to have progressed through the entire trajectory, thus rendering it a *non-reduction biface*. Its invasive retouch does not typically involve all edges equally, usually favoring one or two margins and leaving the rest relatively unmodified.

While the specific reduction stage of many bifaces can be determined through the model outlined here, some are too small or incomplete to be able to make a definitive assessment. They may be fragments of broken bifaces or large flakes that possess significant portions of the original biface on their dorsal surfaces or striking platforms (usually reduction errors)—which it may be useful to designate separately. Some of these elements record events at the end of the reduction process, which are occasionally quite informative. In the model they are called *biface fragments* or *biface flakes*.

Some bifaces were transformed into thin cutting or scraping tools but were not shaped into any other form. These are the generic "reduction stage III" bifaces. Other pieces such as projectile points, drills, burins and scrapers had been modified into specific shaped tools ("finely shaped objects").

The reduction model can provide a useful structure for describing the retouched portion of a chipped stone assemblage and ultimately for comparing assemblages. It is worthwhile to inspect its application to a specific assemblage, for which I have chosen the Middle Woodland Smiling Dan site in west-central Illinois (Figure 4.9). Smiling Dan toolmakers employed a blade technique, which has been added to the basic reduction model. The principal element to notice about applications is that generalized concepts presented in the original model are thereby made specific. In the case of Smiling Dan, four trajectories are presented, each with its specific types. This model deals quantitatively only with modified pieces—unretouched flakes and shatter are analyzed separately and through other models, as are ground stone artifacts.

The biface trajectory at Smiling Dan was complex. All three reduction stages, as well as several types of non-reduction stage bifaces, are represented in the Smiling Dan Middle Woodland chipped stone assemblage. A few of the non-reduction specimens were relatively non-descript, while several were judged to have been pièce esquillées and wedges. Most middle-reduction stage (II) pieces could not be typed more specifically, though a few hoes and an adze were noted. On the other hand, generic stage III bifaces were outnumbered by specific shaped forms such as drills, scrapers, burins, and especially projectile points. The model places biface fragments and flakes near reduction stage II, but this placement was done mostly for convenience, since biface fragments (by far the more frequent of the two entities) were so termed because a specific stage identification could not be made.

Retouched tools in the flake, blade and blocky fragment trajectories all emanated from similar-looking blank forms, manufactured from chunks in the case of blocky fragments and from cores in the case of flakes and blades. The similarity of blank forms in each of these trajectories meant that similar tool types could be manufactured in all three. In each trajectory blanks have been classified into shaped and unshaped objects. Shaped objects at Smiling Dan include burins, scrapers, gravers and unifaces, whereas unshaped objects include pièces esquillées, retouched flakes, retouched blades, and wedges.

Reduction trajectory modeling is an efficient way to characterize a chipped stone assemblage, because at a glance one can derive a clear impression of the numerical strength of each of the trajectories present. A more detailed perspective reveals the typological composition of each trajectory in the assemblage, as well as the lesser-studied elements (e.g., retouched pieces, wedges) that are often overlooked in ordinary lithic analyses. Since only one assemblage

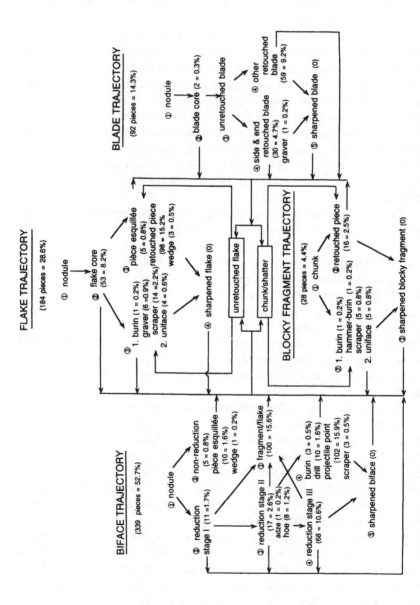

Figure 4.9.   Application of the chipped stone reduction model to the Smiling Dan type collection (taken from Odell 1996: Fig. 9.2).

can be comfortably represented at one time, this method is not usually employed for comparing assemblages visually. On the other hand, tabulations that result from trajectory models can profitably be compared with other similarly derived chipped stone collections through graphics and statistical algorithms.

Morphology: Characterizing Shape

Artifact morphology has frequently served to distinguish one artifact from another, often providing the principal variable by which types such as scrapers and projectile points are classified. Morphology is not easy to characterize, and several systems have been devised to embody at least certain elements of it. Descriptive terms have been used, sometimes with reference to standard geometric shapes, but these systems tend to be subjective and not easily verifiable. John Parkington (1967) improved on this idea by projecting the silhouette of an object on a screen of gridded squares and recording intersections of the silhouette with specific square numbers.

Metric attributes have also been employed for this purpose. A simple shape measure is the ratio of length:breadth, or taking a series of width measurements along the length axis (e.g., Roe 1964). A more comprehensive system, called *attribute analysis*, was devised for Upper Paleolithic tools by Hallam Movius et al. (1968). Requiring measurement of several dimensions of individual tools within an artifact class, the result would allow the researcher to accurately reconstruct the form of the original tool. Unfortunately, there is no compelling evidence that the information gained in this process is worth the considerable effort involved, explaining why few researchers have pursued this line of inquiry.

Instead of focusing on characteristics of shape *per se*, archaeologists have usually preferred to combine morphology with other attributes into a heterogeneous classification system whereby each node is defined on the basis of a slightly different arrangement of attributes. Most lithic classification systems require the breakdown of an assemblage into divisions that have already been discussed—notably, those categories in which elevated cultural input has been encoded, earlier referred to as the type collection. The assemblage is further partitioned into chipped and ground/rough stone components. Let us inspect these classification systems in greater detail.

Although logically a classification could arrange material on an ordinal or interval scale, most systems employ a nominal scale. That is, they place objects into categories, which simplifies the process by reducing the amount of elements to keep track of. Once the type collection has been constituted, a useful research question is:

Q13: What are the most effective criteria to use for creating categories in a lithic assemblage?

Type-Variety Systems

The principal purposes of a classification are: 1) to characterize the collection; and 2) to discriminate among different parts of it. The most common way to accomplish these tasks is to arrange artifacts into mutually exclusive groups based on possession of shared attributes. These groups represent variation of artifact manufacture within relatively large units of time and space, and are known as *types*; variations within the type may be responsive to smaller spatio-temporal units and are known as *varieties* (Phillips 1959; Dunnell 2000). A classificatory system employing the type as the central unit of construction is known as a *typology*. The concept of type has been employed almost since the inception of the modern discipline of archaeology, though in the early days, not in a very formalized manner.

The type-variety system contains weaknesses that scholars have sought to rectify. One of these is that, in contradistinction to biological taxonomies, archaeological types are usually non-hierarchical—essentially because the contributions of underlying attributes to the type structure are relatively unknown. The only quasi-hierarchical typology of which I am aware was constructed by Georges Laplace (1964, 1974). Its inability to gain popularity among prehistorians attests either to the insolubility of the attribute hierarchy problem and/or the obstinacy of prehistorians themselves.

Another weakness of the type-variety system is its subjective and intuitive nature. The types I construct for a collection will probably not be the same as ones you construct. And even if we do agree on the typological structure, it is unlikely that the specific objects that each of us places into the several categories so created would be exactly the same. Read (1974) has improved classificatory objectivity by clustering attributes rather than types; his latest foray (Read and Russell 1996) applied these techniques to unretouched flakes. While the cause is laudable, the results are not very intuitively satisfying, and researchers face similar problems in defining attributes consistently as they do with types. In any case, for our purposes the issue is moot, because almost no archaeologists use such a system, anyway.

A third weakness of the type-variety system, as it pertains to stone tools, is its questionable utility for addressing functional issues while continuing to employ historically derived functional names for objects. Most regional typologies come down to us through historical trajectories initiated by untrained avocational archaeologists, as most archaeologists were in the old days. The categories they used were often functional in tone and included types such as arrowheads, dart points, drills, scrapers, gravers, and so forth. These categories were based loosely on perceptions of the use of similar objects in traditional societies, rather than on studies of the artifacts themselves. Subsequent use-wear analyses have established that the actual utilization of artifacts is often quite different from the proposed usage as suggested by the type name (Wylie 1975; Odell 1981b; Yerkes 1987:128-129).

Typologies could be fashioned to address both components of this problem. On the one hand, one could simply eliminate functional names for objects—an end scraper might become a distally retouched, elongated uniface, for example. Descriptive labels such as this were employed for projectile points/knives from the Normandy Reservoir Project, though functionally charged names were retained for the principal types (Faulkner and McCollough 1973). Although this approach would alleviate functional ambiguities, the labels would be unfamiliar to other archaeologists many of whom, in my experience, are quite resistant to change; I suspect this is the principal reason that Faulkner and McCollough's projectile point/knife labels have not seen more widespread usage.

On the other hand, one could base a typology not only on morphological but on functional criteria, as Ahler and McMillan (1976) have done for Archaic assemblages from Rodgers Shelter, Missouri. Functional classes were based primarily on careful macroscopic observations of the entire collection and an intensive use-wear analysis of a sample of projectile points (Ahler 1971, pers. commun. 2002). In this kind of classification, types bear a closer correlation to the activities in which the pieces were engaged than is the case with traditional, morphology-based typologies. The principal problem with it is that very few lithic assemblages have been subjected to the sort of techno-functional analysis conducted by Ahler. Therefore, it is difficult to compare types such as "Hafted Cutting Tool," "Generalized Cutting Tool," "Irregular Scraper," or "Transverse Scraper/Grinder" with categories in any other system.

The typological systems described above—Read's, Faulkner and McCollough's, Laplace's, Ahler's—contain elements that are not very popular among archaeological practitioners. More subjective or non-hierarchical systems have caught on because they yield intuitively satisfying categories, spring more directly from the well of historically accepted concepts of tool use and nomenclature, and require no special expertise to employ. The best known of these systems were constructed for the European Paleolithic by François Bordes (1961) and the Mesolithic by de Sonneville-Bordes and Perrot (1954–56).

Criteria for Classification

There is a general perception that typological systems are "morphological" because they rely on characteristics of shape to classify objects. This is only partly true. Shape certainly contributes to classification, but other factors do, too. Consider a biface, which is distinguished primarily by the technological trait of having been worked on opposing faces. Though bifaces may be oval, rectangular, or tear drop-shaped in form, this quality does not enter into the definition. Projectile points and drills are often bifacially shaped and have a strong morphological component, but even these types rely to some extent on technological factors for their definition. They must, to at least some extent, have been purposely worked into shape; a flake that appears naturally in the form of a projectile point would seldom be classified as one.

Type and location of retouch on a piece can also help determine its typological designation. One may think of an endscraper as a completely formal entity, as we all have a mental template of one. But what if a piece that looks like an endscraper was modified slightly on the proximal end and not at all on the rounded distal end (the "scraper edge")? Because the principal working edge was not shaped, most typologists would probably not call this piece an endscraper—even though it superficially looks like one. The location of retouch is important for defining other types, as well. A graver is distinguished by its graver spur, a portion that projects from the rest of the tool and was often employed for engraving things. But in order for that specimen to be defined as a graver, at least part of the spur must have been shaped by retouch; otherwise, it is just a flake with a projection.

Many ground and rough stone types are also only partly distinguished on morphological criteria. As discussed in Chapter 3, categories such as hammer, mano, metate, and abrader are defined on the basis of utilization traces from pecking or grinding. Common use of these objects does lend a certain formal homogeneity to a type, however. Hammers and manos must fit in the hand, after all, so they must conform to certain practical constraints. And size plays at least a minimal role—distinguishing manos from metates, for example.

The classes of tools that most fully conform to morphological criteria for inclusion are those whose surfaces have been most completely modified, usually through grinding and polishing. I am referring to tools finely crafted for extensive use, such as ground axes, adzes, hoes and discoidals; or for decorative or ceremonial purposes, such as gorgets, bannerstones, and effigy pipes. Because these types are carefully abraded to shape, there is less ambiguity about form than with most chipped stone types; proximity of modification is not necessary for gauging intent.

These rare and well-made types do not contradict the contention that shape is only one of several criteria used to classify archaeological stone tools. Other important criteria are technology, type and location of retouch, and use-wear. If we place these criteria at four equidistant poles on a piece of paper, we could arrange the principal lithic types according to the importance of any criterion in their type definition (Figure 4.10). A type placed close to Technology would indicate that the principal (or only) criteria for this type were technological; a type placed midway between Technology and Shape would indicate that both criteria are equally important in their type definitions, etc. No quantification of these categories is offered here, so they remain perceptions of how most archaeological lithic classificatory systems are constituted. However, such a graph illustrates the

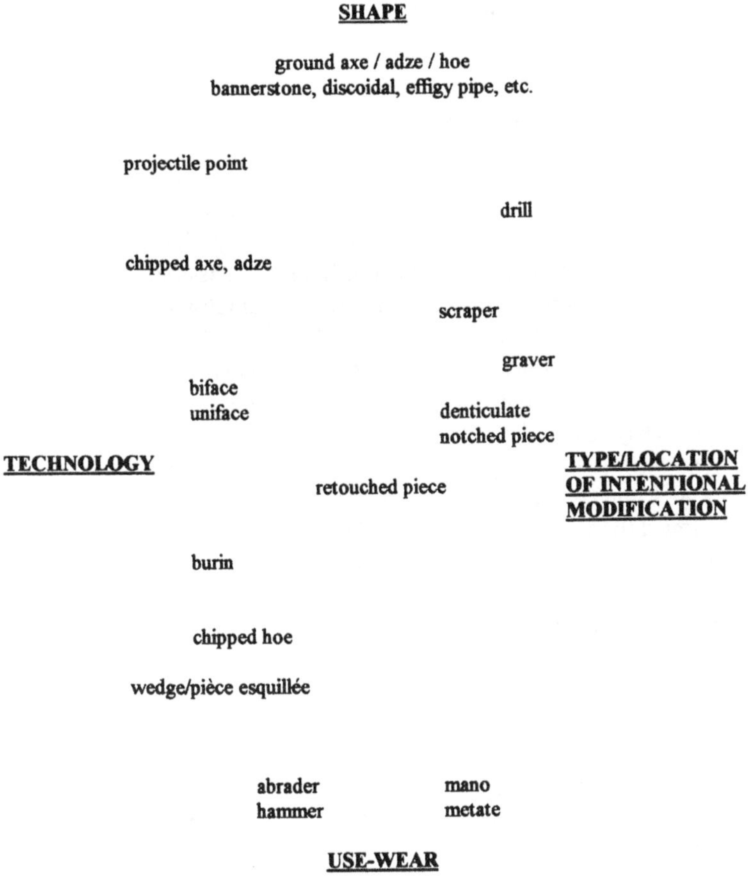

SHAPE

ground axe / adze / hoe
bannerstone, discoidal, effigy pipe, etc.

projectile point

                                                    drill

chipped axe, adze

                                        scraper

                                            graver
            biface
            uniface   denticulate
                                        notched piece
TECHNOLOGY   **TYPE/LOCATION**
                            retouched piece   **OF INTENTIONAL**
                                                        MODIFICATION

            burin

            chipped hoe

    wedge/pièce esquillée

                abrader   mano
                hammer   metate

                    USE-WEAR

Figure 4.10.   Type criteria chart: at the sides are four principle criteria for inclusion of a lithic type into
a typological system. Major types are arranged according to the importance of each of these criteria to
its own type definition.

impressive range of variability inherent in all typological systems and the important
contributions of non-morphological criteria to the normal type structure.

The qualities of intuitive satisfaction, historical continuity, and minimal required expertise are powerful reasons for using a typological system, but such
a system must have at least one other quality to be maximally useful: a capacity for discriminating between assemblages. Bordes' (1961) system does pretty
well in this regard, because it continues to be employed for assemblages not only
in southwestern France, but throughout Eurasia; for chronologically later assemblages, the same is true of de Sonneville-Bordes and Perrot's (1954–56) typology.
These systems are popular for discriminating between assemblages because they

accommodate traditional types, rendering them relatively easy to compare with one another.

Choosing a Classificatory Structure

My purpose in this manual is not to sell one system over another, but to define common problems, identify variability where it exists, and propose common-sense solutions. All classification systems are fundamentally regional and should be constructed to deal with the local situation. If such a classification system exists in the region in which you work, you may wish to employ it, at least initially—for its familiarity and comparability value, if for no other reasons. Remember that morphological classification systems represent only one vector of variation; plumbing other vectors requires devising other systems.

If no ready-made classificatory system for chipped stone artifacts exists in your region, perhaps Figure 4.11, a flow chart for making decisions on each specimen in a lithic assemblage, may be useful. Such facilitators, or keys, have been employed for several years. One of the first in North America, for instance, was constructed by David Thomas (1970) for use on projectile points in the Great Basin.

The key presented here is a suggested structure, not a directive for typologists. The most basic question to be asked is whether or not a particular piece was manufactured by a human agency. If not, the piece should join the gravel in your driveway (but watch out for your tires). If it is artifactual, the next question is, has it been retouched? If not, it joins the debris to await specific analytical procedures but is not included in classification systems that employ formally typed objects. All intentionally modified specimens join the type collection, from which subsequent types are fashioned.

Since all chipped stone type collection items have been retouched, the next decision concerns the type of retouch. Edge retouched items are those whose retouch scars do not extend more than about 5–8 mm into the interior of the piece. For such a specimen, one can ask whether or not it exhibits standard morphological or locational traits. If so, one can give it a designation as a specific tool type: graver, burin or scraper, for example. A piece that does not exhibit standard formal or locational characteristics is usually referred to as a generic retouched piece, although certain qualities of the modification may suggest classification as a wedge or pièce esquillée.

Non-edge retouched items in a type collection must, by definition, be invasively retouched, i.e., the retouch scars reach toward or attain the center of the surface or beyond. If both surfaces of a piece are invasively retouched, it is a biface; if only one surface is invasively retouched, it is a uniface. Unifaces are not usually typed further, but bifaces were often subjected to a complex developmental sequence from blank to end product. As explained elsewhere in this chapter, this sequence can be divided into stages on the basis of formal characteristics. If no

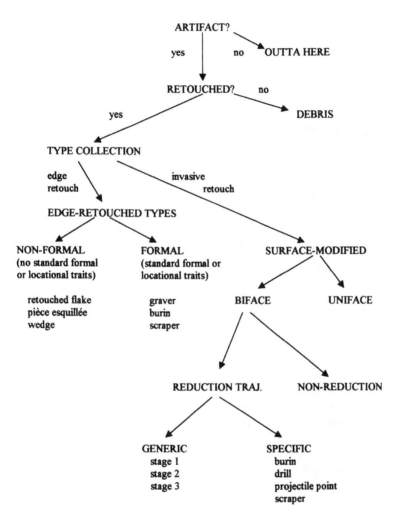

Figure 4.11. A suggested key for guiding decisions related to typing specimens in a lithic chipped stone assemblage.

further shaping is evident, i.e., it retains a general ovoid or rectangular shape, it is classified into a generic bifacial stage. If it is shaped into a distinct form, such as a drill, projectile point, or scraper, it is classified as such. Bifacial burins usually result from the fashioning of a graving implement from a biface that has been fractured through manufacture mistakes or utilization. Non-reduction bifaces are pieces that have been bifacially reduced, but have not gone through the stages of bifacial reduction.

Function

To this point we have assessed how tools were made, what they look like, and where their raw material originated. An additional area of interest, of course, is how they were used. Answering this question requires background information and an explanation of specialized analyses, tasks that will be undertaken in Chapter 5.

COMPARING ASSEMBLAGES

Classification of artifacts into types and sub-types (varieties) results in a partitioning of the collection into a series of nodes (types), each defined on certain criteria. It is wonderful to find that your assemblage has, say, 15% scrapers, 21% projectile points, 25% generic bifaces, and 8% drills, but are these proportions a little or a lot? The only way you will ever find out is by comparing your assemblage with other similarly constituted assemblages, occasioning the following research question:

Q14: What are the best ways for comparing your assemblage classes with others?

This is a rather tricky proposition, as you are comparing not just one type with another, but an entire panoply of types with an array from elsewhere. Statistical algorithms such as X^2, difference-of-proportions, and Fisher's Exact tests are effective in comparing subsets of the data with one another but, despite the commonness of the problem, few simple ways exist to compare entire assemblages. Let us divide the question into two realms: you can consider either the class structure itself and compare the quantities of categories within that structure, or you can compare the specific classes that have been created.

Comparing Class Structure

Comparing class structure is a common activity in disciplines such as psychology, sociology, and biology, which habitually create discrete categories of items. Two important measures have been developed to help interpret biological classes: the *richness* of the class structure, i.e., the quantity of classes in an assemblage in proportion to the total quantity of objects; and *evenness*, i.e., the equitableness of distribution of objects within each of the types.

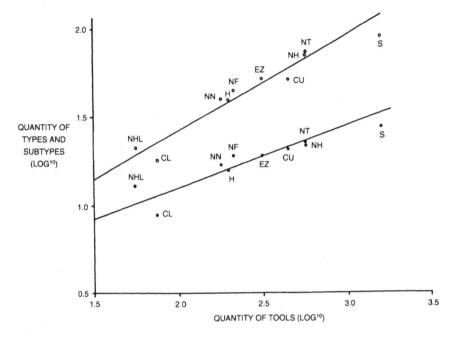

Figure 4.12. Richness of types (lower line) and subtypes (upper line) among 10 prehistoric components analyzed from the Lower Illinois Valley (taken from Odell 1996: Fig. 12.1).

Richness

Richness can be portrayed on a graph comparing quantity of types with quantity of items in the type collection, standardized for sample size (Kintigh 1984). Converting both axes to $\log^{10}$ permits results to be analyzed using linear regression techniques (Jones et al. 1983). Figure 4.12 illustrates such an analysis of types (lower line) and subtypes (upper line) for 10 prehistoric assemblages in the Lower Illinois Valley (Odell 1996). Represented are five assemblages from the site of Napoleon Hollow (NN, NH, NT, NF, NHL), two assemblages from Campbell Hollow (CL, CU), and one apiece from Elizabeth Mound 6 (EZ), Smiling Dan (S), and Hill Creek (H). The quantity of tools in an assemblage increases from left to right; the quantity of types and subtypes increases up the Y axis.

The regression lines represent the best fit for the assemblages on these parameters. Placement of an assemblage above its respective regression line indicates a greater-than-expected quantity of either types or subtypes; placement below the line indicates lesser type or subtype richness. The magnitude of the deviation of any point from the regression line can be displayed graphically as in Figure 4.13.

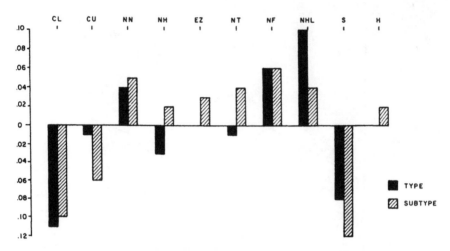

Figure 4.13. Type and subtype deviations from the least-squares regression line for richness of 10 prehistoric assemblages from the Lower Illinois Valley (taken from Odell 1996: Fig. 12.2).

This graph suggests that the Napoleon Hollow Middle Woodland Hillslope and Floodplain (NHL, NF) components exhibit the richest panoply of types, whereas the Campbell Hollow Early Archaic (CL) and Smiling Dan Middle Woodland (S) components exhibit the poorest array of types and subtypes. Since richness was calculated on the basis of a largely morphological classification system, the results reflect deviations in shape and retouch parameters—but only incidentally, if at all, on technology, function, and raw material.

Scores can be compared between assemblages, but more importantly, the relative richness of a tool assemblage can inform on the type of occupation represented by the people who made the assemblage. To a certain extent types can be equated with activities, so an assemblage rich in types should also have been rich in activities—a base camp, for example. An assemblage poor in types may be indicative of a special-purpose or extraction camp.

Evenness

The evenness measure, which assesses whether or not objects are spread evenly throughout the constituted classes, is more difficult to interpret. It may be indicated by the Shannon-Weaver Information Statistic H, though that algorithm does not appear to be very responsive to considerations of sample size (Peet 1974:293; Kintigh 1989) and may blend richness and evenness components into a single measure (Bobrowski and Ball 1989:7). A better approximation of evenness can be derived through the J statistic (Pielou 1966), which divides H by Hmax (the log of the number of categories in the assemblage).

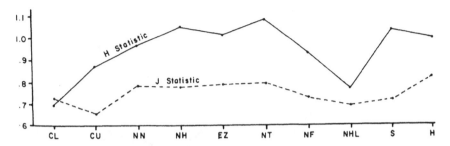

Figure 4.14.   Information Statistic (H) and evenness measure (J) for types from 10 components from the Lower Illinois Valley (taken from Odell 1996: Fig. 12.3).

Figure 4.14 shows the operation of the H and J statistics through the same 10 Illinois Valley components on which richness was computed. It indicates relatively even type composition in the Archaic components of the Napoleon Hollow site (NN through NT) and the Hill Creek Mississippian farmstead (H), but a less equitable distribution in the Campbell Hollow Archaic (CL, CU) and Middle Woodland (NF-S) components.

What these results mean is not entirely clear. Christenson (1987:78) asserted that more generalized sites such as base camps have a more even distribution of frequencies across types. This interpretation agrees with some of the Illinois Valley data but not with entities such as the Smiling Dan Middle Woodland occupation (S)—which, by all other indicators was a base camp or semi-permanent village.

Comparing Specific Classes

Cumulative Graphs

Richness and evenness measures are good for studying the structure of a specific classification, but do not compare the types themselves. For this, a popular tool has been the *cumulative graph*, a device associated particularly with the French use of the Bordian type system but adapted to archaeological assemblages from all over the world. It can be illustrated with Paleoindian assemblages from the American Great Plains, comparing Clovis, Frederick and Cody lithic complexes (Figure 4.15).

To construct a cumulative graph you need to 1) convert type frequencies to percentages; 2) number all types and subtypes sequentially (to conserve space); and 3) display the type numbers in order along the X-axis of the graph. The Y-axis registers the proportion of each type or subtype in the assemblage but it does so cumulatively, starting with the percentage of tools in the first category and progressing to 100% in the last. The resulting curve provides a graphic

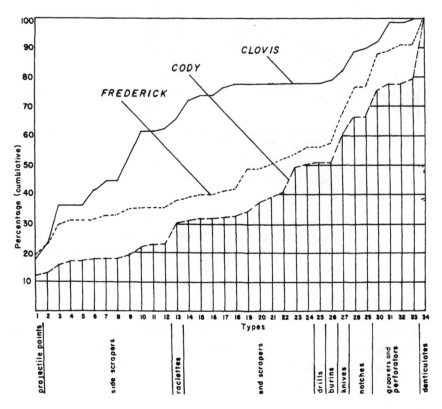

Figure 4.15. Cumulative graph of tools for the Clovis, Cody and Frederick Paleoindian complexes (taken from Irwin and Wormington 1970: Fig. 7).

representation of an assemblage, which can be compared with other similarly constituted assemblages.

In the Paleoindian comparison, notice how the Cody assemblage is light on most of the tools in the first part of the graph—the projectile points, side scrapers, and several end scraper subtypes—whereas the Clovis assemblage contains far greater proportions of these types. The Cody assemblage catches up in the latter part of the graph, particularly through the abundance of other kinds of end scrapers, knives, notches, single-spurred gravers (category #30) and denticulates. From this comparison, we see that the typical Clovis assemblage emphasizes projectile points and side scrapers, whereas the typical Cody assemblage emphasizes knives, notches, gravers and denticulates. (Irwin and Wormington 1970; see also Agenbroad 1978:92).

The cumulative graph provides a quick and easy overview of an assemblage and a visual comparison with other assemblages. It does have problems, however.

First, the system offers no way to quantify differences between assemblages. Although the Clovis and Cody cumulative graphs are quite distinct in this analysis, most comparisons are not so clear-cut. The questions then arise: at what point is a difference significant? And when are two assemblages truly similar? For these questions, one needs to move from the cumulative graph to appropriate statistical algorithms. Second, much of the visual effect of the cumulative graph depends on the placement of categories on the X-axis. A different order would produce a totally different graph (see Kerrich and Clarke 1967).

Snowflake Diagrams

Another way of visualizing the various types in an assemblage is through the *snowflake diagram*, a technique that also works with percentages of items rather than frequencies. Types are amalgamated into a limited number of axes (say, 4–8) based on directions of interest. For instance, Howard Winters (1969) created a structure of generalized functionally charged categories including tool maintenance (Axis I), plant processing (II), animal procurement (III), heavy-duty general utility tools (IV), and light-duty general utility tools (V), into which individual types would be placed. A few years ago I tested this structure with use-wear derived data from an Illinois assemblage and found that the two systems coincided surprisingly well on a general level (Odell 1989b).

Subsequently, I wished to derive a visual impression of a type collection from a Middle Archaic Helton occupation capped by a burial mound at the Elizabeth site in west-central Illinois. This encampment was situated directly above the Napoleon Hollow multicomponent Archaic and Woodland site and a few miles upstream from the famous Koster site. Although a paucity of analytical funding did not permit a functional analysis of the lithic dataset, it was possible that something could be learned by applying Winters' categories in a snowflake format.

The resulting diagram for the Elizabeth sub-Mound 6 assemblage appears in Figure 4.16. The longest (most abundantly represented) axes are heavy- (Axis IV) and light-duty (Axis V) general utility tools, reflecting an abundance of bifaces and retouched flakes, respectively. Tool maintenance (Axis I) is suggested by a relative abundance of burins; plant processing (Axis II) primarily by manos; and animal procurement (Axis III) by projectile points. Most importantly, all of the axes are at least fairly well represented, suggesting that a wide range of activities was conducted at the site—indicative of a base camp.

The Elizabeth snowflake diagrams can be visually compared with assemblages from other sites arranged on the same axes (Figure 4.17). The closest matches are with the two Koster Horizon 6 assemblages, both of which show a relative abundance of heavy- and light-duty generalized utility tools and a moderate representation of the other axes. The Elizabeth diagram is quite different from Foss, which shows a much heavier reliance on light-duty generalized tools, and

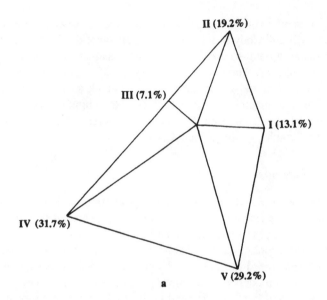

Figure 4.16. Snowflake diagram of the sub-Mound 6 assemblage from the Elizabeth Mounds site,
Illinois (taken from Odell 1996: Fig. 7.4a).

from Modoc, which contains a lot more projectile points but no plant processing
tools at all. Graham Cave and Pabst are similar to one another in having an abundance of heavy- and light-duty generalized utility tools and projectile points but
very few tool maintenance and plant processing implements.

As a way to represent data, the snowflake diagram has some endearing qualities. Like the cumulative graph, it enables a quick visual assessment of an entire
assemblage along certain parameters of interest and it allows limited comparison.
But also like the cumulative graph, there is little more that can be accomplished with
this structure without going back to the individual categories, breaking them apart,
and applying appropriate statistical algorithms to questions that arise from the data.

Brainerd-Robinson Coefficients

Finally, let us investigate a comparative method that has fallen out of favor since it was initiated in the 1950s to seriate pottery assemblages. This is the
Brainerd-Robinson Coefficient (Brainerd 1951; Robinson 1951), a technique that
compares two assemblages on the percentages of tools in each class according to
the following formula:

$$B - R = 200 - \sum_{i=1}^{n} p_{iA} - p_{iB}$$

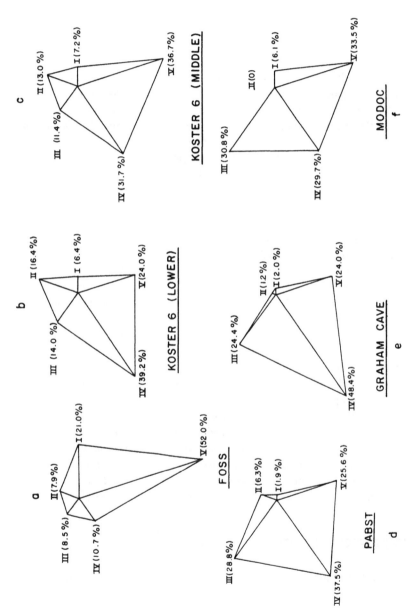

Figure 4.17.   Snowflake diagrams of six midwestern Hellon or Heltonoid occupations: a) Foss; b) Koster Horizon 6 (lower); c) Koster Horizon 6 (middle); d) Pabst; e) Graham Cave; and f) Modoc Rock Shelter (taken from Odell 1996: Fig. 7.5).

To apply the formula, percentages (p) of implements in each class in the type collection are calculated for the two assemblages being compared, A and B. Differences between assemblages on each of the classes are calculated and added together, and the total is subtracted from 200 to derive a similarity coefficient. The higher the B-R score, the more similar the two assemblages are to one another on the parameters chosen.

Although only two assemblages can be compared at a time, calculations are simple and can include a large number of binary assays. In the Lower Illinois Valley, for example, this technique was employed to compare types among the same 10 assemblages discussed previously (Figure 4.18). In this case, each component was compared with nine others, for a total of 90 comparisons on the graphs—but, of course, every result for one assemblage has a reciprocal in another, so the number of calculations was only 45. The resulting graph provides a pretty clear impression of similarity or distance between one assemblage and the other nine (Odell 1996: chap. 11).

In the Illinois Valley example, the assemblages that were typologically least similar to the rest were the Napoleon Hollow Hillslope (NHL) Middle Woodland component and the Campbell Hollow Lower Horizon (CL) Early Archaic component. The components that were similar to the greatest number of other components were three Archaic assemblages at Napoleon Hollow (NN, NH, NT), the Campbell Hollow Upper Horizon (CU) Middle Archaic component, the Elizabeth sub-Mound 6 (EZ) Middle Archaic occupation, and the Smiling Dan (S) Middle Woodland base camp or village. Averages of the binary comparisons provide an overall view of the level of similarity of each of these assemblages to the others in the dataset (Figure 4.19).

The Brainerd-Robinson coefficient is an effective way to compare assemblages on their proportions of commonly defined classes. It is easy to calculate and can be performed a multitude of times with little extra effort. Only two assemblages can be compared at one time and, with a minimal number of comparisons, it may be difficult to derive a clear impression of the extent of similarity within the dataset. With a large number of comparisons, the range of similarity scores is usually broader and more easily interpretable. The individual scores for each assemblage can also be averaged to derive a summary similarity coefficient.

ANALYZING UNRETOUCHED DEBRIS

On habitation sites the world over, retouched tools tend to constitute only about 3–5% of a prehistoric chipped stone assemblage, a proportion that often depends on screen sizes used in the field. This means that at least 95% of all chipped stone on most living sites is classified as unretouched debitage or debris (which, for this discussion, are considered the same thing)—making debitage

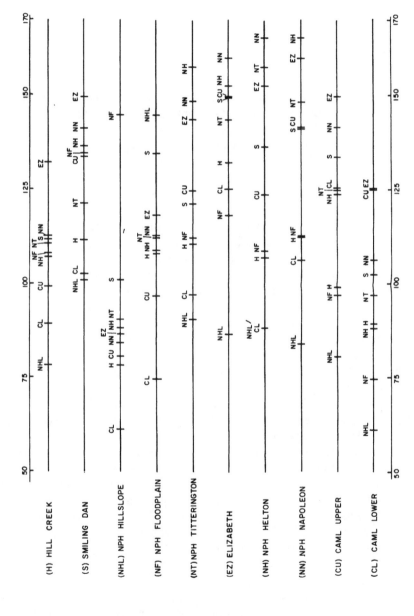

Figure 4.18.   Individual Brainerd-Robinson coefficients of types for each component in the Illinois Valley dataset (taken from Odell 1996: Fig. 11.6).

Figure 4.19.   Means of Brainerd-Robinson coefficients for the Illinois Valley dataset (taken from Odell 1996: Fig. 11.7).

frequently the most abundant artifact class on a site. In addition, a large percentage of the debitage is typically small and unusable and therefore likely to remain in the place at which it was last discarded. This quality is useful when interpreting spatial distributions, particularly in situations involving workshops or knapping areas.

To derive information from this relatively abundant and stable artifact class would be advantageous, but what does one do with a bunch of "waste flakes?" The first imperative is to disavow the notion that all debitage is waste in the creation of some higher goal, like a finely crafted projectile point. We know from ethnographic studies from Australia, New Guinea, and other parts of the world in which hunter-gatherer behavior has been recorded (White 1967, 1968; Gould et al. 1971; Hayden 1977), as well as from relevant archaeological analyses (Ahler 1971; Greiser 1977; Odell 1981b), that stone tool-using people employed unretouched flakes in a large variety of activities. In fact, they often favored unretouched flakes for specific tasks because their edges were sharper; therefore, it is extremely likely that some of the debitage at any habitation site was utilized. But even unutilized flakes potentially contain information about the processes that produced them. It is the goal of debitage analysis to tease as much useful information as possible from these pieces.

The study of lithic debitage can be approached in two different ways. The first is by analyzing each individual flake or piece in a sample; the second is by processing large quantities of flakes simultaneously to derive summary parameters. The following section will be organized by these approaches. It should be kept in mind throughout this section that the success or failure of any debitage analysis depends not only on the analytical techniques, but also on the sampling strategies employed. As noted previously, debitage can be plentiful, often numbering in the hundreds of thousands of items. Even employing techniques of mass analysis, on some sites you simply will not be able to analyze everything. Thus a judicious application of statistics and probability theory will be necessary to assure that the material analyzed is representative of the assemblage whence it came.

Another sampling problem concerns the integrity of the artifact being sampled—in this case, its degree of completeness. Is it all right to use broken flakes, or flakes without striking platforms, or should the sample be limited to complete flakes from which all parameters are measurable? The answer to this question depends on the type of analysis being contemplated, as different approaches have different requirements.

Individual Flake Analysis

Flake Typologies: Interpretive Units

Analyzing every flake in a sample can be an arduous procedure, but one that can yield a considerable amount of information. Three approaches to the study of individual flakes have emerged. Two of these distil information in the form of flake types; the third deals with attributes recorded on individual flakes. The most traditional of these approaches. i.e.. the one that has been around the longest and continues to be popular, is the flake typology using categories that are intuitively meaningful. By this I mean that the categories inform on the specific technique used to produce them or the stage in which they occurred in the reduction process. In a study of interpretive flake types, it is usually not necessary to limit the sample to complete flakes, though an analyst should discard those pieces that do not possess characteristics indicative of having been produced by human beings. Flakes that are so fragmented that it is difficult to determine what they represent can either be omitted or placed in a residual category such as "undetermined flake."

Several flake types are diagnostic of a particular technological strategy. Such a piece is the *lame à crête*, the first blade to be removed from a blade core after a striking platform has been established and a ridge down one side has been prepared (see Figure 4.5). The *biface reduction flake*, characterized by a diffuse bulb of percussion, multi-directional dorsal scar negatives, and platform faceting or grinding, bears witness to the existence of bifacial reduction. The *burin spall* is a distinctively narrow, thick flake, usually terminating in a hinge or step, which occurs as the principal by-product of a burin technique. *Bipolar flakes and cores*, frequently notable by crushing on one or both ends, are difficult to discern but are diagnostic of a bipolar technique. And *hoe flakes* are indicative of the use of hoes on a site, though in this case the distinguishing feature is surface polish from the hoeing activity rather than technological indicators of manufacture.

Other flake categories are indicative of behaviors rather than of specific re- duction strategies or tool types. For example. *cortication flakes*, defined on the presence of dorsal cortex, are generally suggestive of early stages in the reduc- tion process. *Core rejuvenation flakes*, the purpose of which is usually either to flatten the striking platform or to improve the angle between the striking platform and dorsal face of the core, testify to a degree of core maintenance. Similarly, *sharpening flakes*, distinguished by a striking platform-dorsal surface interface that shows evidence of utilization, demonstrates the maintenance of tool edges. And an *outrepassé*, or *overshot*, flake that removes part of the opposite end of the core usually indicates a manufacture failure. In addition to these specialized or diagnostic by-products are generic *interior flakes*, often (though not always) the result of a freehand flake core technique; and *blocky fragments*, sometimes referred to as *shatter*, which lack distinguishable flake characteristics. Other lithic analysts may make slightly different or more fine-grained categories than this, depending on their specific dataset or theoretical inclinations, but these are the principal categories employed by practitioners of this analytical approach. Most applications of this approach seek, at least in part, to answer the following questions:

Q 15: Which stages of tool manufacture occurred on site, and in what form was lithic material imported to this locale?

Let us briefly inspect two studies that apply this technique to a debitage assemblage. One concerns a small sample of Paleoindian debris from the CB-North site in the American Bottom region of the Mississippi River Valley south of St. Louis (Evans et al. 1997:182-183). Employing a series of categories including some of those listed above, the authors recorded 27 reduction flakes (interior flakes), 41 biface thinning flakes, and 35 biface retouch flakes, but only 3 cortication flakes and 3 alternate flakes indicative of early stage bifacial reduction. From these data one can deduce that most early stage reduction activities occurred elsewhere and that bifaces were brought into the site already reduced to preforms. As a material conservation measure, some of the bifaces may also have served as cores for producing sharp-edged flakes. No evidence existed in the Paleoindian occupation of the site for the local procurement or primary reduction of chipped stone tools.

Analysts of the small Paleoindian occupation of the Alder Creek site near Waterloo, Ontario, arrived at similar conclusions (Timmins 1994:178-179). Biface thinning flakes, biface retouch flakes, and channel flakes from fluting Paleoindian points dominated the assemblage, while cortication flakes and other indicators of early stage reduction were absent. The presence of a relatively large quantity of channel flakes suggests that the manufacture or maintenance of projectile points was an important activity, whereas the paucity of uniface flakes suggests that the manufacture and maintenance of scrapers was not.

Flake Typologies: Interpretation-Free Units

In 1985 Alan Sullivan and Ken Rozen proposed a system that simplifies the construction of lithic debris categories. Subsequently dubbed the Sullivan-Rozen Technique, or SRT, it is based not on any inherent diagnostic qualities of the artifacts, but on their degree of breakage. Because type of breakage is the principal criterion employed in the analysis, the sample must consist of all artifactual flakes.

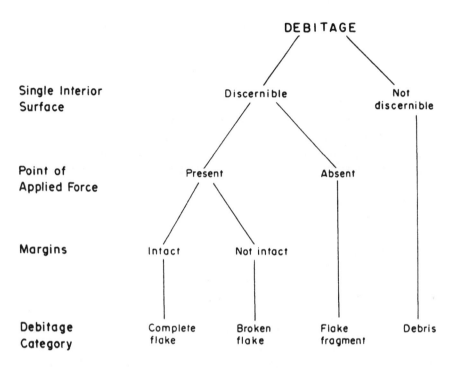

Figure 4.20.   Attribute key employed in the Sullivan-Rozen Technique for the analysis of unretouched debitage (taken from Sullivan and Rozen 1985: Fig. 2).

Four categories of debitage were established: 1) *complete flake* (unbroken); 2) *broken flake* (point of applied force, i.e., striking platform, intact but margins fractured); 3) *flake fragment* (point of applied force absent but ventral surface discernible); and 4) *debris* (ventral surface not discernible, i.e., what other researchers might call *blocky fragments*). Parenthetically, the term *shatter* substitutes for "flake fragment" in some analyses (e.g., Ingbar et al. 1989:123; Mauldin and Amick 1989:83), but for "debris" in others (e.g., Morrow 1997:59). The authors displayed a simple graph that dichotomized the decision-making process on three levels (Figure 4.20).

In the words of the authors, "The categories are interpretation-free because they are not linked to a particular method of technological production nor do they imply a particular reduction sequence" (Sullivan and Rozen 1985:759). Applying these categories to debitage assemblages from eastern Arizona, the authors conclude that assemblages containing relatively large quantities of cores and complete flakes are the result of core reduction, whereas assemblages with large quantities of broken flakes and flake fragments are the result of tool production. The question they were asking was:

Q 16: How can core reduction be distinguished from tool production?

From the moment of its publication, the SRT was a tremendous hit, fostered in part by what Jay Johnson (2001:18) termed the *"American Antiquity* effect" (its appearance in America's most respected journal) and the intractable nature of lithic artifacts in regions such as the American Southwest, where the system was first applied. At last there existed a system for organizing lithic debitage that was simple and direct—and most importantly, it was not even necessary for an analyst to understand lithic analysis in order to achieve results. The euphoria was palpable.

It did not take long for the backlash to occur. Testing these categories independently, Prentiss and Romansky (1989) agreed that tool production could be separated from core reduction by the SRT, but not completely for the reasons given by the original authors. They found that trampling and raw material differences affected the results dramatically, and Shelley (1990) demonstrated that knapper expertise added another significant element of variability. Amick and Mauldin (1997:25) later evaluated raw material within the SRT, concluding "that breakage patterns fail to behave consistently with any variables other than raw material."

The same authors (Mauldin and Amick 1989) had previously recorded debitage from three cores of Georgetown (Texas) chert. They observed that the amount of debitage variability produced by these cores "might be interpreted as reflecting different kinds of assemblages (Sullivan and Rozen 1985; Sullivan 1987), despite the fact that they represent essentially the same trajectories" (p. 84). They isolated percussor type and shape of original nodule as factors contributing to this variability. Morrow (1997) came to a similar conclusion, finding that broken flakes and flake fragments were slightly more frequent than other types in tool production, as Sullivan and Rozen predicted, but not significantly and several different factors could have caused that result. He concluded that the most useful element for discrimination was shatter (Sullivan and Rozen's debris), which correlated with early reduction stages.

The most positive independent tests of the SRT, to my knowledge, have been conducted by Austin (1999) and by Prentiss (1998, 2001). Austin achieved high rates of accuracy by applying discriminant function analysis to the system, but only on pure assemblages. However, when he plotted centroids of mixed assemblages, he was able to tell that they were mixed and in which direction. Prentiss found that the SRT is reliable in the sense that results can be successfully replicated. Where it fails is in validity, or in behaving as the tester thinks it is behaving, i.e., following proposed models and expectations. Separating his data into a series of size classes, Prentiss constructed what he called Modified SRT, or MSRT. Applying these within a principal components analysis, he was able to increase the overall validity of the method, distinguishing consistently between core reduction and tool production.

These successes have not convinced all lithic analysts that even the MSRT is worth pursuing. The most bothersome element of the technique is its very interpretation-free quality. The system is so interpretation-free that it is difficult, in most cases, to determine which series of prehistoric behaviors caused any given set of results. Although Sullivan and Rozen tout this as an advantage, not everyone sees it that way. For example, Magne (2001:28) wrote, "I take great issue with the notion that more should be learned by using arbitrary units of measure. On the contrary, I would point out that the trend is clearly for increasing integration of meaningful units of measure." Magne is not alone in his continuing criticism of the technique, suggesting that more testing will have to be accomplished before the utility of the system can be fully evaluated. Until then, it is best to employ the SRT (or MSRT) in conjunction with other types of debitage analysis, as advocated by Morrow (1997), Root (1997), and Bradbury (1998).

Attribute Studies

The approaches to debitage analysis described so far employ whole flakes or pieces, creating types within a coherently organized system. Types, by their very nature, distil a lot of information into a single analytical unit. The resulting entity has the benefit of being quick and easy to record, once the categories and their underlying causal factors are sufficiently understood. However, the process by which a piece of unaltered stone becomes a tool is frequently complex and is likely to vary along several vectors. Types encode some of the variability discernible in the by-products of the process, but only along certain dimensions. Thus flake types lack the specificity and comprehensiveness necessary to capture more than a moderate portion of the information contained in an assemblage of debitage. In attempting to find out more about what unretouched debris might tell us, several researchers have studied individual qualities of flakes that are considered likely to covary with behavioral parameters.

In the following discussion I will refer to the definable parameter of interest as the *variable*, whose differing values vary according to a scale. The values may be continuous, as in *ratio* or *interval* measurements of, say, the length of a flake; they may be *ordinal*, pertaining to a relational quality such as few or many facets on a striking platform; or they be *discrete attributes*, like the color magenta or the presence/absence of an éraillure scar.

Characteristics of the sample depend on the types of variables being used. If, for example, the nature of the striking platform is chosen as a variable, then the sample must consist of complete flakes or, at the least, platform remnant-bearing flakes (PRBs in the vernacular). If length and width measurements are not crucial to the results, then one might be able to get by with some distal or lateral breakage.

Rigorous variable definition is crucial to the success of this type of analysis. Typically, very little attention has been given to a problem mentioned in a previous section, that of *replicability*—the likelihood that two researchers measuring the same variable (or one researcher measuring a variable at two different points in time) can consistently achieve the same result. This problem is important because, if a measurement cannot be successfully replicated, results may vary depending on who is taking the measurement rather than on the contribution that variable makes in the overall study. The true impact of an unreliable measurement on a computed result can never be known.

For this reason it is a good idea to test the replicability of any variable before using it. This can be done with two or more people, or with one person over time using a small sample (e.g., 20–40 pieces) and submitting the results to an appropriate statistical algorithm at a reasonable level of accuracy. Failure to achieve at least a 90% accuracy level usually means that the technicians are measuring slightly different versions of the variable. If researchers fail to achieve such a standard, the next step is to reconsider those pieces that yielded divergent results, tighten the variable definition, and try again. This process may continue for three or four times before either consistency is achieved or the variable is determined to be too intractable to pursue. For a more complete discussion of the issue, see Fish (1978) and Odell (1989a).

An additional aspect of variable definition worth considering is *validity*, or whether or not a variable is measuring what you think it is. In the previous section we noted that validity was a problem in the application of the Sullivan-Rozen Technique, because the technique was not adequately discriminating between core reduction and tool production. The imposition of size classes has apparently increased the validity of the system. Since the discrimination of different human behaviors—core reduction from tool production, stages of biface reduction, chronological periods, or whatever—constitutes the driving force behind an archaeologist's desire to analyze debitage in the first place, the issue of validity is paramount.

Of all the measurements commonly taken on flakes, the most replicable is *weight* (Magne and Pokotylo 1981; Amick et al. 1988; Mauldin and Amick 1989:77; Odell 1989a). Weight is also a reasonably good predictor of reduction stage, because it covaries with other linear dimensions (Shott 1994:80). Certain qualities of a flake's striking platform also appear to be both replicable and discriminatory (Odell 1989a; Andrefsky 1998). The *number of striking platform facets* tends to discriminate effectively between core and bifacial reduction, because bifacial platforms are typically prepared more carefully than core platforms, yielding more facets (Magne and Pokotylo 1981; Tomka 1989:146-147; Bradbury and Carr 1995, 1999). Striking platform characteristics, including *facet count*, have also been successfully employed for identifying bifacial reduction stage (Dibble and Whittaker 1981; Morrow 1984; Johnson 1989) and type of hammer used (Hayden and Hutchings 1989; Bradbury and Carr 1995).

Other commonly recorded variables are typically less useful than weight or striking platform characteristics, but may be informative when employed with other variables. *Cortex cover* on a flake's dorsal surface, for example, has been used to indicate reduction stage: the less cortex, the more advanced the stage. It appears, however, that the amount of cortex cover typically varies a lot throughout the reduction sequence and is not a reliable indicator of where in that sequence a flake belongs (Bradbury and Carr 1995; Andrefsky 1998:114). Odell (1989a) found this variable moderately useful for discriminating the extremes of a reduction sequence from one another but deficient in determining exact reduction stage, while Mauldin and Amick (1989:70) considered it useful only for determining the early part of the sequence.

The jury is still out on several debitage variables, as accounts of their discriminatory success vary with different researchers and research problems. For instance, Bradbury and Carr (1995) concluded that *dorsal facet count* was a good discriminator among non-platform remnant-bearing (PRB) flakes, whereas Odell (1989a) found that this variable discriminated the middle stages in the production of a Hardin point, but no others. Because the effectiveness of several of these variables has not been established, I am reluctant to come up with a list of "good" or "bad" variables, which would only stifle research initiative. However, my own studies (Odell 1989a), the results of which are largely congruent with results of other investigations, suggest that some variables are better than others for the kinds of questions in which archaeologists are most interested. The best overall discriminators I have found are illustrated in Figure 4.21. Those that are specifically useful

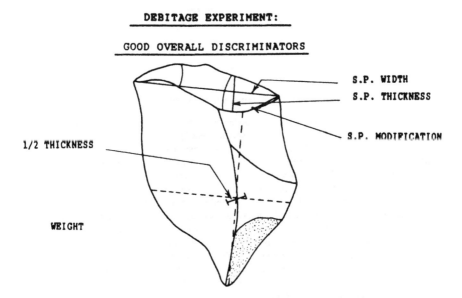

DEBITAGE EXPERIMENT:

GOOD OVERALL DISCRIMINATORS

S.P. WIDTH
S.P. THICKNESS

S.P. MODIFICATION

1/2 THICKNESS

WEIGHT

Figure 4.21. Good overall discriminators among debitage variables (taken from Odell 1989a: Fig. 10).

DEBITAGE DISCRIMINATORS:

CORE VS. BIFACE: BIFACIAL STAGES

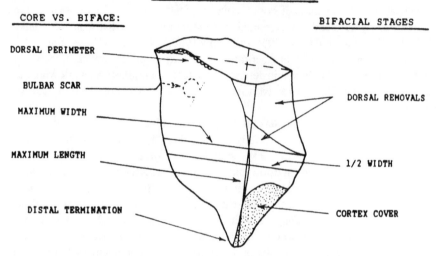

DORSAL PERIMETER

BULBAR SCAR   DORSAL REMOVALS

MAXIMUM WIDTH

MAXIMUM LENGTH   1/2 WIDTH

DISTAL TERMINATION   CORTEX COVER

Figure 4.22.   Variables that discriminate well between core and biface reduction. and among biface reduction stages (taken from Odell 1989a: Fig. 11).

for discriminating core from biface reduction debitage and debitage from different bifacial reduction stages are illustrated in Figure 4.22. Researchers interested in pursuing the subject of flake attributes will find it necessary to consult an additional body of literature. Some pointers in navigating this literature are offered in Box 4.3.

Box 4.3. Flake Attribute Studies

There is little room in this manual to go beyond introducing the concept of flake attribute studies and providing general guidelines for resolving some of the common problems that archaeologists face. For discussions of the effectiveness of variables that have been employed to answer various questions, an interested researcher must delve further into the relevant archaeological literature. This is not a particularly easy literature to access. because most scholars who employ this technique define their variables and then apply them directly to the archaeological record without evaluating their replicability or discriminatory capabilities on an experimental database. Despite the frequent use, in such studies, of multivariate statistical algorithms that show the relative contribution of each variable to the result. the exact behaviors that caused that result remain a mystery. In addition, most archaeologists are more interested in the immediate effects of this application than in evaluating the variables and methodology that got them there.

For elegant detail. it is hard to beat a doctoral dissertation. Indeed, these have provided some of our most cogent and exhaustive studies of technological variables (e.g.. Katz 1976; Phagan 1976; Magne 1985). Getting your hands on a copy of any of these works through University Microfilms or directly from the granting university would be well worth the effort.

Published studies are more accessible. but are usually shorter and do not devote as much space to variable definition and evaluation as dissertations do. In addition. published works tend to report on more restricted problems and datasets than dissertations. Some of the more useful published studies for evaluating flake variables are Dibble and Whittaker (1981). Magne and Pokotylo (1981), Amick et al. (1988). Bradbury and Carr (1995. 1999), and Carr and Bradbury (2001). Useful summaries of work in this area are provided by Shott (1994) and Andrefsky (1998: chap. 5). And if you are one-stop shopping. the volume that contains the most varied and concentrated menu of experimental debitage studies and variable evaluation is a series of articles in Amick and Mauldin (1989). This short section has surely missed several important contributions to this field. but it is designed to get you started so you can discover the rest.

Debitage attribute studies are applicable to a variety of situations, but they seem to be particularly responsive to two research questions, of which the first is:

Q17: How can lithic debitage be used to discriminate among assemblages from different chronological periods?

This question requires a dataset that spans a range of periods and contains assemblages with good chronological control. Such a dataset, which includes assemblages from southern Britain and Italy and spans the Late Paleolithic through Bronze Age, was generated by Michael Pitts (1978). Applying cluster and principal components analysis to a series of breadth:length ratios of unretouched flakes, Pitts was able to document fine blade production in the early Mesolithic, less blade-like forms in the late Mesolithic/early Neolithic, and a late Neolithic/Bronze Age trend also involving less blade-like forms. Chronological boundaries with respect to relative flake breadth differed between England and Italy, suggesting the operation of different tool producing dynamics in the two regions.

Pitts and Jacobi (1979) then applied a similar analytical procedure of length:width ratios to unretouched flakes and obliquely blunted microliths from Mesolithic and Neolithic assemblages of southern Britain. They documented a clear progression from narrower to broader flakes and smaller to larger obliquely blunted microliths through the Mesolithic. Broader flakes were correlated with a diminishing emphasis on controlled blade techniques in the later Mesolithic caused by a dwindling flint supply. The opening of flint mines in the Neolithic increased the availability of flint through a greater dependency on social and economic procurement mechanics. For a time, lithic debitage became narrower as the production of blades and blade-like flakes returned to favor.

A second common research problem to which debitage analysis has been successfully applied can be stated as follows:

Q18: How can debitage analysis be used to discriminate among different types of sites?

John Burton (1980) encountered this type of situation in analyzing debris from two Neolithic sites from southern Britain, Crickley Hill and Grimes Graves. The latter was a famous flint mine and workshop whose products can still be found all over southern England and beyond. It is particularly well known for its "axe factories" that produced implements that were important in field clearance and the construction of permanent housing, activities that were all the rage during the Neolithic. Crickley Hill, located 80 km from the nearest source of flint, was a totally different sort of habitation, lacking the massive workshop debris present at Grimes Graves.

After experimentally replicating two axes, Burton divided the debris into six classes based on size and perceived technology (e.g., biface thinning flakes). Submitting the variables to discriminant function analysis, he was able to characterize the debitage from either settlement. The Grimes Graves assemblage contained mostly large flakes from the manufacture of axes and a less specialized flake industry. The Crickley Hill assemblage contained a preponderance of small flakes, particularly from bifacial thinning, which exhibited a strong emphasis on the maintenance of tools that had been imported to the village from elsewhere. In this case, debitage size was a clear discriminator between these two different kinds of Neolithic settlements.

Mass Analysis

The analysis of individual flake attributes can facilitate the investigation of certain issues, but is quite tedious. The most helpful attributes are often small and/or difficult to measure, and simply recording the data can take a long time. In addition, the extent to which flake attribute analysis has contributed to resolving questions of interest to archaeologists is debatable, as some measurement problems and issues of optimal analytical technique have not been resolved. For these reasons, several analysts have turned to techniques, termed *mass analysis*, that are capable of yielding usable results by processing large quantities of flakes quickly.

Like the last-discussed studies of flake attributes, most mass analyses seek to differentiate site types and manufacture trajectories by differentiating their debris. The dominant assumption is that base camps or villages were characterized by a full range of activities and lithic industrial behaviors, including both on-site production and maintenance of tools. Special-purpose camps, on the other hand, were established for the extraction of specific resources and were occupied for a shorter period than were the base camps. Therefore, tool assemblages at such sites should be restricted to certain technological behaviors or parts of a reduction sequence, though the specific behavior or reduction node varies with the types of activities conducted at the site. For example, tested cobbles and primary reduction flakes tend to dominate lithic extraction sites, or quarries, whereas smaller sharpening and maintenance flakes tend to dominate animal or vegetal processing camps located at a distance from lithic resources.

A size-related problem like this can be approached by measuring each individual flake, but it is more easily accomplished by passing lithic samples through a series of size-graded screens and comparing the resulting distributions. Such a study, by Stahle and Dunn (1984; see also Raab et al. 1979), proceeded from the experimental replication of Afton points from northwest Arkansas in which reduction was divided into four stages and the resulting debris was collected accordingly. Debris was passed through a series of 10 nested screens with effective openings (diagonals) of 4.5–71.8 mm. The authors compared the resulting distributions to theoretical models and found that the Weibull function best fit the resulting flake distributions. Using discriminant function analysis, they achieved fairly good separation of stages when the last two (3 and 4) were combined.

This technique employs average flake values and has a hard time distinguishing mixed samples, as it classifies them to the nearest single stage of reduction (Stahle and Dunn 1984:23). Assigning bifacial reduction stages to unknown flake collections through a generalized least squares solution provided some discrimination, though through a series of rather complicated steps. The generation of data for this approach is simple, as it consists only of collecting flake samples and passing them through size-graded screens. Interpreting the results is not so easy, requiring considerable statistical expertise.

The most extensively documented and tested program of mass analysis has been devised by Stan Ahler (1989a, b). Ahler's system requires a large experimental database. The interpretive core of his experiments revolves around the following technological processes for each major raw material type: 1) freehand percussion cobble testing; 2) hard hammer freehand core reduction; 3) hard hammer bipolar core reduction; 4) hard hammer stage 2 biface edging; and 5) soft hammer stage 3–4 biface thinning. The experiments have been used as a baseline against which to compare archaeological assemblages, interpreting them with the aid of discriminant function statistics and, in certain cases, the relative amount of cortex on sample pieces. Individual experiments are positioned according to their first discriminant function scores in 2- and 3-group analyses. Archaeological debitage assemblages are then compared to the partitioned graph of experimental scores to arrive at an overall interpretation.

Ahler's mass analysis technique has several advantages over individual flake studies—ease of obtaining results and low processing time come immediately to mind. Using discriminant function statistics, an unknown assemblage can be classified fairly accurately even if it is mixed. On the other hand, the technique depends on a substantial series of experiments that took Ahler several years to accumulate. Despite the ability to generally characterize the technology by which a particular debitage sample was produced, technological mixing can still cause interpretive difficulties. And the characterization of general technology may not be the only type of question in which future archaeologists will be interested— aspects of striking platform configuration, dorsal scarring, comparison of raw material with termination types, and heat alteration are just a few potential issues on which this technique remains mute. So mass analysis is not necessarily *the* answer to a lithic analyst's dream, but it can be a useful complement to a battery of analytical techniques that, together, provide a wide range of data from which to render informed interpretations.

SUMMARY

This chapter has dealt with the issue of assemblage variability, or what to do next after you have learned about individual stones and then that big box of rocks is dumped on your lab table. As with other daunting tasks, the most effective way to confront an intractable situation like this is to break it down into smaller, more manageable, units. One immediately useful activity is to isolate those specimens on which special energy has been exerted, i.e., retouched chipped stone and heavily ground or pecked rough stone. This results in two subsets—a type collection and a debris class—that can be analyzed further.

Of the several characteristics of lithic assemblages that archaeologists might wish to know about, two—the morphological and the technological—have been most fully investigated in this chapter. Morphological analyses record the shapes and related attributes in the type collection, usually by creating a system of classi- fication into which individual artifacts are placed. Although classifications may be based on any internally coherent subsets of attributes, the most popular divide the collection into types that may be further subdivided into varieties. Technological attributes describe the ways that tools were made and often record other traits, such as cortex cover, dorsal scar facets, and heat alteration, that are related to their manufacture. The frequencies of classificatory units can be employed to compare one assemblage with another through techniques such as snowflake diagrams, cumulative graphs, and Brainerd-Robinson coefficients.

Unretouched chipped stone debris can also inform on the ways tools were made and the overall function of the site from which the assemblage was ob- tained. Debris can be analyzed through individual flake studies or mass analysis, each of which records slightly different parameters of a collection. Studies of individual flakes may classify whole specimens using interpretive, or value-laden, units such as biface reduction flake, overshot flake, etc., or interpretation-free units such as breakage types. Alternatively, individual flake studies may emphasize spe- cific attributes such as striking platform abrasion or edge angle. Studies of flake aggregates, or mass analysis, employ weights or frequencies obtained by screening the collection through a series of differing mesh sizes. The resulting distributions are interpreted by comparing them to distributions emanating from experimentally produced collections that represent a wide array of manufacture trajectories.

Techniques for analyzing assemblage variability described in this chapter do not exhaust the possibilities, but they provide enough ideas to get you started. In fact, the analysis of lithic material is sufficiently labor intensive that it often does not progress past the techniques mentioned here. The next level of analytical rigor usually entails intensive statistical evaluation, involving techniques that are beyond the scope of this manual.

Chapter 5

Tool Function

The previous chapters have discussed the origins and sources of archaeological stone tools, followed by the most important or diagnostic aspects of morphology, manufacture and technology. Lithic morphogenesis and sourcing are closely associated with geology, and a firm grounding in this area is essential for studying these subjects. Tool morphology and manufacture are best studied through replicative experimentation, close observation, and extensive knowledge of regional archaeological sequences. For most of the history of archaeological research these were the only areas in which stone tools could be interpreted.

During this time there existed a gaping lacuna in perhaps the most interpretively critical parameter of all: how individual tools were utilized. Of course, lots of archaeologists *thought* they knew, from the forms that tools assumed, how they had been used. Thus objects that looked like they had tipped spear points or scraped skins or whatever were considered to have been employed in these activities. The trouble was, these designations were rendered on the basis of limited ethnographic examples and nineteenth or twentieth century views on what these tools *should* have been used for. There was no confirmative evidence that any of them had ever been so employed; in fact, mounting evidence accumulated that modern stone age people in several corners of the world used specific tool types in ways that were dramatically different from traditional Western-oriented notions of tool use (e.g., Heider 1967, 1970; White 1967, 1968; White and Thomas 1972; Hayden 1977). So for most of the time that lithic research has been practiced, until recently very little had been discovered about the actual tasks in which archaeological stone tools were engaged.

This scenario has changed in the past forty years, for several ways to procure functional information from stone tools now exist. Research in this area has developed along two lines: the effects of the utilization process on the tool itself; and additions to the tool surface, or residues, that have accrued through use. This chapter will explore advances in each of these areas and provide information that will get you started if you should wish to pursue these topics.

USE-WEAR ANALYSIS

Background

Interest in stone tool function has never been far from archaeological consciousness, even in remote periods (see references in Vaughan 1985:4), though at this stage techniques for analyzing functional parameters had not been developed. It was apparent early on that stone tools were damaged to varying degrees by the use process, and extensively utilized implements were occasionally commented upon (e.g., Evans 1897:504, 555; Ray 1937; Peyrony et al. 1949; Evans 1957). A tool type that attracted considerable attention because of the spectacular use modification of its surface was the sickle blade, employed extensively in early sedentary and agricultural communities of the Near East (Curwen 1930, 1935). Sickle wear, consisting largely of a bright surficial gloss, was so dramatic and obvious that it could easily be described from observations with a hand lens. Unfortunately, most other types of wear are neither so easily observable nor so characteristic, so this kind of study existed as a sort of anomaly. No attempts were made to assess wear on more than one tool type or on tools with more subtle wear traces.

This situation began to change with the appearance of Sergei Semenov's *Prehistoric Technology*. Published in Russian in 1957 and translated into English in 1964, this study represented the culmination of experimental and archaeological investigations into the processes that caused wear on stone tools from work, later referred to as *use-wear*. Semenov proceeded from a model derived from modern metal implements such as steel knife blades and drill bits. The principal observable wear trace in metal was linear abrasion, or tiny scratches called *striations*. Applying the model to archaeological stone tools from disparate regions and periods, he was able to show that some lithic implements were striated through use, just as the steel tools had been. This study spawned an entire cadre of researchers into stone tool function at the Archaeological Institute in St. Petersburg, and began a totally new trajectory in stone tool research. The book itself became enormously popular in the West: one citations study showed that, of all works published in the decade 1961–1970, it was cited in the pages of *American Antiquity* more than any other source (Sterud 1978). The reason for this was not only because the study was innovative, but also because nobody else was conducting this kind of research yet everyone recognized its importance—hence they felt the need to at least refer to it.

During the period of Semenov's influence and immediately thereafter, interest in functional issues continued to increase. Unlike Semenov, scholars in the West made little attempt to be comprehensive in their treatment of the subject, but selected smaller topics that promised more easily achievable goals. Rosenfeld's (1970), Nissen and Dittemore's (1974), and Brink's (1978) studies of scraping tools, Sonnenfeld's (1962) analysis of hoes, and Hester and his colleagues' investigations of various edge damage types (Hester and Heizer 1972; Hester et al. 1973;

Hester and Shafer 1975) are all examples of these sorts of analyses. During this period Keller (1966) executed a small but comprehensive series of experiments, one of the first such series to be conducted in the West.

During the 1970s three comprehensive experimental series were carried out simultaneously on three different continents. George Odell's (1977) and Johan Kamminga's (1982) studies employed reflective-light, dissecting microscopes within a technique later termed *low-power analysis*. Larry Keeley's (1980) investigation used an incident-light, metallurgical microscope within a technique called *high-power analysis*. These programs were well under way by the time Brian Hayden hosted the first Conference on Lithic Use-Wear in Vancouver, British Columbia, in 1977. This conference for the first time brought scholars involved with disparate research topics and methods together to discuss common concerns and the future of this burgeoning new field, and resulted in the most all-inclusive series of articles ever to be compiled for this subdiscipline (Hayden 1979). There was a general feeling of tolerance, almost euphoria, a sense that many outcomes were possible and divergent approaches were desirable. This happy situation was too good to last.

The principal order of business at this time was to prove the accuracy of the technique—to justify the expenditure of effort involved, to attract practitioners to the field, and to render the results of such studies believable to outsiders. The vehicle of choice was the *blind test*, in which one person would independently utilize a series of implements, then present them to an analyst for interpretation on three parameters: location of wear, tool motion or activity, and material worked. The first blind test conducted (Keeley and Newcomer 1977) indicated that high-power techniques could achieve acceptable accuracy on these parameters; this contention was later verified by Bamforth et al. (1990). Testing the low-power technique, Odell and Odell-Vereecken (1980) also established acceptable accuracy for location and tool motion, but not for exact worked material—a dimension that had never been claimed for this technique. Judged on a 4-part resistance or hardness scale, Odell did attain an acceptable accuracy level for worked material assessment. Subsequent blind tests by Shea (1987, 1988) confirmed these results.

That should have been the end of the matter, particularly since traces observable under low-power magnification, and the technique itself, were subsequently placed on a firmer footing than ever before. John Tomenchuk (1985), employing engineering principles and quantifying use-fracturing along a tool edge at low-power magnification, was able to postdict tool motion and contact material. Despite several sporadic assays during the past 20 years, this remains the only successful use-wear analysis using totally objective, non-interpretive variables and they establish the correlation between fracturing and use-wear. But Tomenchuk's successes were ignored as high-power techniques burgeoned while low-power techniques dwindled in popularity, a victim of misperception and misinformation (Odell 1987).

The high-power technique also suffered some setbacks during this journey. One such situation involved the formation and recognition of *post-depositional surface modification* (PDSM), i.e., alteration of tool surfaces resulting from factors such as soil chemistry, artifact cleaning protocols, etc., which would have affected the tool since its discard (Baesemann 1986; Levi Sala 1986, 1993; Plisson 1986; Plisson and Mauger 1988; Kaminska et al. 1993). A great deal was learned from these exchanges and analysts emerged with a clearer understanding of the extraneous, non-use related forces that act on lithic implements. However, the contentious manner in which parts of the debate were couched and the doubts that were expressed about the method itself appear to have confirmed the worst fears of an already pessimistic audience outside the field of use-wear analysis.

Then there was the brouhaha evoked by the results of two blind tests conducted in the mid-1980s. One of these was an evaluation of 21 flint tools by a multi-national team of four use-wear analysts employing high-magnification equipment (Unrath et al. 1986). The test was difficult and, despite vapid attempts to make them appear acceptable, the results showed substantially poorer accuracy than either of the two previous blind tests.

The second of these evaluations, which involved several analysts and a technician with a hand lens, was orchestrated by Mark Newcomer, who had participated in the original blind test (Newcomer et al. 1986). Observational accuracy in three series of 10 tools apiece was abysmal; in fact, the technician with the hand lens did as well as the use-wear analysts. It was subsequently argued, and probably correctly, that the use duration of 10 minutes per tool that researchers had agreed on beforehand was too short for polish to develop past the initial generic phase (Moss 1987; Bamforth 1988; Hurcombe 1988). Nevertheless, these results sent shock waves rocketing through the use-wear community and further solidified the opposition of external critics.

These events created an ambiguous situation. Problem areas within the field had been encountered, evaluated, and, in most cases, either overcome or deflected, yet the contentious nature of the debate misled the interested but peripheral archaeological audience into believing that all was chaos and that no progress had been made. No matter which side of any particular debate a use-wear analyst was on, he or she was ultimately affected negatively by the process that brought us to our current circumstances.

By the late 1980s and early 1990s, the humbling influence of failure and the creeping realization that use-wear analysis was not being accepted as readily as it should have been by the wider archaeological community finally hit home. Suddenly there were calls to use the most appropriate technique available, to employ all possible wear traces in one's interpretations, and to merge more than one use-wear technique, where feasible (Hall et al. 1989:137; Unger-Hamilton 1989; Grace 1993a:385, 1996:217; LeMoine 1997:15). Ironically, events had placed the field right back in the situation that had existed in 1977, but by the 1990s the damage had been done: far fewer scholars had entered the field than had been anticipated, and the wider archaeological community was still distrustful of use-wear data. And this, despite the fact that use-wear practitioners had been forced to justify their claim to expertise to a far greater extent than any scientific expert brought in to assess pollen, faunal, or paleobotanical remains. On the positive side, the extensive testing and soul-searching encountered and overcame a number of potential problem areas and probably resulted in a more highly trained cadre of technicians than would otherwise have been the case.

Techniques

Techniques for observing use-wear can currently be perceived as following four different pathways, depending on the type of equipment used. In order of enlargement capabilities, they are: macroscopic, low-power, high-power, and scanning electron microscope. The principal question to be addressed in this section is:

Q19: Which technique(s) is (are) most effective for conducting functional studies of archaeological assemblages?

Macroscopic

By *macroscopic* is meant assessment with the naked eye, often aided by a hand lens of 10X magnification or so. Occasionally, use-wear is so obvious that it can readily be observed at a macroscopic level. The use of thin edges on hard materials (e.g., animal butchering) or the bright gloss on sickle blades are cases in point. But alas, these are about the only situations in which use-wear can be accurately assessed macroscopically, because traces more subtle than these are usually not visible or are systematically overlooked. Wear from use on soft materials such as meat, fish and soft vegetables can seldom be detected macroscopically, and even wear on hard substances is undetectable on thicker edges. In addition, practitioners of macroscopic approaches tend to concentrate on edges, which are often thin, rather than on projections, which are usually stout. In general, considerably more use-wear exists than is observable with macroscopic techniques. Since major categories (e.g., wear from soft materials or on projections) are systematically overlooked, it is impossible to put the wear that is observable into any kind of functional context. Conversely, extraneous damage from rock falls, tillage or archaeological excavation and handling can produce damage similar to use-wear, but one needs a microscope to be able to discern the difference.

This point has been supported empirically with respect to the use of the functionally based "utilized flake" category in typological systems, discussed previously. Tests have been conducted to evaluate the ability of researchers to accurately assess whether such a flake had actually been utilized. Results have been uniformly disappointing (Young and Bamforth 1990; Shen 1999), strongly supporting the position that this analytical approach is not accurate enough to be employed for archaeological functional analysis. Therefore, the macroscopic technique will not be described further.

Scanning Electron Microscope

At the other end of the enlargement scale is the scanning electron microscope (SEM), a large machine usually operated with the aid of a technician. The visual image in this machine is not activated by light rays but by a stream of electrons controlled by magnetic or electrical fields. Since the technique is not dependent on light, the visibility of an object is not regulated by the physical laws of light transmission by which the amount of light hitting an object decreases progressively with increases in magnification. Thus the SEM can reproduce an image at high magnification with excellent resolution and depth of field (Hay 1977; Del Bene 1979:169; d'Errico and Espinet-Moucadel 1986). Photography is also simple to operate and very clear.

The principal problem with this technique, from an archaeological point of view, involves the limitations of housing and viewing the objective piece. All machines contain a small stage or compartment into which the object is placed, a constriction that severely limits the size of the object that can be viewed. In addition, many SEMs house the object in a vacuum chamber and require the application of a thin metal coating over the objective surface. It thus becomes either difficult or undesirable to cram a metate, or even a scraper, into an SEM should one be so inclined—not only because of the size of the specimen, but also because of the vacuum chamber and the metallization procedure. Researchers have skirted some of these difficulties by making small synthetic replicas, or acetate peels, of tool surfaces and submitting them, instead of the tools themselves, to the microscope. Image resolution of certain synthetic compounds appears to be quite good even at high magnifications, and the peel has the added advantage of being able to flatten out otherwise curved or undulating surfaces, thus facilitating their observation (Knutsson 1988:26-29).

For a more detailed discussion of procedures involved with observing lithic tools with the scanning electron microscope, consult Box 5.1, which illustrates both the advantages and disadvantages of the machinery. The advantages are obvious: its capabilities of extremely high magnifications with little or no loss of resolution or depth of field mean that it can be used to study phenomena at a depth and clarity unparalleled by any of the other visual techniques considered. Being ideal for observing minute traits, its most effective application is in studying the development and genesis of wear. As described in Box 5.1, it enabled Knutsson to formulate and test a model of wear genesis.

Box 5.1. An SEM in the Boreal Forest

A notable study of experimental quartz tools was conducted in Sweden by Kjel Knutsson (1988). Although he employed an older JEOL JSM U-3 model scanning electron microscope (SEM) built in 1970—a model that has been modernized and upgraded greatly since that time—differences between the machine he was using and more modern ones are a matter of degree rather than of kind; the general principles and limitations of the technique still apply. This machine employed a low voltage mode of scanning and enabled magnifications in the range of 1000X to 10,000X.

Knutsson was interested in evaluating the wear on quartz, from which an abundance of prehistoric Swedish tools had been manufactured. In addition, he was concerned with understanding processes of abrasion in order to formulate a more effective wear model than existed at that time. Out of several hundred experimentally utilized tools he chose 28 for analysis with the SEM. After use, the experimental tools were placed in a detergent solution at room temperature for 24 hours, cleaned under running water, soaked in a 5% HCl solution for another 24 hours, cleaned again with running water, and finally placed in an ultrasonic tank containing distilled water for 30 seconds.

The specimens to be viewed with the SEM were broken into smaller pieces and a suitable portion of the utilized edge about 1 × 1 cm in size was glued onto a stub for viewing. Parts of the specimen that were not slated for analysis were sheathed in colloidal silver to enhance conductivity, after which the piece was covered with a 600 A thick gold layer. The specimen was now ready for scanning with the SEM. Although Knutsson employed broken parts of the actual experimental tools in this analysis, he used acetate peels in other analyses and in previous stages of this one. Descriptions of the preparation of these peels for use-wear analysis can be found in Knutsson (1988:26-29) and Knutsson and Hope (1984). Epoxy casts have also provided replicas of tool surfaces at a resolution sufficiently fine-grained to be usable at high magnification, provided that size of object is not an issue (Plisson 1983; Unrath and Lindemann 1984; Bienenfeld 1995; Banks and Kay 2003).

SEM analyses of the 28 experimental tools were able to concentrate on minute details such as surface flow, dissolution phenomena, and the development of wear from early through late stages, thus acquiring a thorough comprehension of wear formation processes. This success led to the formulation of a model in which most use abrasion in quartz is caused by mechanical processes, but is supplemented by silica precipitation, plastic deformation, and dissolution. The model was tested and confirmed by chemically etching some of the utilized tool surfaces with ammonium bifluoride, which accentuated the characteristics caused by the use-wear.

The very traits that make the SEM effective in analyzing wear formation also make it an inappropriate tool for studying archaeological assemblages. The small size of the objective chamber and the necessity, on most machines, to metalize the surface of the object preclude the possibility of directly observing more than a small percentage of an archaeological assemblage. This problem has been partly alleviated through acetate peels, but these take time to make and, without culling the data by observing tools with another kind of microscope, how does one know which part of an artifact warrants replication? This is the reason Knutsson took, for SEM observation, a small subset of a much larger sample of experimentally utilized tools that had already been observed and recorded with other kinds of microscopes. The SEM can be very effective in lithic analysis, but only for specific questions requiring small sample sizes.

Optical Microscopes

The workhorses of use-wear analysis employ light-sensitive optical micro-scopes in what I have previously dubbed *low-power* and *high-power* modes (Odell and Odell-Vereecken 1980). As I see it now, this is an unfortunate use of terminol-ogy, because the most important distinction between the two analytical types is not their difference in magnification but their use of different kinds of illumination, which facilitate the observation of certain features over others. Nevertheless, the differences in magnification used are generally real and current terminology does capture that distinction.

The pursuit of functional knowledge, no matter which optical technique is involved, has proceeded from a series of experiments in which tools are utilized in various ways on a variety of substances. In order to be relevant to an archaeological situation, the raw materials from which the tools are made should be similar to raw materials prevalent in the archaeological assemblage to be scrutinized. Exper-imental activities should be relatively comprehensive and pertinent to tasks that the studied prehistoric people can be expected to have conducted, with substances that would have been available to them.

Descriptions of experimental series on specialized tasks by researchers em-ploying low-power equipment are spread widely through the literature. They in-clude scraping (Brink 1978; Schultz 1992), graving (Stafford 1977), butchering (Odell 1980a), and projectile use (Fischer et al. 1984; Odell and Cowan 1986). Re-sults of more comprehensive experimental series have been published by Tringham et al. (1974), Lawrence (1979), Ahler (1971:81-87), Kamminga (1982), and Odell (1977, 1996). Comprehensive experimental series produced by high-power prac-titioners include Keeley (1980), Serizawa et al. (1982), Mansur-Franchomme (1983), Plisson (1985), Lewenstein (1987), and Pawlik (1995). Experiments deal-ing with specific activities or tool types have been carried out for agricultural prac-tices (Anderson 1992; Unger-Hamilton 1992), projectile points (Meeks 2000), use on animal horn (Pawlik 1993), fish processing (van Gijn 1986), and several other tasks.

Before encountering an archaeological collection, the analyst should peruse the experimental collection intensively and keep it handy for comparative purposes throughout the observations of archaeological specimens. It is also a good idea to take at least one blind test on experimental material, not moving on until satisfactory results have been achieved. This process is good for the soul, as it highlights areas of weakness and builds confidence in one's ability to interpret wear traces. Such a test need not be as formal as the published versions and may even be self-administered. The important element is that it be honest.

The following paragraphs will argue that low-power and high-power anal-yses are both appropriate for studying archaeological collections, but each has characteristics that enable it to address certain questions more effectively than others. On the level of the individual artifact, two basic functional issues must be confronted, of which the first is:

Q20: Which technique(s) is (are) suitable for ascertaining the dominant tool motion, or activity, in which an individual tool was engaged?

Low-Power

Low-power use-wear analysis employs equipment that has been standard issue for years in biological laboratories. It has been called a "dissecting microscope" because of its frequent use by biological students for inspecting the internal organs of small creatures such as frogs and foetal pigs. These days it is most often referred to simply as a *stereomicroscope*. It was this kind of instrument that was turned to in the early years of wear studies; and after Semenov's publication, this was still the principal type of microscope in use in both Russia and the West. So after Ruth Tringham returned from a visit to Semenov's St. Petersburg lab in 1966–67 (Tringham et al. 1974:178), this seemed like a natural instrument to use for developing some of the ideas that Semenov had promoted.

The stereomicroscope has several endearing features, not the least of which is ease of employment. The type I use, a Nikon SMZ-10, has a zoom lens, removable 10X and 20X eyepieces, and an additional 2X lens that can be attached onto the lower part of the lens tube. Using the 10X eyepieces and no other attachments, the microscope has a magnification range of 6.6X–40X. Use of the 2X bottom lens elevates this range to 80X, and replacing the 10X with the 20X eyepieces raises the limit to 160X. There is no stage as such, though an artifact may be stabilized by placing it on the bottom platform under the lens or securing it with modeling clay and lowering the lens to achieve focus. Most of the time an artifact is focused by holding it in the hands and moving it around under the lens until optimal focal length is achieved. The object is illuminated by reflective light that strikes it diagonally, enhancing shadow effects and depth of field necessary for interpreting topographic features stereoscopically.

An artifact is scanned by systematically observing all edges and surfaces, alternately raising and lowering magnifications as needed to get a good look at the traces and put them in perspective. When viewing an archaeological collection I almost always use the 2X bottom lens and often require the maximum magnification of 80X that this provides; occasionally it is necessary to change eyepieces and raise the magnification, sometimes all the way to 160X. Compared to the SEM and high-power techniques, this remains at the low end of the enlargement scale, but visual enhancement is considerably greater than with macroscopic techniques and is sufficient to see and record all types of wear traces.

If you are shopping around for a low-power microscope, be sure to buy one with either an effective, modern-style adapter to an existing eyepiece or a trinocular head. The third pathway is for a photographic attachment, which makes taking photographs considerably easier than focusing through one of the eyepieces. Having spent a substantial amount of time focusing objects by using cross-hairs in one of the eyepieces of a stereoscopic microscope, I can state categorically that you do not want to attempt this without at least a top-of-the-line adapter. This assertion derives from the practical experience of walking home in the Netherlands after 6–8 hours of microscopic photography, after which my focal length had become so miniscule that I was constantly in danger of taking a dip in a canal.

Each of the wear types mentioned previously, from edge fracturing to rounding, surface polish and striations, is employed in interpreting the function of a stone tool. In fact, it is dangerous to interpret any pattern of wear traces solely on the basis of fracturing without confirmatory evidence from abrasive damage. This point, though consistently adhered to by serious practitioners, was not emphasized in my own publications, which concentrated on the more diagnostic traces on which most interpretations depended (e.g., Tringham et al. 1974; Odell 1980b, 1981a; Odell and Odell-Vereecken 1980). It *was* emphasized, however, in the single most important exegesis of the low-power position, the extensive analysis of experimental material conducted by Johan Kamminga (1982). Kamminga's descriptions of abrasive variables are at least as lengthy and complete as his descriptions of edge fracturing—a fact that has been lost on most use-wear analysts, who either never read his work or conveniently overlooked it in pursuit of a different methodological agenda.

Box 5.2. Low-Power Meets Lowilva

The Lower Illinois Valley (termed "Lowilva" by the Archies who lived there) northwest of St. Louis is a very rich archaeological precinct that has inspired innovative research for years. In the 1960s Stuart Struever, then at Northwestern University, conceived the Foundation for Illinois Archeology (later the Center for American Archeology, or CAA). The Foundation bought up a third of the buildings in Kampsville, a river town, and installed a cadre of assorted archaeologists, biologists and other technical types to work on the plethora of datasets being generated. Fieldwork on the region's most famous site, Koster, continued unabated from 1969 to 1978.

During the latter years of the Koster excavation, the CAA split into a Field School division and a Contract division, the latter a not-for-profit organization designed to promote local archaeological research. One of its first large projects involved the right-of-way for an interstate highway segment between Jacksonville and Quincy, Illinois, on which 92 sites were discovered and surveyed (Farnsworth and Walthall 1983). The significance of each of the sites was evaluated, and several were deemed important enough to warrant extensive excavation. Ultimately, lithic analysis of these assemblages varied from brief typo-technological studies of their modified tools to intensive functional analyses.

I was hired as Director of the CAA's Lithic Analysis Laboratory. During my tenure with this organization, I conducted several low-magnification use-wear analyses using a Nikon reflective-light, SMZ-10 stereomicroscope. Except for assuring that all data were mutually compatible, there was no planning or foresight with respect to the order by which samples were analyzed or their congruence for future comparisons: assemblages were studied if a principal investigator had an interest in doing so and enough money in his budget. It turned out that the first assemblages whose lithic functional attributes were observed were also the weirdest: two components of the Napoleon Hollow site next to the Illinois River that belonged to an ancient Middle Woodland mortuary ritual precinct (see Box 5.5)—although that piece of knowledge was gained only later, through extensive analysis of several datasets. Lithic samples from three stratified Archaic components from this site were subsequently analyzed, as well.

To the Napoleon Hollow assemblages were added samples from three other sites. Smiling Dan, a small Middle Woodland village, provided an interesting contrast to the Napoleon Hollow Middle Woodland mortuary assemblages across the river. On the Smiling Dan side of the river was an earlier settlement, Campbell Hollow, which yielded two stratified deposits: a late Early Archaic component overlain by a Middle Archaic one. These contrasted nicely with the three Napoleon Hollow Archaic components analyzed previously. Finally, remains of a small Mississippian farmstead called Hill Creek were subsequently discovered nearby on another project and this assemblage was thrown into the mix. The lithic dataset whose functional parameters were investigated thus consisted of nine prehistoric components partitioned thusly: 1 late Early Archaic, 3 Middle Archaic, 1 Late Archaic, 3 Middle Woodland, and 1 Mississippian. These assemblages represented 7500 years of Illinois Valley prehistory.

The lithic samples, totaling about 6600 artifacts, were microscopically analyzed and written up, each dataset being employed in a different manner for the interpretation of each individual site. In some cases the functional data became an integral part of site spatial analyses—as with Hill Creek, where artifacts were compared with one another on the basis of their relation to structures and pit features (Odell 1985); or Campbell Hollow, where spatial algorithms were used to help delineate activity areas and clarify the distribution of artifact types (Stafford 1985). In other cases these data served a more peripheral role in the overall interpretation of the site.

As time went by, it became increasingly apparent that the archaeological project for which most of the individual site reports had been prepared was not headed toward any kind of synthesis. Yet it was also apparent that a synthesis of the lithic functional data alone could contribute significantly to our understanding of prehistoric activities for three-quarters of the known human occupation of the region. So it was that the lithic data, spread over five site reports and several other documents, were compiled in a single volume, reinterpreted, and compared by prehistoric component in Odell (1996).

The results of these comparisons were informative and sometimes unpredictable. The incidence of hafted tools is a case in point. One may have supposed that hafting increased through time but, given the typically abysmal conditions of preservation, how would one ever document that trend? It turns out that, in many cases, hafting damage on stone tools can be recognized and described (see Box 5.4). When this variable was plotted proportionally over time in Illinois Valley assemblages, it increased. During the same period, damage attributable to holding tools in the hand decreased proportionally (Odell 1994a,b).

Functional data have also contributed to arguments of economizing behavior on settlements on which it was relatively difficult to procure usable stone for tools—in this region, east of the Illinois River. Comparing Archaic components, tool users at Campbell Hollow, east of the river, showed a greater utilization of broken edges than tool users on the western side of the river at Napoleon Hollow. This finding coincided with a greater proportion of cores and of unbroken bifaces and unifacial tools in the Napoleon Hollow components, as well as some of the only recognized bipolar debitage from nodule smashing in the Campbell Hollow assemblage (Odell 1989b, 1996:202-207).

The foregoing is a sampling of results from the Illinois Valley functional analysis. A diachronic study was able to be pursued and trends detected because the use-wear technique employed promoted the study of large samples and allowed a resolution appropriate for examining broadly defined issues.

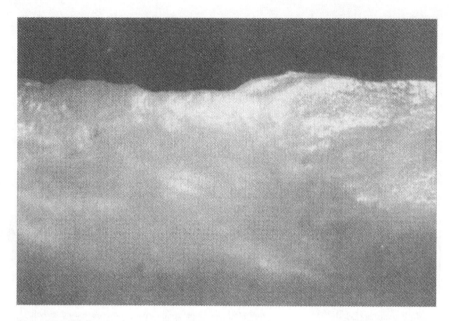

Figure 5.1.   Extensive rounding and polish on edge of experimentally utilized fresh hide scraping tool;
25X magnification.

While all visible use damage should be employed in attributing wear to
specific patterns of traces, it remains true that certain kinds of traces are more
diagnostic than others. For instance, the scraping of animal skin produces rapid
edge attrition ultimately resulting in polishing and extreme edge rounding. These
features are evident on a flint edge experimentally utilized for scraping fresh hide
(Figure 5.1). Polishing and edge rounding are often associated with striations perpendicular to the edge (Gallagher 1977; Brink 1978:101-113; Hayden 1979, 1990;
Kamminga 1982:38-43; Odell 1996:43-45). Edge fracturing remains an extremely
useful indicator of prehistoric task performance, as different fracture sizes, terminations and distributions have been correlated with specific activity/worked material
combinations. Characteristic fractures from butchering are illustrated in Figure 5.2.
Relatively comprehensive task-specific wear associations have been described in
Tringham et al. (1974), Odell (1977, 1981a), Odell and Odell-Vereecken (1980),
and Kamminga (1982). An example of an application of low-power analysis to
archaeological material is provided in Box 5.2.

Blind testing (Odell and Odell-Vereecken 1980; Shea 1987, 1988) has confirmed that the low-power technique is proficient in certain areas but not in others. It
is quite good for distinguishing the presence and location of use-wear, as well as the
activity in which a tool was engaged, or tool motion. Thus in response to Research
Question 20 posed above, blind tests and abundant anecdotal evidence demonstrate

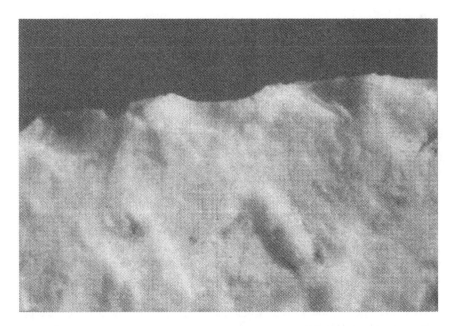

Figure 5.2.   Fracturing on the used edge of a chert dog butchering knife; 20X magnification.

that low-power techniques are successful in accurately depicting tool motion. The next fundamental issue to be confronted on the level of the individual artifact is:

Q21: Which technique(s) is (are) suitable for ascertaining the material with which the tool made contact?

For distinguishing exact contact materials the low-power technique has not proven very accurate, though frequently accurate assessments can be made. Nevertheless, uncertainties on this point have induced low-power practitioners to classify worked material into a restricted number of categories based on the hardness of the substance, or its resistance to pressure from work. For the initial blind tests I employed four categories: soft, soft-medium, hard-medium, and hard (Odell and Odell-Vereecken 1980). More recently I have broken worked material down into seven categories but combined them into a soft-medium-hard structure for statistical analysis (Odell 1996, 1999).

Advantages of low-power techniques are the following: because the equipment is easy to manipulate, protocols are easy to learn. And because focusing is done by hand and magnifications are relatively reduced, the relation between any given wear trace and its edge and overall tool context is usually clear. Despite the necessity to examine all parts of a specimen systematically, scanning can generally be done relatively quickly, with the result that large samples can be processed. This element permits several categories or parts of an archaeological site to be compared using a variety of statistical procedures, a situation that is not possible when sample sizes dip below certain critical levels. Accuracy of wear location and tool motion have been shown to be quite high, and the necessary division of worked material into a limited number of resistance classes does not result in the loss of very much usable information. The categories soft, medium and hard are quite satisfactory for most of the archaeological situations that I have encountered.

One disadvantage of this technique includes occasional difficulties distinguishing use fracturing from extraneous damage and intentional retouch. This problem will never be eliminated, but may be alleviated experimentally by improving the analyst's ability to distinguish these forms of damage. Another disadvantage is its inaccuracy in specifying exact worked material. When the archaeological problem is restricted to a particular class of tools or wear types, this shortcoming can be important. Based on current literature, for example, few if any low-power analysts would have been able to pull off with demonstrable accuracy the study that Yerkes (1983, 1989) produced on the issue of Mississippian shell bead production. Low-power practitioners would have been able to state that the wear on these microlithic drill bits was caused by a resistant material of some sort, but they probably could not have distinguished between bone, antler and shell—all of which have yielded beads.

High-Power

The instrument of choice for the high-power technique is the binocular metallurgical microscope with incident lighting. Directed from above, light strikes the object either at a 90° angle (light-field illumination) or a 45° angle to its surface (dark-field illumination). Dark-field illumination is better for gross surficial and marginal features at lower magnifications, whereas light-field illumination is better for viewing surface topography at higher magnifications, i.e., above 100X (Keeley 1980:12-14; Lewenstein 1987:81). Details of magnification and lens configuration vary from one type of microscope to another. For example, Mansur-Franchomme (1983:83-84) employed lens attachments and eyepieces on a Wild M-20 microscope that provided a series of magnifications up to 500X; later in her analysis she started using an Olympus PME with capabilities of enlargement to only 400X but possessing a stage that could accommodate larger objects.

Most metallurgical microscopes are binocular but lack stereoscopic capabilities. Their strength lies in interpreting subtle changes in surface topography like those caused by different kinds of abrasive forces. With this equipment researchers have been able to discriminate among types of polish associated with specific worked materials, a claim that has held up reasonably well in most of the blind tests. Of the abundant examples of use-polish observed with metallurgical

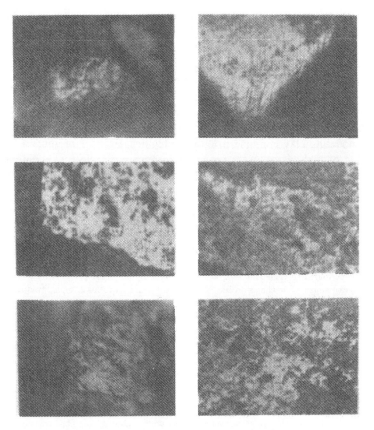

Figure 5.3. Use-polish on chert from working wood, observed on archaeological specimens from Cerros, Belize: *upper left*: sawing; *upper right*: gloss and striations from scraping or planing; *middle left*: perforating/scraping; *middle right*: polish and striae on scraper-plane; *lower left*: perforating; *lower right*: incising (taken from Lewenstein 1987: Figures 95–100).

microscopes, I have selected a set of six experiments of woodworking from the Mayan archaeological site of Cerros in Belize (Figure 5.3). Although many of the characteristics of this type of use-polish appear to be variable, all exhibit the bright, glossy aspect diagnostic of wood polish. Linear striations can also be effectively observed with high-magnification equipment, as shown in Figure 5.3 (upper and middle right) from scraping or planing wood. Some discrimination of striation types has been achieved (Mansur 1982, 1986), but this research is still in its infancy. The ability to discriminate types of polish and striations is most important for distinguishing worked materials; if exact worked material is required, the high-power use-wear technique is the most effective solution.

Another strength of high-power techniques is the ability to employ relatively high magnifications, a quality made possible by the increase in illumination with increases in enlargement provided by the incident lighting technology (Keeley 1980:13; Mansur-Franchomme 1983:84). Finally, high-power techniques may have the ability to identify the type of hammer used to manufacture tools (Veerle Rots, pers. commun. 2002), though supporting data for this assertion have not yet been published. Photography with metallurgical microscopes is generally straightforward, but can entail focusing problems from restricted depth of field. Though digital cameras have alleviated certain aspects of this problem, other issues like observing surfaces with variable topography and leaving tools too long in modeling clay continue to pose difficulties. Box 5.3 presents a typical application of high-power use-wear analysis to an archaeological situation, the French early Magdalenian.

Box 5.3. High-Power High Jinks at Cassegros

Shortly after Larry Keeley initiated his approach to use-wear analysis, a spate of graduate students took up the mantle by developing the technique and applying it to archaeological assemblages. One of the most prominent was Patrick Vaughan, a doctoral student at the University of Pennsylvania, who had prepared himself for analysis by undertaking a comprehensive series of 249 functional experiments. Vaughan's project illustrates a typical application of high-power analysis and one in which the technique was nicely suited to the situation (Vaughan 1985).

The archaeological application in this case was an assemblage from the early Magdalenian level (called Magdalenian "0") from the small cave of Cassegros in southwestern France. The deposits in this level had been heavily stained by red ochre, a phenomenon that readily demarcated them from units above and below. Although the cave had been excavated for seven field seasons, Magdalenian 0 level 10 yielded only 532 flints larger than 1 cm long, a quantity that Vaughan could analyze in its entirety. These flints included a range of Upper Paleolithic tool types, as well as several unretouched flakes and a lesser quantity of blades.

Vaughan's results confirmed a number of points that other scholars had previously established, such as: 1) some tool types correlated strongly with certain activities, but most were used for a variety of tasks; 2) unretouched flakes were utilized for a full range of tasks, just as formal tool types were; and 3) plant-cutting tools have been identified in assemblages vastly pre-dating Neolithic sickle blades. Vaughan found that almost 60% of the utilized tools from the early Magdalenian level had been employed in processing dry hides. Minor components of use on wood, bone, antler, and an unspecified hard material were also present.

A significant contribution of Vaughan's study was in specifying the spatial distribution of functional types at the site. Hide scraping activities occurred throughout the excavated portions of level 10. Unfortunately, no structural elements were recognized, suggesting that the cave may not have been an actual habitation, but rather an occasional or seasonal workshop locale where hides were processed by people who lived someplace else (Vaughan 1985:99).

Vaughan's use-wear analysis contributed substantially to knowledge of the Cassegros site and the early Magdalenian in general. It specified the range of tasks conducted, highlighted hide scraping as the dominant activity, and indicated the types of tools that were associated with specific tasks. From these results functional tool types could be plotted on a site plan and used to interpret the spatial distribution of activities across the site.

Abrasive traces can be subtle and are occasionally confounded by residues left on tool surfaces through a variety of extraneous factors, an issue that has elevated the importance of artifact cleaning processes among high-power analysts.

Keeley (1980:10-11) habitually wiped his implements with white spirits, washed them in ammonia-based cleaners, immersed them in warm 10% HCl and 20–30% NaOH solutions, and finally placed them in an ultrasonic cleaning tank. If mineral deposits survived all this, they were removed by prolonged immersion in hot HCl. If anybody objected that these treatments might alter the surface of the tool or actually degrade it, Keeley's response (personal communication, 1981) was that functional interpretations of archaeological artifacts are based on their similarity to experimentally derived comparative collections. Since the latter had all been treated in this way, it matters little what the chemicals do to the surface of the tool, because it will have affected all tools in the same way.

This justification has not satisfied everybody. First, it is possible that researchers employing divergent cleaning procedures, with possibly differential effects on the various flint surfaces, were actually observing different phenomena (Moss 1986). And second, some of the chemical treatments used had the potential to alter or degrade the surface of flint (and, supposedly, any polish on that surface), a point supported by several experimental assays (Plisson 1986; Plisson and Mauger 1988; Rodon Borras 1990). The result of these studies is that the use of chemical cleansers has declined in both submersion time and intensity since the early days of the technique; several practitioners these days employ few, if any, chemical solutions in cleaning their artifacts.

The popularity of the high-power technique is a result of its capacity for postdicting the exact worked material with which an individual implement made contact. This increment in accuracy is not without cost. First, some metallurgical microscopes possess stages that can accommodate only small artifacts or parts of artifacts. This problem has been alleviated through the use of acetate peels or by switching to a microscope with a different stage setup (Mansur-Franchomme 1983). Second, the artifact is not handled with the hands but is manipulated by a series of knobs. The higher the magnification and the further into the interior a given observation point is, the more difficult it becomes to comprehend the orientation of the wear at that locale with respect to the closest margin and the overall tool configuration. Third, there is typically a short working distance between the instrument lens and the surface of the object being observed. Keeley (1980:12) first noted that "it may be difficult to observe features at the bottom of a hollow because the objective lens apparatus will not fit between the adjacent high points." But once Keeley presented the problem, he dismissed it without offering any resolution and it continues to plague some analysts. On the other hand, technical improvements to many microscopes have included objectives that are able to operate at long working distances (Veerle Rots, pers. commun. 2002), so this may no longer be a problem for most practitioners.

A fourth problem area is the inability of most metallurgical microscopes to reproduce an image stereoscopically. This is not a problem when one restricts oneself to observing surface abrasive phenomena, but contributes to inaccuracies when trying to interpret edge fracturing. Inconvenient details of this nature have not always impeded some of our colleagues from making far-reaching pronouncements on fracturing when using non-stereoscopic microscopes (e.g., Vaughan 1985; see reply in Odell 1986). An advancement in high-power technology involves Nomarski optics. Providing three-dimensional views of tool surfaces, this addition improves the clarity of both polish and edge fracturing (Kay 1996:319).

Finally, the issue of analysis time must be confronted at some point. In the early days some high-power practitioners were in denial: Mansur-Franchomme (1983:37) even doubted that there was any difference whatsoever in processing time between low- and high-power techniques. But this variable has been recorded by some analysts and can be verified. In the first series of low-power blind tests, the average observation time, not including variable recording, was 5 minutes/tool (Odell and Odell-Vereecken 1980). In contrast, participants in the Tuebingen blind test took an average of 1.5 hours/tool (Unrath et al. 1986:165). The late Irene Levi Sala, one of the researchers at the London Institute, has gone even further, stating, "It is my experience that it can take much longer than one or two hours for complex pieces" (Levi Sala 1996:2).

These days the issue of appropriate equipment has induced some researchers to employ both dissecting and metallurgical microscopes in their analyses (Grace 1993b; Brass 1998:21; Clemente and Gibaja 1998; van Gijn 1998; Rots 2002). Combining the two techniques compensates for the deficiencies of using either method alone, and allows the analyst to select tools under lower magnifications that can receive extensive treatment under higher magnifications.

Summary

The purpose of this section is to provide an overview of functional techniques currently available to contemporary lithic researchers. It is argued that each technique is useful for certain purposes but less so for others. On the other hand, many of these traces can be studied effectively with both techniques, witnessed by observation of prehensile traces, i.e., damage from holding the tool in a hand or haft (see Box 5.4).

Box 5.4. Prehensile Traces

The literature of use-wear analysis is full of descriptions of the damage that accrues to tool edges and surfaces from contact with a worked material. Yet this "active" area is not the only portion of the tool that was in contact with something or that received pressure of some kind during the utilization process. If the tool was held in the hand, the fingers or palm surely exerted pressure on certain parts of the stone. The hand may have been wrapped in leather to protect it, thereby being able to exert even greater pressure on the tool. If the implement was hafted, it may have been immobilized by the hafting mechanism, but just as probably the handle allowed some movement, however slight. In most of these situations, contact between the tool and the hand or a haft may have been intense enough to cause friction or edge fracturing, and if so, that damage may be recognizable as such. The generic term for either holding a tool in the hand or securing it in a hafting device is *prehension*.

I am interested in this process because, in trying to develop workable use-wear techniques in the early days after Semenov's study, my own experimentation produced prehensile damage all over the place (Tringham et al. 1974; Odell 1977, 1980a). In addition, I was seeing the same types of damage in archaeological collections (Odell 1977, 1978, 1980b). During blind testing the discrimination of prehensile wear became an important element in accurately assessing the forces to which these experimental pieces had been subjected, and was accordingly described in detail (Odell and Odell-Vereecken 1980:102-108; Odell 1981a:207).

Imagine my surprise when, in subsequent years, the entire issue of damage from prehensile forces was totally ignored by almost every use-wear researcher on the planet. But not without consequence. In 1984–85 a multi-national cadre of four analysts took a blind test administered from Tuebingen, Germany (Unrath et al. 1986), the results of which were not encouraging. Of the difficulties that could be highlighted specifically, the most pervasive were those in which either prehended portions were mistaken for use-wear or use-wear was interpreted wrongly as prehensile damage (see Owen and Unrath 1989:674). In evaluating the results, the experimenters opined,

> It is remarkable that very few attempts were made in this blind test to distinguish hafting traces. Tools nos. 18 and 20 clearly show that there is a large gap between the search for use-wear traces on the edge areas and prehension and hafting traces on the surfaces of the dorsal ridges. Remarks on the answer sheets indicate that the analysts believe hafting wear traces exist but that they are undiagnostic, infrequent or too problematical to analyze within the framework of a blind test. Hafting is a task, and it is a significant technological feature archeologically. Its appearance in prehistory has been reported through microwear analysis (e.g., Keeley 1982), but experimental documentation and quantification of the wear traces ... are woefully few. As a result of the general lack of experimental hafting, confident recognition of hafting in the archeological record is undoubtedly low. (Unrath et al. 1986:172-173)

Problems in the prehensile realm stimulated a conference attended by many of the prominent use-wear researchers of the day (Stordeur 1987). Despite a program designated specifically to deconstruct hafting traces and make them interpretable, the general conclusion of that conference seems to have been that, on evidence presented to that point, prehensile traces were too subtle to be assessed accurately. The limited research on this topic conducted subsequent to the hafting conference (e.g., Owen and Unrath 1989) indicated that prehensile traces could indeed be interpreted, but this research was quickly forgotten.

Well, almost. Veerle Rots, a graduate student at the Catholic University of Leuven (Belgium), became interested in this subject and persisted, despite being told by several use-wear researchers that hafting wear could not be accurately discriminated. After an extensive experimental program, intensive analysis, and application to collections from Upper Paleolithic and Neolithic sites in Belgium and France, Rots determined that: 1) hafting and other prehensile damage was produced experimentally; 2) it was interpretable as such; and 3) it was observable in the prehistoric samples analyzed (Rots 2002).

In her analysis Rots employed several microscopic techniques and recorded the kinds of traces that were interpretable by each. Interestingly, given the history of research on this topic, she concluded after analyzing the prehistoric samples that, in almost every case, macroscopic and low-power analysis were sufficient for making a reliable interpretation of prehensile traces, which was usually confirmed by observation with high-power equipment. The upshot of this research is this: the world's first and only doctoral dissertation devoted entirely to prehensile traces on experimental and archaeological stone tools has concluded that prehensile traces are interpretable, after all. What goes around, comes around.

This section is meant to be a guide through the literature, indicating the potential usefulness of each of the possible technical modes for analyzing archaeological assemblages. If you should decide to further evaluate one of these techniques, you should procure and try out the appropriate equipment, then delve more deeply into technical studies in that analytical mode. Citations in this chapter should be enough to get you started.

To summarize: the least useful analytical technique is macroscopic analysis, because most of the diagnostic wear types are either invisible or unlikely to be accurately assessed in their appropriate context. Use of the SEM is viable, but only for specific issues. Its superior depth of field at high magnifications makes it ideal for investigating the origins and genesis of specific wear types. On the other hand, its severe limitations on object size and its processing requirements, usually involving metallization and a vacuum chamber, assure that sample sizes will always be low, restricting the types of research questions that can reasonably be assessed. This is not the type of technique that one would wish to apply to an entire assemblage of stone tools.

The two analytical modes that are most applicable to the investigation of prehistoric assemblages are the low-power and high-power techniques. Low-power analysis is accurate in assessing the presence and location of use-wear, as well as tool motion and worked material on a 3- or 4-part resistance scale. It is not accurate in assessing exact worked material. The ease and speed by which artifacts can be analyzed make it suitable for the examination of large samples and their manipulation by an array of statistical algorithms. This analytical mode facilitates the investigation of large research questions such as long-term, diachronic patterns of tool use or the comparison of several portions of an archaeological settlement.

The high-power technique enables the accurate assessment of all important functional parameters including the specific substance with which a tool made contact. It has proven to be popular for investigating archaeological assemblages or parts thereof, and developments in appropriate artifact cleaning techniques, post-depositional surface modification, and other matters have increased its methodological rigor substantially. Certain microscopes have characteristics or requirements, such as a non-stereoscopic image or small objective stage, that limit their usefulness; and prolonged analysis time remains a limiting factor. High-power techniques can be employed conjunctively with low-power ones, or they can complement each other through separate analyses. An example of the latter is presented in Box 5.5.

Box 5.5. A Congruence of Techniques

As explained elsewhere in this chapter, low-power and high-power use-wear techniques developed simultaneously but grew apart in the 1980s as they increasingly came to be perceived as competing with one another. This is no longer the case, and many analysts now employ both systems in studying a body of stone tools (Grace 1993a,b; Pawlik 1995:19; Hudler 1997:26-27;

van Gijn 1998; Kooyman 2000:151). Each technique has strengths and weaknesses in different areas and can complement each other effectively.

Occasionally a low-power and high-power analysis converge to provide insight on a particular topic. A case in point concerns production of prismatic blades in the Middle Woodland period of the North American midcontinent. This technique appeared out of nowhere about the same time as the mortuary/ceremonial overlay known as "Hopewell," lasted for perhaps 500–600 years, and disappeared as mysteriously as it had come. For decades scholars have been seeking clues to the function of these blades, but that knowledge has been elusive, to say the least.

One thing is certain: to inform on the function of the blade phenomenon in Middle Woodland society, it would help to know the functions of individual blades. A breakthrough in this matter occurred with the excavation and analysis of the Murphy site, a small Hopewell habitation in central Ohio located near the famous Newark Earthworks and Flint Ridge quarries. As part of a larger study, Richard Yerkes (1990) applied high-power use-wear techniques to a sample of 456 retouched and unretouched blades from the Murphy assemblage. He found that the blades had been used for 12 different tasks, including cutting, graving and scraping. High-power techniques thus established that Middle Woodland blades at this small habitation site were not specialized tools; indeed, there was no evidence at all for craft production at this site.

During the same period George Odell completed the analysis of several prehistoric assemblages from another hotbed of Hopewellian culture, the Lower Illinois Valley (see Box 5.2). Included in these assemblages were three Middle Woodland components. The analysis of several datasets established that one, Smiling Dan, was a Hopewell habitation; the other two were a circular ritual structure next to the river (Napoleon Hollow floodplain component) and a dumping area (Napoleon Hollow hillslope component) halfway up the bluff between the floodplain below and the Middle Woodland Elizabeth Mounds on top. Odell's data from each of these components included a large sample of retouched and unretouched blades, which he inspected using low-power equipment (Odell 1994c).

Analysis of the Smiling Dan habitation showed the same phenomenon that Yerkes had witnessed in Ohio: the blades had been used for a number of different activities—as wide a range, in fact, as the unretouched flakes or most of the retouched tool classes. Whatever social processes governed the use of prismatic blades on habitation sites, they apparently operated similarly in both Ohio and Illinois.

The surprise came in analyzing the two Napoleon Hollow components. Both were associated with a ritual context: a circular structure probably occupied sporadically by a priestly elite, and a dump for material evacuated from the mounds on top of the bluff. In these assemblages the blades had much more restricted purposes. Unretouched blades were used almost exclusively for cutting, mostly of soft materials like hides, skins and soft vegetal substances. A large proportion of the retouched blades had been employed for scraping soft substances like hide. These activities appear to have been related to preparation for ritual or ceremonial activities, either of foodstuffs, or bedding, or hides.

This analysis established that, when a component was associated with a ceremonial context, Hopewell blades were related in some way to that context. When the blades were associated with living quarters such as a camp or village, they operated according to a different dynamic, being used for a much wider range of activities. A ritual connection may still have existed, but it was a different kind of connection. From a methodological standpoint, the Yerkes and Odell studies demonstrate that the low-power and high-power techniques overlap significantly, they augment one another effectively, and the knowledge gained in one is ultimately transferable to the other.

It cannot be stressed strongly enough that use-wear analysis does not simply add a nice supplement to the meat-and-potatoes of typology and technology. It provides an entirely different vector on which to assess lithic assemblages, a point made several years ago by Semenov (1970). Consider the lithic analysis of Lasley Vore, a large protohistoric settlement in eastern Oklahoma that yielded 10 discrete feature clusters, five of which were subsequently compared with one another in quantitative terms. Despite extensive testing, no typological or technological variable exhibited the slightest tendency to favor one part of the site over another. In other words, all portions of the settlement yielded the same tool types manufactured by the same processes. But when these clusters were compared on use-wear criteria, clear differences were discernible. The central part of the site was characterized by domestic activities such as food preparation and the construction of facilities; other locales were distinguishable as areas of tool maintenance, woodworking, weapons repair, and light industry (Odell 1999). This study demonstrates that functional types operate on a separate plane from types defined on the basis of morphology and technology. Typological systems can be applied to functional questions only in the broadest sense.

RESIDUE ANALYSIS

Residue is the non-soil stuff that clings to a stone tool. It can be organic or inorganic and it may have gotten there through precipitation, meaningful contact with the origin of the substance, or because a cave bear sauntered through and sat on the tool for awhile. In other words, the association of a substance with the surface of a stone does not necessarily tell you how that substance got there. Arguments of origin are necessarily inferential and probabilistic. This does not render residue analysis less significant, but it does require the researcher to establish probable cause for the association.

At least four lines of evidence can be used to test whether or not a residue was produced through utilization of that material by stone tools. First, finding the same type of residue on non-utilitarian or non-cultural objects in the site as is present on the tool renders a cultural or tool-use origin of this residue unlikely (Briuer 1976:482). Second, finding in the soil bits of the same material contained in the residue and at a similar intensity renders the soil a more likely contributor of the residue than utilization processes. Third, on the other hand, a distribution of residue on the tool that is aggregated and coincides with areas of use strengthens the argument that utilization produced the residue. Finally, finding spatially associated use-wear of a type consistent with the residue also strengthens its causal link with utilization (Hardy and Garufi 1998:179).

Plant Remains

Once a plant residue can be associated with the use of a particular stone tool, other questions immediately arise. The most basic can be phrased as follows:

Q22: Do plant residues on archaeological stone tools reliably indicate the principal substances on which these tools made contact?

This question will be posed for three common types of plant residue analysis.

Compound Structures

People have noticed residues on archaeological stone tools for a long time, but the scientific investigation of them is relatively recent. An early study of residues was Frederick Briuer's (1976) examination of 37 tools from two prehistoric rock shelters in Chevelon Canyon, northeastern Arizona. Briuer conducted a low-power use-wear analysis of each of the specimens, and attempted to identify the adhering material through microscopic observation and a series of chemical reagents. Most, perhaps all, of the residues that could be identified were of vegetal origin. Though the author was quick to note that these results did not necessarily mean that vegetal materials were worked by these implements, the specific locations of residue on the tools and the correspondence of the residue results with the use-wear analysis render this conclusion likely.

Shafer and Holloway (1979) followed up on Briuer's work with a similar study of 11 Archaic-period chert flake tools from Hinds Cave in southwest Texas. Low-power use-wear analysis indicated that most of this sample consisted of sharp, multi-purpose cutting and slicing tools. Microscopic observation of the residues revealed phytoliths, starch grains, plant fibers, rodent (especially lagomorph) hairs, and epidermis fragments from Agave lechuguilla, sotol and yucca. Figure 5.4 illustrates the wide range of residues that were observed on these tools.

Although the association between the residue and the task in which a tool was engaged was not established conclusively, the study suggested that these tools were used in activities such as butchering hare and slicing desert succulents. These conclusions were later corroborated by a similar study of 55 tools from Hinds Cave by Sobolik (1996). Along with the research on soft plant materials such as yucca, the working of wood has been identified at other sites through the preservation of tiny bits of cellular tissue preserved on tool surfaces (Hardy and Garufi 1998).

Although these kinds of studies are useful in any region and period, they are particularly beneficial in creating a baseline for tool use or resource exploitation. This has been a driving force in ethnographic studies of Australian Aborigines, some of whom still use stone tools (Fullagar et al. 1992). Establishing patterns for the ethnographic present provides a range of practices that serve as a referent that extends for many years into prehistory.

The common denominator of these studies is the identification of plant parts through microscopic investigation of the residues. Attempting such an analysis for the first time entails preparation along several lines. The most basic requirement

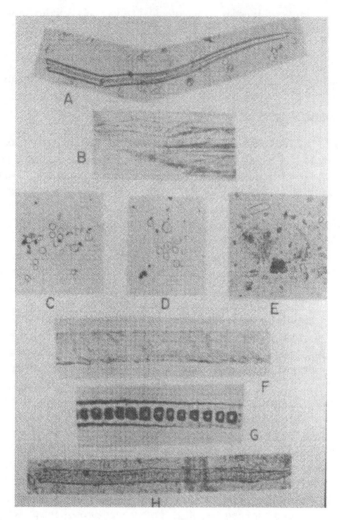

Figure 5.4.   Residues identified on stone tools from Hinds Cave in southwest Texas: a,b) plant fibers; c,d) starch crystals; e) phytoliths; f) lagomorph hair; g,h) rodent hair (taken from Shafer and Holloway 1979: Figure 4).

is to be able to identify plant tissue under the microscope. Published photos of anatomical features (e.g., for wood, see references cited by Hardy and Garufi 1998:180) are helpful, as are replication experiments of tools used on materials likely to be encountered among prehistoric residues. The Hardy and Garufi study also included a 50-item blind test for identifying residues. If the edges on which residues are observed are to be examined for use-wear, then preparation for this kind of analysis, described earlier in this chapter, must also be completed.

Starch Grains

A panoply of plant parts, including stellate hairs, conifer tracheids, raphides, hair vessels, fibers, and calcium oxalate crystals have been recognized in archaeological deposits, and most of them in stone tool residues. Chapters have been written on their identification, but I will concentrate here on two plant elements that have proven most useful to archaeologists: starch grains and phytoliths.

Starch is a solid food material formed in plant cells. More specifically, it is produced by chloroplasts in leaves, but does not last very long there. It is also produced by amyloplasts in seeds, tubers and roots, and can be stored there as a reserve food source for several years.

Starch forms as grains that are usually oval or spherical but can assume other shapes. Grains grow by apposition, exhibiting layers or lamellae from this process. They often cluster in specific ways and, in this form, are known as compound grains. They can also appear as semi-compound grains that have at least one apposition layer around the aggregated grains. The crystalline properties of the internal structure of individual grains make them birefringent and thus readily identifiable using a microscope with cross-polarized illumination. With this equipment a characteristic cross-shaped pattern appears on individual grains or on aggregations. Although interplant and intergrain variation exists, grain formation is genetically controlled and starch can be identified to at least the family and sometimes to the species level (Hall et al. 1989:139-141).

Much of the development of starch grain residue research has occurred in Oceania. Here considerable effort has gone into addressing basic issues of contamination and taphonomy that must be resolved before archaeological work can proceed. An issue we have already encountered is, how does one know that a particular residue was deposited as a result of tool use and not through other means? In Oceania residue research has developed in tandem with use-wear research, frequently on the same projects, so the question has often been confronted on the same artifacts. For instance, Barton et al. (1998) studied obsidian artifacts from an open site in Papua New Guinea, as well as sediment samples in contact with the artifact (but not on it) and away from the artifact (general soil samples). In addition, use-wear observations were conducted on all artifacts containing residues. The results turned out well. Although the site soil was full of starch grains, frequencies of starch were considerably greater in the tool residues; moreover, the use-wear analyses corroborated the residue analyses.

Experimental work has been conducted on the movement of starch grains through different-sized sediments. Therin (1998) established that little starch grain mobility can be expected to occur. That said, the limited mobility that does occur is greatly influenced by irrigation level. In general, the smaller the particle size of the sediment, the less easily starch grains can move through it. This study offers some assurance that artifacts deposited in lower stratigraphic layers of a site are not likely to be inundated from above with starch grains from subsequent horticultural

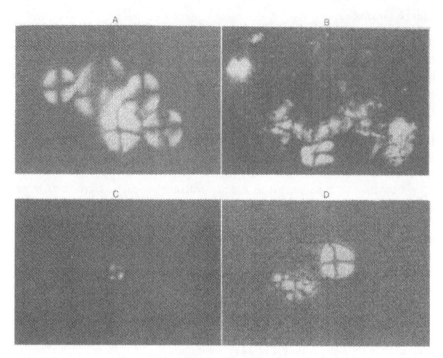

Figure 5.5.   A selection of starch grains found on pounding implements and from spits excavated from Jinmium Rock Shelter, northwest Northern Territory, Australia (taken from Atchison and Fullagar 1998: Figure 5).

communities that may have occupied the same land. Taphonomic studies such as this are establishing a firm foundation for future starch residue investigations. In fact, starch grain studies have occurred in several research domains—even its intrasite distribution has recently been explored to delineate loci of specific activities (Balme and Beck 2002).

Research into starch grains has now been applied to stone tools from several sites in Australia, from which I will choose one example: the stratified Jinmium Rock Shelter, located in a remote area of northwestern Northern Territory and into which four trenches were excavated. Three cobbles that possessed use-wear from pounding or grinding were recovered, and the investigators were curious whether or not they had been employed in processing starchy roots or tubers (Atchison and Fullagar 1998). To this end they created a local reference collection of 11 edible plant species still exploited by local Aborigines. They extracted starch from the cobbles and took 17 bulk sediment samples from elsewhere on the site to use as a control. Figure 5.5 presents a selection of grains from this site, extracted from the surfaces of two tools (a, b) and from two of the excavated spits (c, d).

Starch grains from the tools were not able to be identified definitively, but grasses and palms have been ruled out on size considerations and the most likely candidates remain starchy tubers. It is clear that, for future identification, the local reference collection needs to be expanded and should include phytoliths and raphides. Despite the taxonomic uncertainty, the study established that the grains extracted for this analysis were probably not contaminated from the sediments through processing, and that starch grains survive in these conditions down to a depth of at least 120 cm.

This kind of research has also been applied to tropical environments, facilitated by the fact that starch grains preserve better than other plant parts in such an ecosystem. In one such study, Piperno and Holst (1998) were concerned with edge-ground cobbles similar to the Australian tools just discussed, as well as boulder milling stone bases and metates. Starch grains were extracted from cobbles from four sites in Panama dating to preceramic (ca. 8000-5000 BP) and early ceramic (5000-3500 BP) occupations. Their identification demonstrates that a variety of tubers, palms, legumes and maize were processed throughout these cultural stages. Maize starch analyzed from a grinding stone base from the site of Aguadulce supports other evidence for late preceramic maize cultivation in central Panama. Starch from arrowroot also suggests an early and possibly extensive exploitation of this tuber as a food crop. Abundant maize starch from a more recent site supports the connection between social complexity and maize dependency in this region. Studies such as the two discussed here document a technological trajectory in its infancy, but one that has already demonstrated considerable validity and worth.

Scholars interested in pursuing starch residue studies need to prepare themselves along certain lines. First, prepare a reference collection of representative modern starch grains from the region in which future archaeological research will take place. Piperno and Holst (1998:768) describe a method of macerating the plants, adding water, and filtering them through cheese cloth, whereas Atchison and Fullagar (1998:114) recommend cutting a piece from a specimen, drying it in an oven, and grinding it into a powder. It would be difficult to imagine two less similar methods of sample preparation, but both are viable and other variations on these themes also exist. In addition, Hall et al. (1989:141) suggest making slides of both raw and cooked specimens, storing dried and pounded specimens in jars for use in testing for range of variability, and keeping a photomicrographic record of all differentiation tests. These authors also provide detailed pointers on drying and on fixing specimens to preserve the structural integrity of the samples.

Methods for extracting residue samples from stone tools exhibit some variation, but are explained in Loy (1994), Atchison and Fullagar (1998:115), and Piperno and Holst (1998:768). Extraction of starch grains from bulk sediment samples is explained in Atchison and Fullagar (1998:115) and Fullagar et al. (1998:52-54). Methods for differentiating types of starch grains through chemical reagents, reactions with dyes, histological examination, etc., are discussed in Hall et al. (1989:143-148) and in Briuer (1976:481-482).

Phytoliths

Phytoliths are opaline silica bodies that have been deposited in epidermal and other cells of a growing plant. The silica from which they were made is transported from groundwater in the form of monosilicic acid. In some plants the silica body assumes the shape of the cell in which it is formed and retains that shape after the organic structural material around it has decomposed. In other types of plants the silica body does not assume the shape of the cell, but instead forms an undiagnostic, amorphous mass (Pearsall 1982:862, 2000:356). A seminal article by Irv Rovner (1971) brought the potential of plant phytoliths to the attention of archaeologists and induced substantial subsequent development. By 2000 Deborah Pearsall, one of the world's leading phytolith specialists, could state:

> that phytoliths are produced in many, not a few, plant families; that there are often one-to-one correspondences between diagnostic phytoliths and genera, and in some cases species, of plants; that phytoliths are highly redundant in a few, not in many, families; that even in families characterized by high redundancy, such as the grasses, genus-level diagnostics do exist, and species-level identifications may be possible through application of multivariate statistical techniques. (Pearsall 2000:355-356)

Phytoliths are not designed to be dispersed widely like pollen rain, but are isolated as individual entities in sediments by the burning or decomposition of the organic tissues that surround them, or by their ingestion by animals and subsequent incorporation in excrement or gut contents. Some researchers maintain that, once deposited, phytoliths tend to stay put. Others have postulated a more complex scenario involving transport by fire or by aeolian or alluvial processes (Pearsall 2000:393-395). This is obviously an area that could use some research. From an archaeological point of view, the most appealing characteristic of phytoliths is their longevity and relative indestructibility. They survive in mid- and low latitude conditions with abundant moisture, regions in which most other types of botanical remains have long since decomposed (Pearsall 1982:862; Kealhofer et al. 1999:529).

Because of phytoliths' resistance to decay, much of the recent phytolith research in archaeology has been conducted in tropical and semi-arid regions. There it has proven useful in elucidating the onset and development of early domesticated species such as maize, barley, and emmer wheat. The process of identifying domesticated maize phytoliths and discriminating them from wild grasses has entailed painstaking studies by Pearsall and Dolores Piperno of the size of various cross-shaped phytoliths and their three-dimensional morphology. The examples of grass phytoliths presented in Figure 5.6 relate to the research on the development of cultigens in Central and South America. These studies do not, for the most part, involve stone tool residues, but other studies do (e.g., Figure 5.4e). On a wide array of characteristics these studies have pushed back our knowledge of

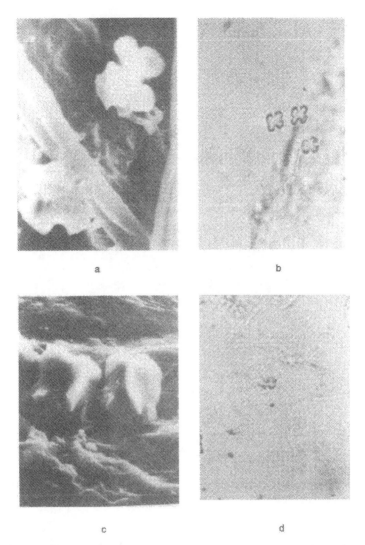

Figure 5.6.   Grass phytoliths from Central America: a,b) *Zea mays*; c) *Tripsacum dactyloides*; d) Bambusoid grass #1 (taken from Piperno 1984: Figure 1).

the earliest maize domestication to at least the fifth millennium BC in Panama and Ecuador (Pearsall 1978; Piperno 1984; Piperno et al. 1985; Pearsall and Piperno 1990). Phytolith research by Arlene Rosen and others (e.g., Rosen 1992, 1993; Rosen and Weiner 1994) has aided in interpreting the developmental effects of early grass domestication in the Near East.

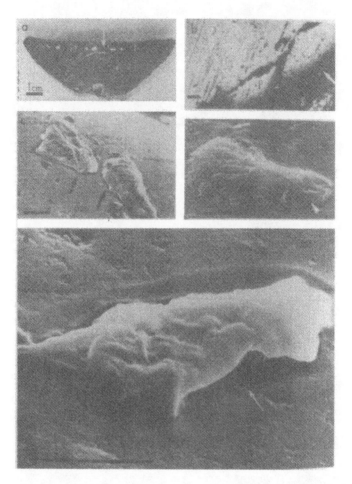

Figure 5.7. Danish Neolithic sickle blade (a) that was heavily abraded (b) and exhibited phytolith bodies in varying stages of dissolution into the surface of the flint (c–e) (taken from Anderson 1980: Plate 8).

One of the earliest cases of the involvement of phytoliths in stone tool research was Patricia Anderson's (1980) microscopic study of experimental pieces and archaeological artifacts from several sites in Europe. She interpreted use-polish as an additive phenomenon that has the capability of enclosing within it particles of the material being worked. Her photos suggest the presence of grass phytoliths and other plant structures seemingly "melting into" the polished surfaces of experimental and Neolithic sickle blades (Figure 5.7).

This is pretty heady stuff and Anderson's photos are compelling, but they have failed to convince everybody. For example, Romana Unger-Hamilton (1984) observed surficial structures identical to Anderson's phytoliths, caused by rubbing one flint against another. Instead of phytoliths, Unger-Hamilton interpreted these as components of the flint itself—perhaps relict organic tissues or skeletal calcite of organisms that occur in the flint. She accepted that the "melted" appearance may have been caused by a non-mechanical component of polish formation such as amorphous silica filling in interstices around the projecting objects. Other scholars have argued against the entire idea of formation of a silica gel, i.e., the layer that the silica bodies were "melting" into (Yamada 1993; Grace 1996:211; Levi Sala 1996:3-4).

A phytolith residue study that does not emphasize the issue of use-polish formation has been conducted at two sites in Australia by Kealhofer et al. (1999). The authors first established that the phytoliths from the residue were associated with tool use by extracting samples from the tool, then comparing them to site samples and to samples in close proximity to the artifacts. The latter two samples contained a substantially smaller density and greater variety of phytolith types than the residue. Use-wear analysis of the tools distinguished contact materials to the level of woody plants and non-siliceous starchy tubers. Analysis of phytolith residues was able to refine these results by specifying that the tools were utilized on bamboo, palm, arboreal species, or mixed species.

A scholar interested in pursuing phytolith residue research would be well advised to consult the abundant literature of phytolith identification and extraction. Excellent manuals for phytolith analysis now exist, notably Piperno (1988) and Pearsall (2000). The latter, for example, provides detailed advice on setting up a phytolith laboratory, processing soil samples and comparative plant materials, scanning slides, and counting individual phytoliths (Pearsall 2000:411-460). Pointers for processing residue samples from lithic artifacts are provided in Kealhofer et al. (1999:533).

The dominant research issue in plant residue analysis is whether or not plant residues are reliable indicators of the substances on which the tools made contact. The answer is affirmative for each plant structure studied, as long as the residue can be shown to have been associated with the use of the tool.

Blood Residues

About the same time that phytolith research on bulk sediment was being established, Tom Loy was devising methods for analyzing relict blood caught on surfaces and in interstices of stone tools. Loy's early work involved tools from several sites in British Columbia estimated to have been occupied between 1000 and 6000 years ago. The earliest of these to be associated with a radiocarbon date (2830 +/− 210 BC) tested positive for grizzly bear and caribou. Along with microscopic evidence of hair fragments, plant and animal tissue, and feather barbules, a variety of tests revealed the presence of amino acids, haemoglobin and

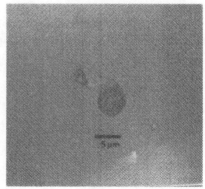

Figure 5.8.   Red blood cells extracted from the surfaces of archaeological tools suggesting the presence of *Bison bison* (a) and *Ovis dalli* (b) (taken from Loy and Dixon 1998: Figure 4).

red blood cells (Loy 1983). Two examples of red blood cells extracted from the surface of archaeological tools, shown in Figure 5.8, suggest the presence of bison and Dall sheep. The principal issue here is similar to that posed for plant residues:

Q23: Do blood residues on archaeological stone tools reliably indicate the type of animal with which these tools made contact?

Loy has continued to develop blood residue analysis and to publish his results. One example of these studies involves a group of complete bifaces eroding from the bank of the Toad River in northern British Columbia (Loy 1993). Initial examination of tool surfaces revealed hairs that appeared to have been from bison— a real surprise, as the closest record of bison habitation at any time in history occurred 500 km south of there. A purified sample of a residue from one of these tools subsequently yielded an Accelerator Mass Spectrometry (AMS) date of 2180 +/− 160 BP (Nelson et al. 1986).

Detailed microscopic investigation of tool surfaces revealed traces of red blood cells, fat cells, lymphocytes, hair, feather barbules, wood cells, and skin. The presence of haemoglobin (Hb) and myoglobin (Mb) was confirmed through the Ames Hemastix test (see Loy and Wood 1989:451). Likewise, the presence of mammalian Immunoglobin type G (IgG), a major component of mammalian immune systems, was confirmed on all tools through positive tests for Staphylococcal protein A (SpA), which binds with IgG. The presence of haemoglobin and serum albumin (SA) was verified using isoelectric focusing (IEF), an electrophoretic method for separating molecules from complex substances.

The tests discussed above indicated that the residues isolated on the Toad River Canyon bifaces included mammalian blood by confirming the presence of IgG, Hb, and SA. At this point the researcher would normally like to know the source of the blood: did bison once exist in northern British Columbia, or is this what happened to Uncle Charlie? Several techniques exist for identifying the taxonomic character of blood remains—sometimes to the species level, at other times only to the genus or family level. The most popular of these techniques are described in Box 5.6.

Box 5.6. Identifying Blood Residues

Once blood residue on a stone tool has been detected, several ways exist to identify it. The first to be introduced to a rapt archaeological audience was *haemoglobin (Hb) crystallization*, a process derived from the successful identification of mosquito blood-meal hosts. The specific technique used is called "salting out," i.e., precipitating Hb in crystal form, a process influenced by temperature, salt concentration, type of salt, acidity of the resulting solution, and characteristics of the protein involved. Different species possess different amino acid sequences with different electrical charges, which result in crystals with diagnostic characteristics. Examples of the variety of haemoglobin crystals that one might run across in such a study are illustrated in Figure 5.9. Effective Hb crystallization requires a sizable blood sample; lesser samples result in a lower level of detectability (Loy 1983; Loy and Wood 1989:453-455; Hyland et al. 1990:106; Loy and Dixon 1998:28-30).

Other techniques of identification are called immunoassays because they relate to the ability of cells to produce antibodies that are used to repel foreign substances, or antigens. Because of the strong affinity between antibody and antigen, the positive reaction of a blood sample to a specific antibody is indicative of the antigen represented by that sample. The underlying theme of this series of identification procedures, then, is the introduction of known antibodies to the sample. Procedures can take several forms, of which only the most widely used will be discussed here.

Cross-over immuno-electrophoresis (CIEP) employs an agar gel into which are cut paired basins or wells. Antigens (tool residue) are placed in wells along one side, antibodies in the wells on the other side. The molecules involved are electrically charged and, when an electrical current is passed through the gel, particles from the two wells migrate toward each other. If there is a positive reaction, they bind to form a solid precipitate, which may need to be stained in order to be identified (Newman and Jullg 1989; Downs and Lowenstein 1995:14; Shanks et al. 1999:1184; Kooyman 2000:162). CIEP is simple, it does not require expensive equipment, and it can be used on multiple samples, but it is less sensitive than alternative techniques.

In *enzyme-linked immuno-absorbant assay (ELISA)*, the antibody being tested is placed on a hard surface, or plate. The residue and an additional sample of the antibody are mixed, then placed on the surface with the antibody. A lack of reaction on the plate indicates a positive assay. That is, the reaction with the antibody had already occurred; thus none remains to react with the antiserum on the hard surface. Reaction can be detected by a color-producing enzyme. ELISA is considered more sensitive to reaction than CIEP (Eisele et al. 1995:37-38; Tuross et al. 1996:290; Kooyman 2000:163).

The most sensitive of the immunological techniques is *radio-ammunoassay (RIA)*. This is a double-antibody method that, unlike others, can be quantitatively measured. The residue sample is placed in a small plastic well, some of its proteins bonding with the plastic and stabilizing.

An antibody developed in a rabbit is added, binding to some extent with the antigens if they are of the appropriate species. A second antibody, radioactive and known as goat anti-rabbit gamma globulin, is then added to the concoction. If any of the first antibody reacted with the antigen, there will be a reaction at this point and the remnant radioactivity can be measured by a counter. This measurement reflects the amount of rabbit antibody remaining and thereby the strength of the species relationship (Downs and Lowenstein 1995:14; Kooyman 2000:163). Because the second antibody amplifies the initial reaction, it is inherently a stronger technique, but this increment does not come without disadvantages. Its reagents have a short shelf life and are consumed rapidly by the plastic, the equipment for counting radioactivity is expensive, and there is radioactive waste to consider (Hyland et al. 1990:106).

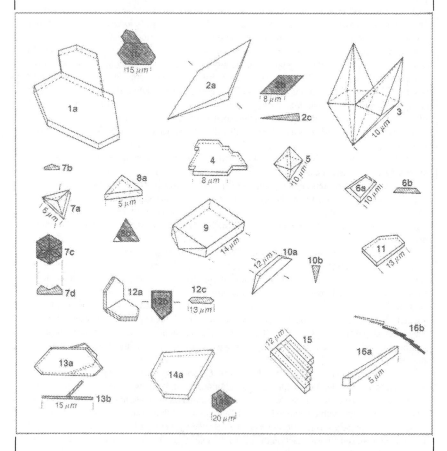

Figure 5.9. A variety of haemoglobin crystals, from 1) woolly mammoth; 2) *Bos primigenius*; 3) human; 4) *Capra* sp.; 5) wapiti; 6) *Bison bison*; 7) *Ovis dalli*; 8) *Ovis* sp.; 9) moose; 10) caribou; 11) *Bison priscus*; 12) musk ox; 13) California sea-lion; 14) mule deer; 15) brown bear; 16) timber wolf (taken from Loy and Wood 1989: Figure 3).

Finally, a non-immunological method known as *isoelectric focusing (IEF)* takes advantage of the ionic charge of proteins, which ultimately depends on the structure of the protein molecule and the amino acid sequence. As these sequences change genetically from one species to another, so does their ionic charge. Molecules are separated by placing a liquid residue sample in a polyacrylamide gel that is buffered to create a pH gradient when a high-voltage electric current is passed through the gel. Each molecule has an isoelectric point (pI) where its pH is neutral. When a current is applied to the gel, the molecule will migrate to the place that corresponds to its pI and stabilize, forming a band visible after staining. The location of this band is compared to similar assays for known species to identify the residue. In this way species can be separated on the basis of their protein molecules, though the general position of the different species' bands in the gel can be quite similar. Comparison with modern samples is accomplished by transferring the gel to a densitometer and calculating coefficients of similarity of the various pI values. These calculations can yield ambiguous results, suggesting the existence of additional variables to which IEF may be sensitive—perhaps racial or geographic variation, drying or ageing of sample proteins, or other elements in the soil that may also constitute a portion of the residue (Loy 1993:50; Loy and Dixon 1998:27-28). It seems that "While this last method [IEF] has been used with success, further development will be required before it routinely can be used in the study of archaeological materials" (Hyland et al. 1990:106).

Loy applied to the Toad River Canyon biface collection four identification techniques; three of the tools received the entire suite. Isoelectric focusing showed isoelectric point (pI) values different from non-bison comparative specimens, radio-immunoassay (RIA) identified residues on two of the tools to the Bovidae Family, and Hb crystallization produced crystals typical of *Bison bison*. The most powerful technique used was DNA analysis through the polymerase chain reaction amplification method (PCR), which can deal with extremely small samples (see explanation in Loy 1993:52-53; Bonnichsen et al. 2001). Testing revealed bovid DNA strands of a sub-Family whose only native North American representative is *Bison bison*. Thus the four identification techniques converged to either confirm bison as the origin of the residue (DNA, Hb crystallization), or to support the claim at a lower order of specificity (RIA, IEF).

In a more recent study, Loy and Dixon (1998) applied a suite of seven tests to a series of 36 fluted points from eastern Beringia. Twenty-one of these yielded microscopically visible residues, and all of those contained mammalian IgG. Various assays yielded evidence of mammoth, bison, sheep, caribou, and musk ox—the first associations of fluted points with specific fauna in the entire region.

Scholars other than Loy have conducted blood residue analysis, with variable rates of success. Among the most persistent advocates of this type of study have been researchers from Calgary. One of their principal responses to critics of blood residue analysis is that modern experiments that try to replicate a prehistoric situation duplicate neither the processes or conditions that prevail on archaeological sites nor the passage of time. Therefore, it is better to evaluate techniques through known archaeological samples than through modern simulated ones (Newman et al. 1996:680; Kooyman 2000:164).

To this end they have analyzed several tools from the 5600-year-old Head-Smashed-In buffalo kill site in southern Alberta. Their immediate goal was to evaluate a standard immunological technique, cross-over immuno-electrophoresis (CIEP), on real archaeological conditions with the probability that only one species was involved. The technique elicited positive reactions to bison and elk antigens for 9 of 31 stone tools and 6 of 16 soil samples. Since it is known that cross-reactions between elk and bison are frequent, the elk determinations are probably spurious. Thus it appears that, as predicted, all immunological reactions from the Head-Smashed-In residues pertained to bison (Kooyman et al. 1992; Newman et al. 1996).

Chipped stone is not the only kind of prehistoric tool to have been investigated for residues. Ethnographic reports from California and parts of Baja California recount the pulverization of small animals such as mice, snakes, and lizards on large grinding stones, the remains to be cooked up in a stew. To test whether or not this process is detectable on archaeological material, 6 manos, 3 metate fragments, a core hammer, a mortar, and a pestle from two sites in southern California were submitted for CIEP analysis. With the exception of asphaltum, no residue was visible on the grinding surfaces of any of these tools. One of the manos reacted to rat and mouse antisera, while a second mano reacted to rat only. The mortar and pestle both reacted strongly to mouse and weakly to rat antisera (Yohe et al. 1991). All other tests were negative. This study is interesting both prehistorically and methodologically: prehistorically in demonstrating that, at least in southern California, grinding stones were not just plant pulverizing implements; methodologically in showing that these techniques are possible on rough, as well as chipped, stone tools.

Box 5.7. Does Blood Residue Analysis Work?

In this chapter a few of the successes registered by blood residue analysis have been recounted—a remarkable ascent in a mere 20 years. If this were the entire story, it would have a happy ending and our most pressing question would be how to add the technique to our own repertoire. Alas, like good ice cream, concocting a tasty blood residue analysis that pleases all palates is not that simple. This text box, an abbreviated version of Odell (2001:57-59), explores the dark side of this analytical trajectory. For a less compromising account, see Fiedel (1996).

Archaeology can be perceived as the study of history through material culture to which scientific principles have been applied. Here we are concerned with the nature of scientific application, which usually involves evaluating any new technique for reliability and validity. This is first accomplished in the laboratory, but in archaeological applications two additional dimensions must be accounted for: geological/taphonomic conditions and the passage of time. A technique that works fine in the lab may not necessarily operate at all when time and burial conditions are imposed on the situation.

In the laboratory, electrophoresis, immunological and other techniques employed in blood residue analysis have generally fared pretty well (e.g., Downs and Lowenstein 1995:14; Newman et al. 1996:681; Shanks et al. 1999:1186). Indeed, they were developed for medical research and crime labs and have been tested for years. Yet even under controlled laboratory conditions, adequate reliability has not always been achieved. For instance, a recent series of 54 experimental tools was sent to a lab in which the blood identification technique of choice was cross-over immuno-electrophoresis, or CIEP (Leach and Mauldin 1995). The laboratory's success rate for this series at a species level (i.e., naming the experimental species correctly) was only 37%, of which several of the errors represented cross-reactions between closely or more distantly related species. This result was probably caused either by shoddy lab procedures (e.g., inactive antisera) or by protein degradation, the samples having been refrigerated and stored for 1–2 months before submission to the laboratory. Similarly disappointing results of another experimental series were reported in Mauldin et al. (1995).

Testing archaeological residues is less straightforward than testing experimental residues because animal of origin is unknown, but there are ways of evaluating at least some parameters of the process. One of these is whether or not laboratory results coincide with what is known about the archaeological record. Consider, for example, a study of residues on projectile points from northwestern Australia, where ethnographic evidence indicates that projectile points there were manufactured to kill animals. Surprisingly, the quantity of blood residue on the analyzed collection was dominated by evidence for plant processing, an activity that was not supposed to have involved projectile points (Wallis and O'Connor 1998). Stuart Fiedel (1996) recounts a litany of such incongruities—from bovids in New Jersey at 700 BC to chicken in the Archaic of Oregon.

Another way to evaluate archaeological residues involves the fact that perception of accuracy increases geometrically with the number of independent techniques that can be marshaled to show the same thing. Of course, if the techniques fail to coincide, perception of accuracy declines in the same proportion. As a case in point, Downs and Lowenstein (1995) conducted blind tests in which participants were sent modern and archaeological residues that they subjected to the same technological analyses. Whereas agreement on the modern samples was total, agreement on the archaeological samples was almost nil, a result that the authors attributed to protein degeneration. Garling (1998) noted the same effect for samples from the 30,000-year old Cuddie Springs site in Australia. And in correlating blood residue with use-wear analysis where both were applied to the same body of stone tools from northern Virginia, Petraglia et al. (1996) recorded very little correspondence.

A multitude of studies have established that some proteins degrade quickly, but they do not degrade in regular fashion (Gurfinkel and Franklin 1988; Hyland et al. 1990; Smith and Wilson 1992; Cattaneo et al. 1993; Downs and Lowenstein 1995; Eisele et al. 1995; Tuross et al. 1996; Garling 1998). There is currently little information on which proteins degrade more easily or under which conditions, though both time and local burial situation appear to be involved. This is the principal uncertainty under which blood residue analysis currently operates, and is the obstacle that must be overcome if this technique is to be perpetuated.

When blood residue analysis was first introduced, it was greeted with both euphoria and skepticism. Those attitudes continue to prevail 20 years later. Its successes, some of which have been recounted above, offer hope of an ultimate microanalysis that would reveal the most salient activities engaged in by prehistoric peoples. Many of the results already achieved are intuitively satisfying, in some cases supporting behaviors suggested from other evidence (e.g., rodent pulverization in California), in others introducing innovative ideas useful for further testing (e.g., bison exploitation in northern British Columbia). Yet critics have always existed, and in a few areas they have become more strident with the passage of time (see Box 5.7). In evaluating the research question whether or not blood residues are reliable indicators of the animals on which their associated stone tools made contact, the answer is a firm maybe. With more research in key areas, notably protein degradation, perhaps a less ambiguous response to this question will be forthcoming.

A researcher electing to pursue the investigation of blood residues should be aware that it is a highly technical undertaking to be conducted only in fully equipped laboratories by trained technicians. The extent of one's involvement in the process therefore depends on adequate equipment, the level of training in this area, and the means to acquire and maintain appropriate chemicals, reagents and antisera. Interested researchers without these capabilities should contact one of the labs currently established for the interpretation of blood residues rather than set up their own operation.

Researchers desiring more involvement may find the following sources useful. For detecting the presence of blood residue on individual artifacts, see Loy (1983:1269; 1993:48-50), Fredericksen (1985), Custer et al. (1988), Gurfinkel and Franklin (1988), Loy and Wood (1989:451), Hyland et al. (1990:108), and Loy and Dixon (1998:24-25). For extracting residue, see Newman et al. (1996:680), Tuross et al. (1996:291), and Shanks et al. (1999:1186-1188). For identification of the source of the residue, most of the references contained in this section provide some detail of the specific detection technique employed for that study. Particularly helpful overviews can be found in Cattaneo et al. (1993), Downs and Lowenstein (1995), Eisele et al. (1995), and Tuross et al. (1996). These by no means exhaust the useful sources, but they should provide a suitable starting point. Whatever one's position on the ultimate worth of blood residue analysis, it is apparent that the final verdict has not yet been rendered. Further development and testing of the technique will elucidate relevant variables, delineate boundaries between techniques, and refine our perceptions of its possibilities.

Summary

Different kinds of residues produce different kinds of relict traces and require specific and unique strategies for analysis. For any kind of residue, a good place to start is with a microscope. Microscopic observation can reveal compound structures such as hair, starch grains, phytoliths, red blood cells, oxalate crystals, and a host of other remnant parts of plants or animals.

Starch grains often preserve well and may represent the only direct evidence for the exploitation of root or tuber crops. The most extensive development of archaeological starch grain research has been in Australia and the tropics of Central and South America. Some attention has been paid to taphonomic issues such as the migration of starch grains through sediments and the strength of association of starch with the tools on which they have been observed.

Like starch, phytoliths, which are composed primarily of inorganic silica, are often preserved in sediments in which organic compounds have totally degraded. These include tropical environments, explaining why much phytolith research has been conducted in Panama and Ecuador. Phytolith studies are dominated by the examination of bulk sediments, whereas the investigation of these bodies in tool residues is in its infancy. Phytolith preservation on tools has been confounded by their possible incorporation in amorphous silica gel developed through use polishing, but neither this type of polish formation nor the reputed incorporation of phytolith bodies into it have yet been established to everyone's satisfaction.

Research on blood residues has followed a different trajectory, because blood rarely leaves relict structures like starch grains or phytoliths. The detection and identification of blood involves a suite of chemical and electrolytic techniques developed in medical and crime labs. In several studies the various techniques converge to support a coherent interpretation, suggesting that this type of analysis has considerable validity. In some cases it is capable of identifying blood to the species level, and it can be applied to both chipped and ground stone tools. However, experimental testing of blood residues has fared much better in the laboratory on modern samples than it has when the passage of time and natural environmental conditions have been imposed. These work to degrade proteins at differing rates, and at present there is little solid information on which proteins degrade more quickly and which conditions are responsible. Until these problems are resolved, the application of blood residue analysis to archaeological stone tools will remain controversial.

Chapter 6

Encountering Prehistoric Behavior

The foregoing chapters have laid the groundwork for most forms of lithic analysis practiced today, either by discussing concepts and analytical options or by introducing literature that can be accessed to provide more detailed coverage than is appropriate in a manual like this. Questions that have been addressed so far concern how to conduct specific analyses, which techniques are most effective, and whether or not certain indicators are reliable; in other words, procedural issues. But no matter how important the acquisition of methodological proficiency is, the ultimate goal of archaeology should involve the acquisition of knowledge about prehistoric lifeways and cultural processes. Accepting that methodological refinement is a lifelong endeavor, once a researcher is familiar with the range of technical options available for appropriate archaeological questions, it is time to apply these techniques to issues of human behavior.

Chapter 6 attempts to build on the previous chapters by introducing a suite of human behavioral questions that have been addressed through lithic analysis. By human behavior I refer to prehistoric decisions involving the type of life to be lived—not, in this case, to the manufacture of implements that provide for that lifestyle. These issues will be arranged in a rough order, from more basic and individual questions such as the acquisition of food and shelter to more interactive and communal issues like trade and the organization of mobility.

The goal here is not comprehensive coverage of these topics, but a notion of boundaries and possibilities, to provide a vision of the limits of the database and the range of issues that can be addressed by these methods. I will not be concerned about mentioning all of the studies that have addressed these problems, and I extend my apologies to authors whose brilliantly conceived analyses have been overlooked. The primary purpose is to introduce a suite of human behavioral issues for which lithic analysis has proven appropriate, and in each case to specify the kinds of analytical techniques that have been employed. The reader is then urged to seek out other examples, to be imaginative, and to ultimately travel beyond the vision of research capability that these studies provide.

SUBSISTENCE

Food Procurement

Perhaps the most basic human concern is, Where's dinner? Progressing to the level of acquiring that dinner, one could ask,

Q24: How were stone tools used to procure and process food resources in prehistory?

Plants

The procurement of vegetal resources usually does not require the use of stone. Collecting seeds or fruits can be accomplished with the hands and appropriate containers, while tubers and roots can be extirpated with the aid of a digging stick. Only two lithic tool types have figured prominently in prehistoric plant procurement: sickles and hoes. Either was manufactured to a specific shape, but substantial variation exists within those shapes. For instance, sickles in Near Eastern Natufian and Neolithic societies were made predominantly on blades, but by no means were all blades used as sickles. Sickle blades are characterized by a distinctive bright surficial polish known as sickle gloss or phytolith polish, caused by friction of the blade with silicates in the plant stems (Curwen 1930, 1935; Unger-Hamilton 1989, 1992; Anderson 1992; Clemente and Gibaja 1998). The presence of sickle gloss, combined with other associated wear characteristics, is the principal way that this type of plant procurement can be distinguished.

Hoes are agricultural implements that were employed for digging furrows in the soil. They were usually bifacially manufactured, but again, most bifaces were not hoes. By encountering silicates in the soil, hoes acquire a surficial gloss similar to that formed on sickle blades and can be distinguished through similar criteria (Sonnenfeld 1962; Witthoft 1967; Odell 1998a).

Good chipped stone hoes had to possess qualities of endurance as well as knappability, a combination of characteristics that did not occur in most raw materials. Substances suitable for this task were therefore prized and found their way into trade networks that distributed them widely from their original location. A case in point is the extensive trade of hoes made of kaolin and Mill Creek cherts from southern Illinois in the Mississippian period of midcontinental North America (Kelly 1991; Cobb 2000). A similar situation occurred among the Maya of Belize. In this region oval bifaces were manufactured in workshops at the site of Colha and were shipped throughout the region for use in agricultural activities and field clearance (Shafer 1983, 1985; Shafer and Hester 1983; Dockall 1994).

Animals

Like collecting, animal procurement does not require that stone be a part of the procurement facility. For example, most prehistoric animal traps and snares do not possess a lithic component (e.g., Nelson 1973). The wood or other material of which the trap was made may originally have been fabricated with stone tools, but stone itself is not usually part of the device and the lithic use-wear evidence accrued from fashioning the apparatus would look like any other kind of woodworking wear. The same is true for fish traps and weirs. Fishing equipment, such as fishhooks and leister prongs, may have been fashioned using stone tools, but they were usually made of shell, bone or antler—rarely of stone.

The most common use of stone in animal procurement was at the business end of a spear, dart or arrow. The most direct evidence for projectile use is contextual: finding such a weapon tip in indisputable association with animal remains. A nice example of such a situation occurred in the early years of the twentieth century, when a Preboreal (i.e., immediately post-glacial) aurochs was discovered in a Danish peat bog. Initial analyses (Hartz and Winge 1906) produced evidence of flint projectile points embedded in two ribs. Since one wound was healed and the other unhealed, the animal had been hunted at least twice. Re-analysis of the Vig bull (Noe-Nygaard 1973) showed spear holes in both scapulae. Different clues on the scapulae enabled Noe-Nygaard to surmise that one spear, perhaps ejected from a trip-mechanism, was projected through both scapulae and exited the other side. This was undoubtedly the fatal blow to this unfortunate creature, which staggered to a nearby lake and breathed its last.

Plenty of other associations between projectile points and animal bones demonstrate that prehistoric people from all over the globe hunted their prey (including fellow humans) with stone-tipped weapons. The most famous North American example was the discovery of a Paleoindian point in direct association with bones of extinct bison at Folsom, New Mexico (Figgins 1927). This discovery was followed by several additional findings, including a broken Paleoindian point at the Lindenmeier site that had nicked the interior surface of a bison's vertebral column and had lodged in its neural canal (Roberts 1936:Figure 2; Wilmsen and Roberts 1984: Figure 145); and an impact-damaged Folsom point found inside the rib cage of a bison at the Cooper bison kill in Oklahoma (Bement 1999: Figure 32).

In most cases an association of weapon with prey cannot be established, yet direct evidence of projectile use is frequently preserved in the form of impact damage and hafting traces on specific artifacts (Ahler 1971; Greiser 1977). In an early study in this genre, Odell (1978; see also Odell 1980b) investigated use traces on a large assemblage of microliths from the Friesian Mesolithic settlement of Bergumermeer. The microliths exhibited a complex array of use traces, but in the end all were attributable either to impact or to the movement of the piece under the haft. Such movement produced interpretable damage, as with the short

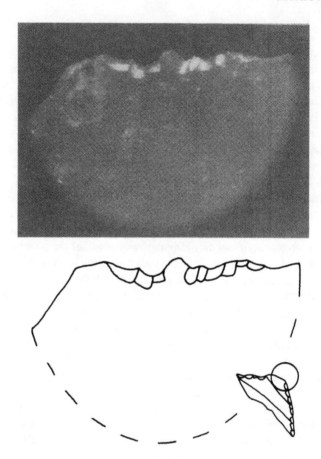

Figure 6.1. Microscopic removals (enlarged 34X) from the shorter side of an asymmetrical trapeze that figured prominently in the reconstruction of the hafting of this arrowhead, shown in Figure 6.2k (taken from Odell 1978: Fig. 10).

unretouched side of the asymmetrical trapeze photographed in Figure 6.1. This portion was apparently fastened to the shaft by narrow ligatures that broke off tiny pieces of the edge when under stress, but left one small portion unscathed. Patterns such as this allowed reconstructions of probable hafting configurations of a variety of microlithic types including triangles, trapezes, and Svaerdborg points (Figure 6.2). Studies conducted since then have revealed similar types of projectile damage in an assortment of prehistoric assemblages (Moss 1983; Odell 1988; Shea 1988b; Woods 1988; Cox and Smith 1989; Plisson and Schmider 1990; Kay 1996). Experimental testing of projectile points has confirmed the patterns exhibited in the prehistoric collections (Fischer et al. 1984; Odell and Cowan 1986; Dockall 1997).

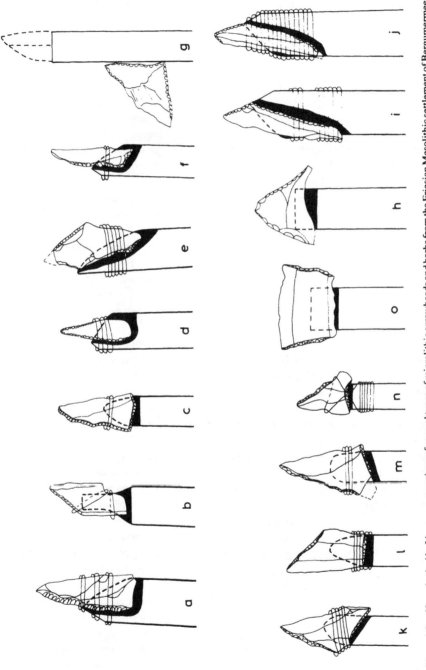

Figure 6.2.   Hypothetical hafting reconstructions of several types of microlithic arrowheads and barbs from the Friesian Mesolithic settlement of Bergumermeer (taken from Odell 1978: Fig. 11).

Projectile tips associated with animal kills have also yielded blood residues, thus supporting the causal relationship between weapon and prey. One well-known example has come from the Head-Smashed-In bison kill site in Alberta, from which several projectile points have retained evidence of 5600-year old bison or elk blood (Kooyman et al. 1992; Newman et al. 1996). It is not always easy to tell whether a particular tool acquired a residue because it was shot into the prey or was used to butcher it. In my experience, larger tools, such as the Archaic points from Head-Smashed-In that retained blood, may have been employed as either weapons tips or processing tools. Small, often geometrically shaped projectile tips, such as North American late prehistoric Madison or Fresno points or western European Mesolithic microliths, were almost universally arrowheads, not processing tools (Odell 1978, 1981b, 1996: chapter 10).

The foregoing studies recount ways of determining prehistoric animal procurement practices using specific tools, usually projectile points. Information on hunting and predator-prey relations can also be gleaned using entire assemblages. One way is to record associations between tool types and faunal remains, a tactic that Clark (1989) employed at the Upper Paleolithic La Riera Cave in northern Spain. Of the two species that were most intensively exploited, ibex was associated with one set of lithic types, red deer with another. These differential associations suggest that each of these species was procured or processed differently with a specific suite of tools.

In chronologically recent assemblages such as the one from La Riera, observed patterns can safely be attributed to hunting activities. For much earlier assemblages one cannot make this assumption, as the possibility that humans scavenged already felled animals is just as great as that they actively hunted live ones. Employing faunal and lithic data from Middle Paleolithic deposits in West-Central Italy, Mary Stiner and Steve Kuhn established criteria for evaluating prehistoric procurement practices. Faunal assemblages interpreted to have been accumulated through scavenging exhibit an incomplete list of body parts with a small proportion of limb bones and a large proportion of cranial bones. Associated lithic assemblages are characterized by a large percentage of nonlocal raw materials, extensive modification of tools, heavy use of blanks, and radial Levallois or disc-core reduction techniques. In contrast, faunal assemblages attributed to hunting show a more complete representation of body parts and a higher proportion of limb bones. Associated lithic assemblages were made predominantly on local raw materials and consisted of smaller flakes, less frequent retouching of tools, and cores with opposing or parallel platforms.

A primary difference here is that Middle Paleolithic scavengers appear to have been more far-ranging and nomadic, bringing lithic materials long distances and economizing their tools. Middle Paleolithic hunters stayed closer to home, perhaps provisioning their base camp through small hunting forays. Hunters were more knowledgeable of local raw material sources and therefore less careful to conserve their tool material through intensive use of preforms and retouching;

Table 6.1.   Types of lithic analysis that have addressed issues of plant
and animal procurement.

Kingdom	Tool type	Type of analysis	References
Plant	Sickle	Use-wear: silica polish	Curwen 1930, 1935; Unger-Hamilton 1989, 1992; Anderson 1992; Clemente & Gibaja 1998
Plant	Hoe	Use-wear: silica polish	Sonnenfeld 1962; Witthoft 1967; Cobb 2000; Odell 1998a
Animal	Projectile point	Use-wear: polish, striae, fractures	Ahler 1971; Greiser 1977; Odell 1978, 1988; Moss 1983; Shea 1988b; Woods 1988; Cox & Smith 1989; Plisson & Schmider 1990; Kay 1996; Dockall 1997
Animal	Projectile point	Blood residue	Kooyman et al. 1992; Newman et al. 1996
Animal	Various tool types	Association with animal remains	Clark 1989
Animal	Preforms, cores, various tool types	Technology: core types, retouch, etc.	Stiner & Kuhn 1992; Kuhn 1993, 1995a

they were also able to secure more optimal cuts of meat (Stiner and Kuhn 1992; Kuhn 1993, 1995a:144-149). The types of lithic data that were amassed to establish these relationships were predominantly technological, including variables such as core type, frequency of retouching, and artifact size. Table 6.1 encapsulates the types of tools involved and analyses conducted for this and other studies of food procurement presented herein.

Food Processing

Tools for the processing of food were not usually very distinctive nor, in many cases, were they used exclusively for that purpose. Skinning animals, fileting fish, cutting up vegetables—tasks such as these required only knives, which could be obtained from the chipped stone debitage or could be unifacially or bifacially fashioned for the situation. The most distinctive processing tools were the mano/metate and mortar/pestle combinations, but even here, the existence of these tools does not necessarily indicate what was being processed.

Plants

Plant processing has been practiced for thousands of years, driven by the toxicity or inaccessibility of the edible portions of certain high-intensity wild resources such as nuts or seeds. A well-known example of grain processing found throughout the Mediterranean region is the *threshing sledge*, also called a *tribulum* or *dhoukani*. It consisted of a flat wooden surface in which several rows of flint flakes had been inset. This apparatus was tied to a draft animal such as an ox or mule and dragged around a floor of grain, separating the seeds from the chaff (Hornell 1930; Crawford 1935; Bordaz 1965). Threshing sledge technology was still in use until quite recently, so ethnographic accounts of the production of flint flakes for inserts exist (e.g., Fox 1984; Whittaker 1996). Descriptions of wear accruing to the flints through this activity have been offered by Whallon (1978).

The processing of nuts has also received some attention. A Middle Archaic camp in the uplands near the Illinois River Valley provides insight into the dynamics of nut processing before societies grew dependent on domesticated plants (Stafford 1991). At the Buckshaw Bridge site 49 pit features, apparently filled with organic material, were discovered. Archaeobotanical analyses revealed that more than 95% of the nut-shell fragments were thick-shelled hickory (*Carya* sp.). The extremely low quantities of wood charcoal in the pits indicated that the site's occupants had accumulated so much offal from nut processing that they did not need to rely on local deadwood for their campfires. The lithic assemblage from this site was different from most other assemblages in consisting of 81% hardstone/groundstone tools. Most of these exhibited evidence of battering, grinding or pitting—a very specialized assemblage indeed.

As long as societies exploited wild plant resources, processing could be conducted by small parties away from the society's base camp at the locations at which these resources naturally occurred. With increasing sedentism and dependence on domesticated starchy seed crops, food processing increasingly tended to occur at the village where most of the members of the society lived. A lengthy occupation span at some of these villages induced changes in grinding techniques, which affected motor responses and are encoded in the shape of grinding tools and the wear on their surfaces. These tools can be compared with earlier wild food grinding tools to record changes over greater time depths.

Describing temporal changes in motor behavior over time in the American Southwest, Morris (1990) noted that grinding tools at Archaic sites like Ventana Cave were dominated by one-hand manos with distinctive and differential patterns of abrasion on their surfaces. Two-hand manos and trough metates eventually replaced the earlier style. As sedentism increased, smaller grinding tools were replaced by larger ones that could process corn more efficiently. Adams (1993) explained how grinding efficiency is positively correlated with grinding surface area. The increase in intensity and efficiency necessary to process corn for increasingly sedentary populations induced a progression in the shape of metates from basin to trough to flat.

Analyses of tool shape and gross wear pattern differential work well in the American Southwest, because archaeologists there have a good idea through macrobotanical analysis and direct ethnographic analogs which resources were being exploited prehistorically and how they were processed. In other parts of the world macrobotanical remains are rarely recovered and historical continuity in food processing practices is hard to demonstrate; in these areas a different suite of techniques must be employed.

This was the situation on the southeastern coast of Queensland, Australia, where ethnographic evidence of aboriginal exploitation of the fern, *Blechnum indicum*, exists. Aboriginal peoples there processed the rhizome of this plant (locally known as bungwall) by pounding or bruising it, but there is no ethnographic description of the types of tools employed in this activity. Kamminga (1981) hypothesized that processing was accomplished through use of *bevelled pounders*, which were made from a wide variety of lithic materials. On archaeological examples Kamminga observed microscopic use-smoothing in areas lateral to the beveled margin, wear that he hypothesized was caused by light abrasive contact with these rhizomes. Subsequently, Gillieson and Hall (1982), utilizing experimentally manufactured bevelled pounders to process bungwall, reproduced the dominant wear patterns observed by Kamminga.

This work was followed by residue studies. Pulling out Gillieson and Hall's experimental tools after they had been carefully cleaned for the manufacture of latex moulds and stored for five years, Hall et al. (1989) were able to extract an abundance of starch grains. Initial observations of prehistoric collections have shown promise in that starch grains from *Blechnum indicum* have been observed on prehistoric tools as well as on experimental ones. This research presents a classical example of archaeological argumentation the structure of which has been outlined in Figure 6.3 and dissected in Box 6.1.

Starch residue analysis has begun to figure prominently in tropical and arid regions in which the inhabitants developed a lengthy dependence on starchy food staples. One of these regions is Panama, where starchy plants such as maize, arrowroot and possibly manioc were pulverized by edge-ground cobbles on milling stone bases. Starch grains from a variety of plants have survived on tools from sites in several different environments (Piperno and Holst 1998). Starch grains have also been extracted from the surfaces of obsidian artifacts from Papua New Guinea. These tools yielded a strong correlation between high frequencies of starch and the presence of use-wear, strengthening the assertion that the tools on which the residues were found served to process those plants (Barton et al. 1998).

Another important type of plant residue that has successfully been extracted from tool surfaces is phytoliths. In a recent study of obsidian artifacts from two sites in Papua New Guinea, Kealhofer et al. (1999) compared phytoliths recovered from utilized tool surfaces with those recovered from site sediments. Phytoliths taken from utilized surfaces were present in greater frequencies and lesser variety than those taken from other contexts, supporting the hypothesis that the tools were used to process the plants that yielded the phytoliths. It is becoming clear that, in

Box 6.1. Associating a Tool with an Activity

Lithic analysis sometimes entails figuring out what kind of tool was employed to perform a specific task in a prehistoric society or region. Tools were often multi-functional, rendering determinations of specific tasks problematic, but some tool types served a dominant functional mode. This seems to have been the case with the Australian *bevelled pounder*. The argumentation by which tool and activity are associated is classical archaeological reasoning and will be deconstructed here, following the outline in Figure 6.3.

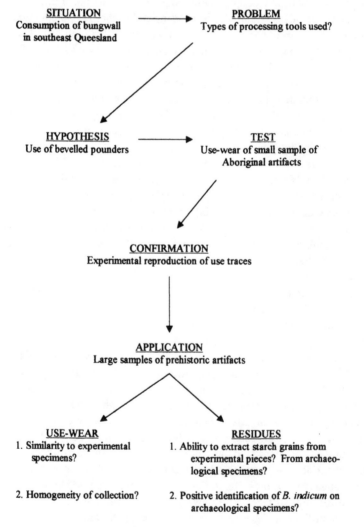

Figure 6.3.   Argumentation used in associating a specific tool type, bevelled pounder, with a specific activity, procuring *Blechnum indicum*.

Questions concerning the prehistoric record usually emanate from a perceived situation which, in this case, concerns the consumption of the rhizome of the fern *Blechnum indicum* (bungwall) by Aborigines of southeastern Queensland. The problem is that, although there is ethnographic evidence that Aborigines processed this resource, neither ethnographic accounts nor archaeological remains provide any obvious clues as to which types of tools may have been used. The analytical process for approaching this problem begins with a hypothesis of a prehistoric tool type that may have been utilized for rhizome processing—in this case, the bevelled pounder. Archaeological examples of this tool were inspected to see if they possess attributes consistent with the proposed hypothesis, and in this case some experimentation was also done (Kamminga 1981). Since the hypothesis is functional, the application of use-wear criteria was considered appropriate and the hypothesis was ultimately confirmed at a low level.

The fact that the designated use-traces are logically consistent with what one might expect does not necessarily render the association valid, however. The connection is strengthened by controlled reproduction of the same kinds of use traces on experimental tools as had been hypothesized for the prehistoric tool. This Gillieson and Hall (1982) accomplished by replicating bevelled pounders and using them to bruise bungwall.

Having experimentally confirmed the hypothesized use-wear pattern for a small sample of tools, criteria established in this process could be applied to the greater archaeological record of southeast Queensland. A number of questions were posed at this juncture: do all prehistoric bevelled pounders exhibit the same type of wear as the replicated tool? Are these patterns homogeneous throughout this tool type? Do other tool types show the same type of wear? Did processing behavior or technology change through time? Etc. Resolving questions of this nature requires large and representative archaeological samples from securely dated contexts.

Archaeologists in southeast Queensland introduced a second set of confirmatory criteria to the bungwall processing problem: residue analysis. Since the *B. indicum* rhizome contains starch, some of that starch may have been retained on the tools used to process it. To find out whether or not starch is preserved on a tool after use and can be extracted, it makes sense to turn first to experimental tools—the tactic employed by Hall et al. (1989). Failure to observe or extract residues from experimental tools after only five years of storage in a lab would have cast considerable doubt on the analyst's ability to extract starch from archaeological tools that have been weathered and are much older. The ability of the researchers to do so was encouraging, but the rate of starch degradation and the conditions in which it is preserved are still unknown. As with use-wear traces, the next step in the confirmatory process is to apply starch residue analysis to well controlled archaeological samples. Since use-wear and starch residues are independently acquired datasets, a hypothesis that is confirmed by both is more strongly supported than an hypothesis that has been confirmed by only one or the other.

the future, both phytolith and starch residue analysis will play an important role in evaluating the processing of plant materials in prehistory.

Animals

Depending on the size and nature of the animals and the uses to which their remains were to be put, prehistoric processing of animals could take many forms, some rather unconventional. For example, Yohe et al. (1991) made a good case that small rodents and perhaps reptiles captured in prehistoric southern and Baja California were pulverized with milling equipment for inclusion in soups, stews, and other concoctions. This contention was tested by submitting equipment from two archaeological sites to phytolith and immunological residue analyses. Although the phytolith analysis was inconclusive, crossover electrophoresis (CIEP) detected rodent immunoglobins from both sites. Armed with this knowledge, to consider rough stone artifacts such as manos and metates found in these regions as purely plant processing implements would probably be mistaken.

The processing of fish and larger animals for food can generally be considered butchering (or fileting, in the case of fish), though this activity is often difficult to separate totally from hide working (Frison and Bradley 1980:127). A considerable amount of effort has been expended in attempting to understand prehistoric butchering activities on the American Plains, a situation caused by the dominance of one resource—bison—in the economy of the region's prehistoric occupants and the relative abundance of point-specific capture locales, or kill sites, on the landscape. Observations on butchery will be limited here to bison, but to some extent they are generalizable to the processing of other large animals.

Butchery equipment was simple and functional and was not limited to stone tools. In fact, once an animal is cut open with a sharp knife, it is just as easy to separate the hide from connective tissues with a pronged bison humerus tool or pound it loose with a hammer as it is to continue to perform these functions with a stone knife. In any case, the essential bison stone processing tool kit included sharp cutting tools, as well as heavy chopping and bone breaking tools.

This is messy work, and the tools quickly gum up with grease and sinew. Hafting such a tool may have been counter-productive, because this kind of intensive labor put a huge strain on the bindings, such that a large portion of the tool needed to be placed under them. This configuration decreased the percentage of cutting edge available for work and increased the likelihood of fouling up the bindings and breaking them. In contrast, an unhafted stone tool had a greater proportion of its periphery ready for use, could be rotated in the hand, easily sharpened, and readily discarded when no longer effective (Frison 1978:301-328, 1979; Frison and Bradley 1980:127-130). These considerations would have intensified on the American Plains in late summer/fall when much of this kind of processing was accomplished, rendering speed and efficiency a necessity. Temperatures at this time of year can be oppressive even when rocking on the front porch tossing down a mint julep; meat left unprocessed in such conditions can stand no more than a day or two before it will spoil (Frison 1979:260).

This scenario of bison processing may not be totally accurate. Steve Tomka (2001) has noted that expedient tools are more difficult than formal tool types to control at higher pressures, they enable less leverage to be maintained, and they often cause considerable discomfort in use, suggesting that tools employed for processing sizeable quantities of medium-to-large mammals would have been hafted. Proceeding from the assumption that most formal tools on the North American

Plains were hafted, he argued that formalization of tools (not well defined, but seemingly related to shape or intensity of retouch) may not have been a function of residential mobility, as argued by others, but of meat processing requirements.

Techniques employed in investigating these relationships and analyzing prehistoric butchery tools have relied heavily on experimental replication and technological analysis (Frison 1978, 1989; Frison and Bradley 1980). Use-wear analysis may prove useful in discriminating butchery wear (e.g., Kay 1996), but not much of this has been done yet. And blood residue analysis may yet have a role to play in confirming animal processing activities (Kooyman et al. 1992). A summary of the food processing issues discussed in this section is presented in Table 6.2.

Table 6.2. Issues of plant and animal processing that have been addressed through lithic analysis.

Resource	Research question	Tool types	Types of analysis	References
Wild nut	Identification of plant processing	Ground & pecked stone tools	Type frequencies; use-wear: grinding, battering, pitting	Stafford 1991
Domesticated grain	Manufacture processes, identification	Threshing sledge flints	Technological; use-wear	Bordaz 1965; Whallon 1978; Fox 1984; Whittaker 1996
Domesticated maize	Grinding efficiency	Manos, metates	No./loc. of grinding surfaces; surface area; shape	Morris 1990; Adams 1993
Wild fern rhizome	Tools used for processing	Bevelled pounders	Use-wear; experiments; starch residues	Kamminga 1981; Gillieson & Hall 1982; Hall et al. 1989
Starchy plants	Identification of plant processing	Obsidian tools, milling stones, edge-gd. cobbles	Use-wear, starch residues	Barton et al. 1998; Piperno & Holst 1998
Grasses	Identification of plant processing	Obsidian artifacts	Use-wear, phytolith residues	Kealhofer et al. 1999
Small rodents, reptiles	Pulverizing animals	Milling equipment	Phytoliths; blood immunological analysis	Yohe et al. 1991
Bison	Types of processing	Bifacial tools, chopping tools, flakes, hammerstones	Technological; metric; use-wear; blood residue	Frison 1978, 1979, 1989; Kay 1996; Bement 1999; Tomka 2001

SHELTER, FACILITIES, AND CLOTHING

A dominant theme of this book involves the vast amount of information about human cultures that stone tools *cannot* impart. Lithic data are, by nature, particularistic; they can be interpreted only in context. Rarely does one discover a tool, such as a projectile point embedded in the rib of an aurochs, whose context is both indisputable and causal. More often, causes for an association are determined by the general situation in which an artifact was found. This point is nicely illustrated by the tools that were used for building structures and facilities, for which the following general research question applies:

Q25: How were stone tools employed for the fashioning of shelter, facilities, and clothing?

Structures and Facilities

At the end of the last glacial period in northern Europe glaciers receded and forests encroached on what had been tundra. The hunter-gatherers who inhabited this increasingly closed territory felt that their survival depended on the management of this changing environment. A new lithic type that appeared in the early Mesolithic of northern Europe was the chipped stone axe, a tool that was clearly designed for working wood and cutting down trees (Schwantes 1923; Clark 1975:106). Axes would have been useful for clearing the forest to create settlements or forest edge environments for browsing animals; for building houses; for constructing facilities and handles for tools; or for a variety of other tasks. Although these are all activities for which this tool type was suitable, it is practically impossible to know precisely which activity a particular early Mesolithic axe was engaged in. The same can be said for axes and adzes of the early agricultural Linearbandkeramik colonizers of central and western Europe, milling equipment of Natufian complex foragers, or a host of other prehistoric tool types from around the world.

This ambiguity is true even of tools that have been subjected to intensive functional analysis. For instance, the Lasley Vore protohistoric settlement in eastern Oklahoma yielded a clustered distribution of features that served as the basis for site spatial analyses. Use-wear studies of stone tools indicated that the middle of the site constituted the principal domestic unit, a conclusion reinforced by the concentration of chopping and wedging tools found at this locale (Odell 1999). This wear type was interpreted as relating to the construction of dwellings, which would have been concentrated in the principal domestic area.

Although this is a reasonable conclusion, no individual tool could be attributed to any task more specific than a percussive activity on a material of medium resistance.

Relating specific tools to the construction of facilities poses a similar problem. Facilities such as windbreaks, traps and snares for small animals, and traps and weirs for fish were usually made of wood in temperate and tropical climates. Implements used in their manufacture may be distinguishable as generalized woodworking tools, but exactly what they were involved in working is beyond the current capabilities of lithic analysis.

Facilities dug into the earth, such as storage or hearth pits, required digging tools. Excavation was an activity that involved a highly abrasive substance (earth), often containing an abundance of phytoliths or other silicates. Stone digging tools frequently acquired specific wear traces related to the abrasiveness of the medium (i.e., deep striations) or its silica content (i.e., gloss). Functional distinctions of this nature are discernible through use-wear analysis but usually not through typological and technological analyses, as the types of tools used for this activity were often generalized in form and varied from one cultural group to another. Of course, digging tools were frequently not made of stone at all, witnessed by the abundant tibia digging sticks and scapula hoes present in late prehistoric North American Plains contexts.

Clothing

Clothing can be made from vegetal materials, such as the fiber skirts and sandals worn by peoples of the Great Basin (Kelly and Fowler 1986:373; Thomas et al. 1986:269; Kehoe 1992:367), the woven cedar bark hats, aprons and blankets worn by Northwest Coast Indian groups such as the Kwakiutl (Codere 1990:366), and so forth. The manufacture of these items involved pointed and spatulate organic tools, but rarely stone. Any involvement of stone tools would probably have occurred early in the process in cutting reeds or slicing cedar bark, activities that would be difficult to associate directly with clothing manufacture.

The manufacture of hide clothing is a different story as stone tools did contribute to hide processing, though perhaps not as prominently as many archaeologists believe (see review of Plains ethnographic literature in Schultz 1992). Certain assemblages exhibit clear evidence of hide scraping in a context that suggests that the goal of this process was to produce clothing, blankets, rugs, and other items that could be used for warmth, cover, or household furnishings. This was the case with the early Magdalenian assemblage from Cassegros in southwestern France, in which an intensive use-wear analysis by Pat Vaughan (1985) detected an abundance of hide scraping wear (see Box 5.3).

It would be foolish to equate all hide scraping wear with the production of locally consumed clothing or household accoutrements, however. As an example to the contrary, the protohistoric period of the North American Plains and Eastern Woodlands featured an active trade between Native Americans and Europeans in the hides of several mammals, including beaver, deer and bison. Deer hides provided buckskin shirts and breeches for Indians and settlers alike, and beaver pelts furnished the top hats fashionable in seventeenth and eighteenth century Europe.

Likewise, bison hides were used locally on the Plains for warmth during cold winter months (e.g., Stewart 2001:340 for the Hidatsa) and for the round "bullboats" used by the Hidatsa and Mandan (Stewart 2001:339; Wood and Irwin 2001:353-354). But sites like Ferdinandina, or Deer Creek, in Oklahoma (Sudbury 1975; Wedel 1981) bear witness to a flourishing trade in bison hides—not only with other Plains Indian groups, but also with Europeans. Yet these hides were probably not being used by Europeans in the same way they were used by Indians—it is a bit of a stretch to imagine a Parisienne or Lyonnaise adorning herself in the latest style of bison robe for an evening at the opera. The popularity of bison hides for European consumers lies not in clothing, but as the belts that turned the wheels and lathes that propelled the Industrial Revolution.

ORGANIZATION OF MOBILITY AND TECHNOLOGY

Most hunting-gathering people were mobile to at least some extent as they exploited naturally occurring resources. This form of resource use entailed making a series of interrelated decisions concerning not only the nature and location of targeted resources, but where and how long to camp, which segments of the total group to involve, how the group would be supplied logistically, and which kinds of technologies would be needed to extract the necessary resources. In a series of seminal articles, Lewis Binford analyzed several aspects of the hunting-gathering decision making process (e.g., Binford 1977, 1979, 1980).

Exploiting resources when they were available and conducting all the social, ritual, political and economic obligations to which a social group was beholden entailed adherence to a strategy for movement from one part of the landscape to another known as the *organization of mobility*. Binford conceptualized two basic forms of organization. In one, *foragers* moved from one resource to another as availability permitted; in the other, *collectors* moved as a unit from one base camp to another, provisioning these camps through smaller groups that targeted specific resources and brought them back to the settlement. In theory, groups following a collecting strategy were larger than those that pursued a foraging strategy and they tended to stay longer in one place. This conceptualization of hunter-gatherer mobility has proven to be a useful heuristic device, although Chatters (1987) and others have pointed out that the variability inherent in hunter-gatherer mobility strategies is more accurately depicted as continua on a series of multivariate axes than as a simple dichotomy.

Successful mobility strategies were facilitated by technologies that enabled the accomplishment of immediate goals such as providing warmth, clearing the forest, constructing houses and facilities, and procuring and processing food. Stone tools played an integral role in these technologies and, by extension, in the society's seasonality and mobility strategies. Although some scholars have distinguished the technological organization of tools from the organization of mobility, the two concepts are interrelated and difficult to separate at lower levels. The discussion in this chapter will center on the lithic assemblage while recognizing the tight connection that exists between the assemblage and the overall organization of mobility.

Tool Design

Tools are responses to specific tasks that must be accomplished to overcome environmental constraints. A general model focusing on activities and the performance characteristics relevant to specific activities has been articulated and applied to prehistoric pottery by Schiffer and Skibo (1997). Peter Bleed (1986) articulated the situation specifically for stonetools by proposing two principal axes along which tools in any assemblage might vary. One is *maintainability*, sometimes called *flexibility*, or the capacity of a tool to be usable under a variety of circumstances. The other is *reliability*, or the capacity of a tool to always function when needed. Shott (1986), Nelson (1991) and others have expanded on this dichotomy to include opportunistic behavior, versatility, and related qualities.

These concepts are devilishly difficult to operationalize on a body of stone tools, because 1) most tools possess *both* qualities, though usually to varying degrees; 2) appropriate surrogate characteristics on stone tools are difficult to establish; and 3) frequently a lithic artifact did not constitute the entire tool as originally conceived and utilized. The former presence of a handle would have altered the manner in which such a tool would have been used from its unhafted state, yet evidence for a handle on previously hafted tools is usually not obvious. Furthermore, a lithic artifact may formerly have been part of a larger composite tool, but in most instances there is no way an analyst could be certain of this.

Despite the analytical difficulties, these qualities of tools were very real to the people who made and used them; therefore, an approach to assemblage variability that incorporated these concepts might bring the analyst closer to understanding the way specific tool types functioned within the rubric of prehistoric society than by pursuing more traditional artifact analyses. This type of study emphasizes the design of tools for specific prehistoric situations and can be applied to a particular tool type or to an entire assemblage. An appropriate archaeological question can be framed as follows:

Q26: How were prehistoric tools designed for specific situations, and how can an archaeologist ascertain differences in tool design?

Root et al. (1999) applied design analysis to a unique tool type within the assemblages of three Folsom period camps in the Knife River quarry area of western North Dakota. The authors noticed a finely crafted, bifacially reduced artifact type that they dubbed the "ultrathin biface." Technological studies allowed them to distinguish the reduction trajectory through which ultrathin bifaces were manufactured, and use-wear analysis suggested that they were employed as butchery knives. Made for transport, many of them were manufactured from Rainy Buttes silicified wood, found 100 km away. These studies indicate that ultrathin bifaces were essentially Folsom butchering tools, primarily for bison, that were made for extensive reuse and resharpening. They were carried great distances before being discarded in favor of freshly knapped Knife River tools at the quarry.

Hayden et al. (1996) applied design analysis to an entire lithic assemblage from the Keatley Creek settlement in interior British Columbia. The advantage of applying design analysis to this region is that Native Americans there were practicing traditional hunting-gathering subsistence economies until relatively recently and extensive ethnographic observations of their lifeways have been published. Thus the subsistence and seasonal patterns of these people, as well as the tools they used for various tasks and the nature of the constraints on those activities, are generally understood. Armed with this knowledge, archaeologists have been able to direct their analysis of lithic assemblages to the prehistoric strategies facilitated by these tools rather than solely to the characteristics of the tools themselves. Examples of technological strategies employed include expedient block core, bifacial, portable long-use, quarried bipolar, scavenged bipolar, and ground stone cutting.

Considerations of tool design have figured even more prominently in recent studies of ground stone tools, as recounted in previous chapters. They include tests of grinding efficiency (Morris 1990; Adams 1993, 1999; Hard et al. 1996) and the influence of raw material, which can produce effects that confound models of grinding efficiency (Stone 1994). Tool design also figures prominently in considerations of the appropriateness of grinding equipment for processing specific products such as maize (Stone 1994) and seeds (Wright 1994; Fullagar and Field 1997). A brief outline of a few of the lithic analyses that have addressed issues of tool design is presented in Table 6.3.

Table 6.3.   Issues of tool design addressed through lithic analysis.

Organizational response	Tool types	Types of analysis	References
Designing tools for specific situations	Ultrathin bifaces	Reduction analysis; measurements; use-wear	Root et al. 1999
Designing tools for specific situations	Entire assemblage	Reduction analysis; raw materials; use-wear	Hayden et al. 1996
Designing tools for efficiency	Grinding stones	Extent of grinding surface; wear	Morris 1990; Adams 1993, 1999; Stone 1994; Hard et al. 1996
Designing tools for specific products	Grinding tools	Typology; residue analysis	Wright 1994; Fullagar & Field 1997

Raw Material Procurement, Supply, and Use

Retooling Models

Just as the design of tools in hunting-gathering cultures was responsive to considerations of seasonality and mobility, so was the procurement of raw material for these tools. After all, that hard stuff had to be picked up from somewhere, and that somewhere usually had to bear some relation to the landscape a people passed through on a yearly basis. There has been some debate about whether an individual society would tend to commission quarrying parties to provision the rest of the populace or simply embed a trip to a raw material source in its seasonal round. This question is usually not resolvable with the types of data archaeologists normally work with; either way, the presence of a particular material in an assemblage bears witness to its transportation by some mechanism to the location at which it was found. Even if the specifics of its procurement are unknowable, the structure or pattern of acquisition can sometimes be deduced. One way of framing this issue is:

Q27: In what ways was lithic raw material provisioned and utilized in prehistory, and which archaeological methods are appropriate for investigating issues involving raw material?

A group would normally provision itself according to its perceived tool needs at the time of provisioning. Ingbar (1994) produced a useful simulation of a hypothetical hunter-gatherer group that visits three lithic source areas in the course of a seasonal round. In all simulations the proportions of material from each

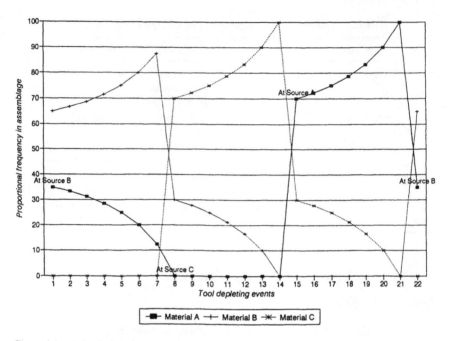

Figure 6.4.   A simulation of frequencies of raw material from three widely spaced lithic source areas in the tool assemblage of one mobile foraging group (taken from Ingbar 1994: Fig. 2).

source are dependent on where the group is situated with regard to that source. A group that has recently visited a specific quarry is likely to have a lot of material from that quarry in its inventory, whereas material from quarries visited several months before is likely to have been greatly diminished or depleted. Hypothetical frequencies of each raw material type that might result from such a situation are illustrated in Figure 6.4.

Like Ingbar, Hofman (1992) has suggested that the most important variable in assemblage composition (at least for projectile points in the Folsom period of the North American Plains) is not distance from raw material source, but number of retooling events since visiting a source. *Retooling*, or the refurbishing of hunting and butchering equipment, affected the elements from which tools were made. As the number of retooling events since visiting a lithic quarry increased, the proportion of bifacial cores decreased and the proportion of blank preforms (large flakes) increased. Using the points themselves, Hofman introduced a *retooling index*, a ratio of the percentage of reworked tips to mean length of complete points, under the assumption that the more points were reworked, the shorter they would become. His comparison of seven Folsom assemblages on this index, presented in Figure 6.5, suggests that the Elida assemblage had experienced the greatest

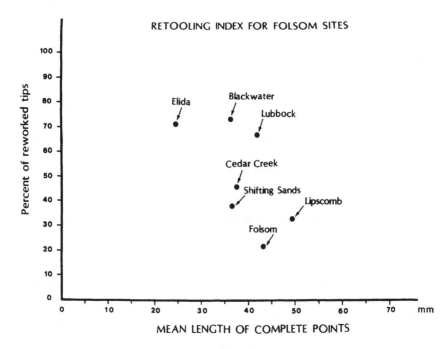

Figure 6.5.   Retooling index for Plains Folsom sites (taken from Hofman 1992: Fig. 6.9).

number of retooling events among the sites studied, the Folsom and Lipscomb assemblages the least. Bement (1999:141) later employed this index to analyze points from the Cooper bison kill in Oklahoma. Points from the three separate kill episodes at the site registered differently on the retooling index, indicating that the hunters involved in each episode had passed through different tool refurbishing trajectories on their way to this location.

Earlier, Judge (1973:199-203) had attempted to distinguish kinds of sites that served specific technological niches within the subsistence trajectory. For this he used point:preform ratios. Assemblages with high proportions of points (especially bases) were interpreted as base camps, where game was returned after a kill. Assemblages with high proportions of preforms were armament stations where weapons were refurbished and tool manufacture focused on the production of finished points. Amick (1994) later surmised that this pattern was strongly affected by the availability of tool raw material (see discussion below).

Using the whole assemblage from the Middle Paleolithic settlement of Wallertheim D in Germany, Conard and Adler (1997) concluded that at least part of the settlement bore witness to a retooling and recycling episode whereby red-brown rhyolite tools were replenished by gray andesite tools. This conclusion was derived from careful refitting, distribution, and reduction sequence analyses of tools of each raw material type. Most of the artifacts arrived on-site in already finished form and were maintained and refurbished at that location.

Responses to Mobility

The composition of raw material types in a lithic assemblage was influenced by a number of factors, one of which was mobility organization. The concept of mobility organization has been discussed in a variety of publications and earlier in this manual and will not be reiterated here, except to note that it has stimulated several research questions, one of which is:

Q28: How can prehistoric hunter-gatherer mobility organization be clarified through lithic data?

Mobility organization was operative in the Epipaleolithic of southern Jordan (Henry 1989), where seasonal mobility patterns varied from small ephemeral upland summer camps near flint sources to large lowland winter camps located at some distance from flint sources. The markedly greater ratio of blanks:cores in lowland than in highland assemblages indicates exportation of flint downslope to areas deficient in this resource. This scenario was strengthened by measurements of variables related to tool manufacture. Although the principal thrust of prehistoric lithic technology in both areas was the production of bladelets, the average length of primary elements and blade core facets in lowland assemblages was shorter than comparable measurements on bladelets from upland sites. In addition, primary elements and facets on cores from lowland sites were substantially shorter in maximum length than their counterparts on upland sites (see Figure 6.6). These results suggest that the initial preparation of cores occurred at or near their origin and before they were exported to lowland settlements.

The influence of mobility organization on lithic technology has also been documented by Blades (2001) for the Aurignacian culture of southwestern France. Blades proceeded from an ecological model whereby very mobile early Aurignacian foragers living in a cold period practiced encounter hunting of herd animals such as caribou, whereas later Aurignacian people living in warmer climes subsisted on a wider range of resources and became less residentially mobile. Employing variables such as raw material, tool types, intensity of retouch, amount of dorsal cortex, and core and blank measurements, he established that lithic assemblages associated with the more mobile early Aurignacian people contained raw materials obtained at greater distances from their source than those from the later Aurignacian period. In addition, early Aurignacian tools exhibited greater retouch

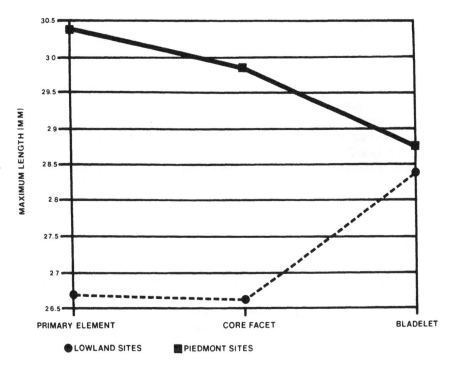

Figure 6.6. Average maximum lengths of primary elements, core facets, and bladelets from lowland and piedmont Epipaleolithic sites in southern Jordan (taken from Henry 1989: Fig. 7).

intensity, whereas later Aurignacian assemblages showed greater intensity of core reduction.

In North America there is some evidence that tool assemblages of mobile hunter-gatherers tended to be fairly standardized, a response to technological uncertainty and a result of the frequent hafting of these implements (Keeley 1982; Shott 1986:39-43; Young 1994; Amick and Carr 1996). In the long term, this trend was reflected in the progressive decline of formalized bifacial technologies and increased use of expedient tools throughout the Holocene (Koldehoff 1987; Parry and Kelly 1987; Odell 1996, 1998b). In addition, Odell (1994b) noted an increase in hafting use-wear traces through time in a series of Illinois assemblages. Increase in hafting was deduced from the increase in average proportion of tools under a hafting device, which caused a decrease through time in the average quantity of functional units per tool and different activities and worked materials per tool. Utilized polar co-ordinates per tool increased slightly as use intensity increased on sites that were being occupied on a more permanent or semi-permanent basis than ever before (Odell 1994a).

Interestingly, residentially mobile Paleolithic cultures of southern Europe may not have responded to tool portability considerations by making more bifaces or formal tools, but by carrying smaller tools. By calculating and comparing a tool's potential utility to its mass, Steve Kuhn (1994) found that the most efficient artifacts were those whose length was approximately 1.5–3.0 times their minimum usable length. This formulation has been criticized by Morrow (1996a), who emphasized that small tools would be quickly expended. Nevertheless, mobile hunting-gathering tool kits in Europe were constituted differently from those in North America. Reasons for these differences may have included optimal size, efficiency, availability of toolstone, intended function, or simply the historical technological trajectory pursued on either continent.

Responses to Raw Material Availability

Effects on lithic assemblage variability attributed to mobility organization are often difficult to separate from the effects of other factors, such as the availability of raw material for tool production. Sometimes these two elements simply operate at different levels, e.g., a less residentially mobile people would have fewer opportunities than more mobile people to pass through lithic source areas, so their resource options and technologies would be more severely constrained. Let us continue to explore the issue of assemblage variability by focusing on raw material availability, keeping in mind that this element may also be associated, on another level, with mobility organization or other pertinent factors. A general question to consider in this regard is:

Q29: How can differential responses to lithic raw material availability be discerned in the prehistoric record?

In regions in which good quality tool materials were not plentiful or were unavailable altogether, a common solution was to import better resources from outside the area. The intrinsic qualities of these substances rendered them more suitable than local materials for the manufacture of certain items. For instance, Andrefsky (1994) found that local materials from the resource-poor Calispell Valley, Washington, dominated the expedient tool inventory, whereas finer imported raw materials were employed for the manufacture of formal tool types. MacDonald (1995) has recognized similar relationships in Oregon. In fact, throughout the American West, later Paleoindian Folsom tool users often preferred non-local materials for the production of technically refined objects like fluted points, burins and drills, and local materials for more easily fashioned items like flakes and scraping tools (Ingbar 1994; Amick 1999).

Formal tool types are not the only lithic elements that can reflect differences in the availability of raw material. Dibble (1995) investigated several technologically based variables from both the retouched tool and debitage components of two Middle Paleolithic assemblages from southwestern France. Combe-Capelle-Bas, a Typical Mousterian site with a preponderance of denticulates and notched tools, was located on a raw material source, whereas Combe Grenal, a Quina Mousterian shelter characterized by scrapers, was located 35 km away from the nearest source of toolstone. Dibble showed that material constraints at Combe Grenal caused its assemblage to reflect smaller average core, flake and tool lengths, flake surface areas, and flake length:core length ratios, as well as larger average blank:core and tool:flake ratios, than Combe-Capelle-Bas. All of these effects were attributed to economizing behavior at Combe Grenal as a result of its greater distance from raw material sources.

Technological variables of a different nature were employed by Odell (1989b, 1996) in comparing the Archaic components of the Napoleon Hollow site, located in an area of chert abundance, with those of Campbell Hollow, located just across the Illinois River in an area of chert scarcity. Economizing behavior at Campbell Hollow took the form of trying to make usable tools from every available piece of lithic material. Consequently, the Campbell Hollow assemblage was left with almost no cores, as the cores that previously existed had been obliterated in an effort to extract as many usable edges as possible. Tool users at Campbell Hollow were also compelled to employ bipolar techniques to conserve toolstone, and their discarded tools were more frequently fragmented than tools in areas of greater raw material availability. This pattern of economizing behavior has been recognized elsewhere and was probably a common response to lithic resource scarcity.

In assemblages from sites at which suitable toolstone was scarce or unavailable, economizing behavior can often be recognized from patterns of tool utilization that exhibit extreme or anomalous characteristics. Kazaryan (1993), for example, attributed the abundance and intense wear on Middle Paleolithic flakes and convergent scrapers from Armenia to this phenomenon. And in central North America, Odell (1989b, 1996) observed substantial utilization of broken edges on tools from resource-poor areas, and considerably less of this trait on tools from areas well supplied with good quality toolstone.

Unfortunately, these economizing characteristics do not appear to be consistent across the board and must be established on a case-by-case basis. A case in point is Kuhn's (1991) comparison of two Mousterian assemblages from west-central Italy: Grotta Guattari, situated amidst a coastal plain full of pebble flint; and Grotta di Sant' Agostino, located in a similar environment but with no known deposits of flint nearby. Like the studies in the Illinois Valley and southwestern France cited above, Kuhn found that the distance of a site from the nearest source of good lithic raw material had a profound effect on the rate at which cores were consumed: chert-rich Guattari contained a considerably higher frequency of tested cobbles and casual cores than Sant' Agostino. But these constraints are not reflected in the intensity of tool reduction, i.e., the relative amount of retouched tools in an assemblage and the average proportion of intentional modification along the periphery of an individual implement. Guattari actually contained a larger percentage of retouched flakes, higher mean indices of reduction, and greater proportion of retouched tools with multiple edges than Sant' Agostino. Thus whatever economizing behavior existed at Sant' Agostino, it apparently did not involve intensive retouching. It may have involved intensive utilization, but this proposition was not tested through functional analysis; and it certainly involved the maximization of cores by making more unretouched flakes from them.

In a study of late prehistoric sites in southeast Texas, Ricklis and Cox (1993; see also Hester and Shafer 1975:182) related several of the economizing traits mentioned previously to a falloff, or gravity, model of chert acquisition. Their research region near Corpus Christi Bay contains only one lithic source area, located a few kilometers up the Nueces River. Prehistoric tool users in this region tended to procure their flint from this source rather than to trade for toolstone from outside the region, a contention supported by falloff curves of chert frequency from the material source and the relative homogeneity of the flint itself.

The authors observed several characteristics of the lithic assemblages that were directly associated with the distance of a particular site from the lithic source area. As distance from source increased: 1) the flake:formal tool ratio decreased; 2) the average flake length decreased; 3) the average length of Perdiz points decreased; 4) the proportion of bifacial thinning flakes increased; and 5) the proportion of utilized flakes increased. These relationships held constant across several environmental zones and two very different site types.

Behaviorally, as late prehistoric occupants of this region traveled greater distances from their lithic resource, they were increasingly forced to sharpen and reshape their implements, causing their projectile points to decrease in size and their other formal tools to increase in number at the expense of unretouched flakes. This tendency is clearly shown in the falloff of flake:tool ratios with distance from source (Figure 6.7). The two Aransas River sites demonstrate this distance-decay pattern even more acutely than the other sites, as costs of chert procurement for people living in the Aransas Valley would have been higher than for people living in the Nueces Valley. As lithic supplies dwindled away from the source area, the size of flakes that could be removed from cores decreased and the amount of use to which tool users had to subject these flakes increased. This increase in proportion of flake utilization with distance from chert source is reproduced in Figure 6.8. Eventually people in this region began to favor the production of long-lasting bifacial tools and cores at the expense of their core-flake technology. This and other issues discussed in this section have been tabulated in Table 6.4.

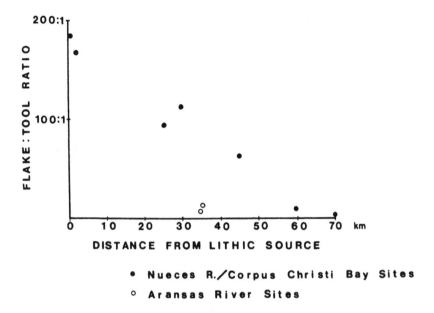

Figure 6.7.   Falloff of flake:tool ratios with distance from chert source, of Rockport phase sites near the Central Texas Coast (taken from Ricklis and Cox 1993: Fig. 3).

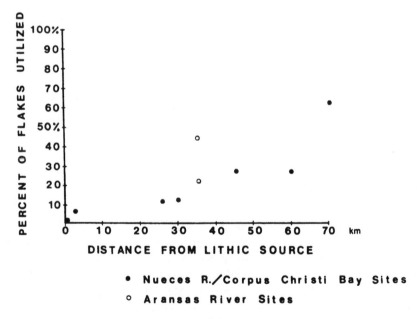

Figure 6.8.   Increase in percentage of utilized flakes with distance from chert source, of Rockport phase sites near the Central Texas Coast (taken from Ricklis and Cox 1993: Fig. 5).

Table 6.4. Issues of raw material procurement, supply, and use addressed through lithic analysis.

Organ. response	Tool types	Types of analysis	References
Pattern of procurement	All	Typology; simulation; raw materials	Ingbar 1994
Retooling	Projectile points	Metric; blanks; cores; reworking	Judge 1973; Hofman 1992; Bement 1999
Retooling	Whole assemblage	Refitting; tool distribution; raw material; reduction	Conard & Adler 1997
Influence of mobility org. on lithic technology	Blades, tools	Typology; blank & core meas.; raw mat.; cortex; retouch intensity	Henry 1989; Blades 2001
Standardization of tools	Bifaces	Measurements; technology	Shott 1986; Amick & Carr 1996; Odell 1996, 1998b
Tool portability	All	Use-wear; efficiency ratios	Kuhn 1994; Odell 1994a, b, 1996; Morrow 1996
Influence of raw mat. availability on lithic technology	Formal tool types	Raw materials; typology	Amick 1994, 1999; Andrefsky 1994; Ingbar 1994; MacDonald 1995
Influence of raw mat. availability on lithic technology	Debris, tools, cores	Measurements; reduc. techniques; breakage; technological types	Odell 1989b, 1996; Kuhn 1991; Ricklis & Cox 1993; Dibble 1995
Influence of raw mat. availability on lithic technology	Scrapers, butchery tools, whole assemb.	Abnormally intense use-wear	Odell 1989b, 1996; Kazaryan 1993; Ricklis & Cox 1993

COMPLEX SOCIETIES

Most of the examples of lithic resource manipulation discussed previously could have been drawn either from hunting-gathering or from more complex societies though, for obvious reasons, the former tend to dominate lithic studies. Yet burgeoning, and even developed, complex societies from all over the globe retained their lithic technologies—the Maya, Uruk, and Levantine Bronze Age cultures being only a few of the many examples that could be marshaled (Lewenstein 1987; Pope and Pollock 1995; Johnson 1996; Rosen 1997b). Changing sociopolitical structures altered people's relations with their sources of supply and with the tools themselves to such an extent that studies of lithic resources in these societies must take into account a series of factors that were not as important in simpler hunting-gathering societies. In this section I will discuss a few of these factors as they relate to the lithic database.

Production of Surplus Goods

To have developed the sociopolitical structures that constitute social complexity, a cultural group must have been able to sustain a subsistence economy of relative abundance through all seasons of the year. This is usually accomplished through agriculture, though some foragers that occupied environments rich in natural stable resources also developed characteristics of cultural complexity (e.g., Natufian, Calusa, Northwest Coast Indians). In some instances, societies that produced a subsistence surplus were able to support artisans and craftspeople who created products desired by members of that society or of outside groups. In fact, one reason an artisan might create such a product was to be able to procure something else of value, whether that be food, a different non-subsistence related item, friendship, or prestige. It is not much of a stretch to imagine a progression of craftsmanship from a lone artisan bartering for nourishment, to a household augmenting its corporate wealth, to an entire class of artisans enhancing the prestige of a ruling elite, thereby cementing that class's hold on power.

In analyzing these phenomena it is often difficult to separate cause from effect or one goal from another. For instance, it would be difficult to separate craft specialization from trade or from sociopolitical control when the very purpose of the specialization was to procure specific products from far-flung regions or to enhance the political position of a particular social class. Although it might not ultimately be very effective to separate these influences, I will try to do so here for purposes of clarity and specificity.

Craft Specialization

In this discussion the concept of craft specialization is not restricted to evidence for tremendously high levels of production intensity, large quantities of goods, support by an elite class, or full-time artisans. As used here, it includes any product manufactured by a specific subset of craftspeople over and above the amount needed by the producers of that product. Thus evidence for cottage industries in grinding stones and microlithic drills for making ostrich eggshell beads, found at the Early Bronze Age Camel site in the Central Negev of Israel (Rosen 1997a), would qualify as craft specialization. Though production was not voluminous by Henry Ford's standards, it was created by a specific subset of the population and was meant for export to other areas. Relevant research questions pertaining to this topic would be:

Q30: How can craft specialization be distinguished using lithic data, and how was it organized within ancient societies?

From the perspective of the lithic database, craft specialization can affect either a lithic product or a lithic tool used to manufacture a product of a different material. Let us first consider an example in which the desired end product was made of stone. Such a situation existed at Colha, a small major Mayan center in Belize containing ceremonial structures organized around four or five central courtyards. Colha sat on an important source of high-quality chert that had weathered from marls and limestones or was mined from subsurface marls (Figure 6.9). During the late Preclassic and Classic periods, flint workers at Colha manufactured specific tool types for distribution at other centers in the Mayan world. Some areas of the settlement contained workshop debris more than a meter thick. Deposits in these areas included almost no soil matrix whatsoever, inducing excavators to refer to their spoil as "back-chert piles." The principal tool types produced during the Preclassic and Classic periods at Colha were oval bifaces and tranchet bit adzes, as well as lesser quantities of macroblades and large bifacial eccentrics (Shafer and Hester 1983; Hester 1985; Shafer 1985; Hester and Shafer 1991). Certain locales at Colha contain both household and workshop waste, suggesting that flint working was a cottage industry conducted within individual households. Despite the abundance of workshop debris, flint working was probably not a full-time craft specialization at Colha (Shafer 1985:309) or, for that matter, at any other Mayan site.

Examples of these tool types have shown up at other Mayan settlements of similar periods in contexts that indicate importation. That is, the assemblages exhibit little evidence for initial reduction, their technology was geared toward recycling and maintenance, and their bifaces were shorter than those at Colha and included few broken or aborted specimens. One such chert consumer site was Cerros, which overlooked Chetumal Bay and the mouth of the New River. Tools found at Cerros that probably originated at Colha are illustrated in Figure 6.10 (Mitchum 1991). This *Producer-Consumer model* of Mayan chert distribution has been studied extensively by McSwain (1991), Dockall and Shafer (1993), and Dockall (1994).

A contrasting situation for an analyst occurs when the lithic component of an industry was not the end product, but an implement used in manufacture. Such a

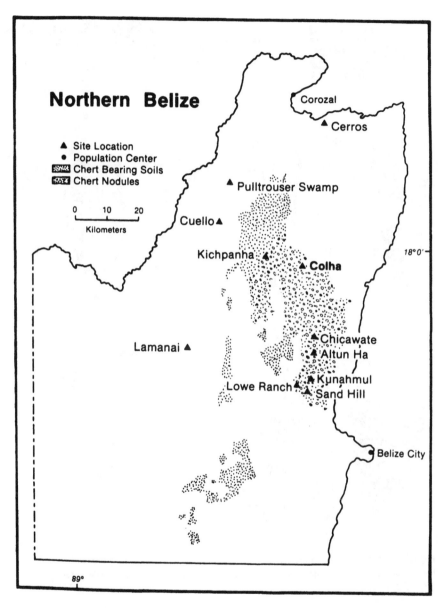

Figure 6.9.   Northern Belize showing Colha and other Mayan sites in relation to chert-bearing deposits (taken from Shafer and Hester 1983: Fig. 1).

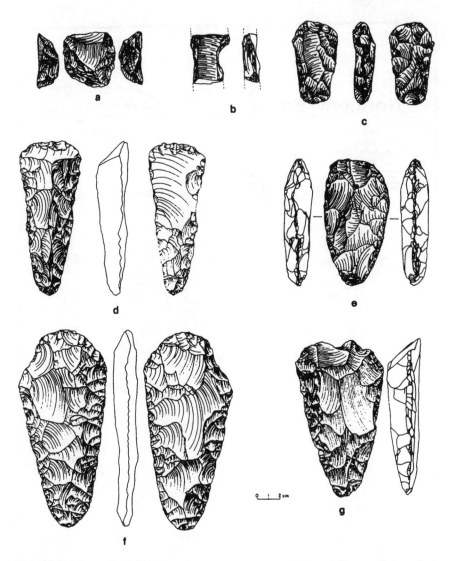

Figure 6.10. A sample of lithic types from Cerros, Belize: a) flake tool; b) macroblade tool; c) hammerstone; d) tranchet adze; e,f) oval bifaces; g) reworked tranchet adze (taken from Mitchum 1991: Fig. 1).

situation occurs in shell bead making, for which an integral part of the process was boring a hole with a stone-tipped drill. A good example occurred in the Channel Islands and adjacent mainland of southern California. Here, active production of Olivella shell beads developed in the Middle, Transitional and Late periods, i.e.,

600 BC–AD 1782. Beads were produced in large workshops on the islands for transport to the mainland, in return for terrestrial products such as acorns, seeds, deer meat and hides, and baskets (Arnold 1992).

An important component of the bead industry was the microlithic drill bit used to bore holes in the Olivella shells. The manufacture of microdrills was a specialist activity located at workshops on eastern Santa Cruz Island. Finished drills were sent to bead-making locales on other parts of the island chain (Arnold and Munns 1994). The drill workshops contained a wide range of lithic manufacture debris, including rejects and pieces broken in manufacture. Assemblages of recipient sites contained spent drills and sharpening debris, but little evidence of direct drill manufacture. However, these sites did exhibit copious evidence for manufacture of the beads.

The Mississippian center of Cahokia in the American Bottom region of the Central Mississippi Valley also yielded a shell bead industry manufactured with the aid of microlithic drill bits, some of which are illustrated in Figure 6.11. In this case the most persuasive evidence for bead manufacture was shell use-wear on almost all of the drill bits analyzed. Production of these microdrills was restricted to the larger sites in the Cahokia settlement system, and much of the manufacture of the beads themselves was carried out by specific artisans at Cahokia.

The earliest shell working in the American Bottom was a household specialization. Later, more households took part in the activity such that it might be called a regional specialization, but full-time specialists in either shell bead or microlithic drill production probably never existed in this region (Yerkes 1983, 1989).

Since all of these specializations involved the manufacture of a specific material item, evidence for such specialization must include detritus from its production. This means evidence for all stages of production—or, if blanks were whacked out at the quarry, then evidence of the middle and late stages. In cases in which the lithic component was not the end product of the industry, as in shell bead making, workshops for the end product (beads) may have existed at locations different from the workshops of tools used in manufacturing the product (drills). The workshop debris at such sites should reflect the nature of the object being produced. Stone tool consumer sites and non-lithic workshop sites that imported lithic implements should contain evidence for the sharpening of these tools, but little evidence for their manufacture.

Trade

Craft specialization in a community can occur without the goods resulting from that specialization ever leaving the community. In fact, most specializations probably started out that way, as one person or unit, such as a family of

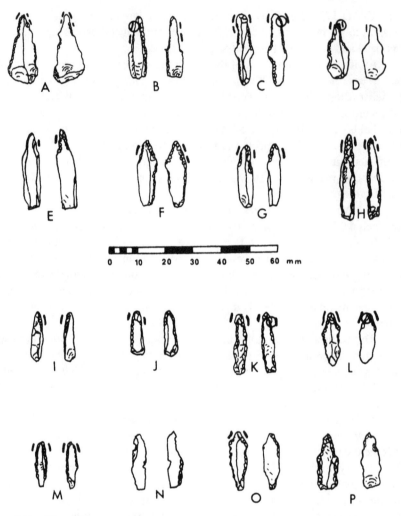

Figure 6.11.   Microdrills from the Powell Mound (A-H) and Dunham Tract (I-P) of the Cahokia site (taken from Yerkes 1983: Fig. 5).

shell divers or a talented creator of Folsom points or fine pottery, became good at the procurement or production of a desirable but dear item. As long as volume remained small and distribution local, the specialization was not likely to be more than a cottage industry practiced by part-time specialists. However, some communities expanded their markets and engaged in medium- and long-distance trade. Such a situation might spawn research questions related to this general issue:

Q31: How can the existence of prehistoric trade be determined using lithic data?

The previously discussed communities that practiced craft specialization were all engaged in at least a region-wide trade that involved the products of those specializations. For instance, chert tools from Colha were transported to consumer sites several kilometers away, and the distribution of this trade appears to have changed with time. In the Late Preclassic these items were transported primarily in a northwesterly direction, whereas by the Late Classic they were shipped by boat in all directions (Santone 1997).

At Cahokia the production of chert microdrills was directly associated with the manufacture of shell beads, and the importance of this industry also waxed and waned with time. The earliest shell working, in the Fairmount/Lohmann phase (AD 900-1050), has been characterized as a household specialization distributing beads within the community. The subsequent Stirling phase (AD 1050-1150) saw an expansion of bead distribution at least throughout the region and perhaps beyond. During this period shell production occurred at the Cahokia and Mitchell sites and a number of outlying settlements in the American Bottom. The Moorehead and Sand Prairie phases (AD 1150-1400) saw a retraction of shell working, as the craft was virtually absent from small outlying sites and became increasingly restricted to Cahokia itself (Yerkes 1989).

A lithic analyst interested in pursuing the topic of prehistoric trade must confront three paramount issues. One must establish, first, the source of the raw material under consideration; and second, the location at which the product was manufactured. At Colha source was never an issue, because the village sat on the geological formation from which the chert for the tools was obtained. And the nature of the workshops at Colha left no doubt that this was where the tranchet adzes, oval bifaces, macroblades and eccentrics were knapped. In southern California shell bead production occurred in an island environment that abounded in shell, and the Santa Cruz microdrill workshops existed close to natural sources of flint. At Cahokia, bead and microdrill workshops were definable through the nature and patterning of their manufacture detritus. The shell and chert employed in these activities were most likely procured from outside the American Bottom.

A third issue to be confronted is the mechanism of material displacement: was trade or another process responsible for the translocation of items from one locale to another? Huge workshops with abundant initial stage debris, rejects, and tranchet bit sharpening flakes at Colha leave no doubt as to its role as primary lithic tool production center. Conversely, the lack of early stage debris and production rejects and the abundance of sharpening flakes of this chert type at outlying sites imply that the occupants of these settlements must have received their original chert tools by trade with Colha.

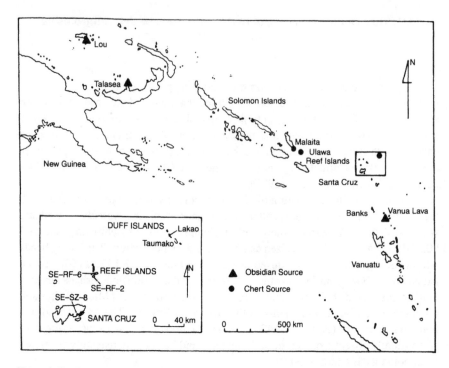

Figure 6.12. Locations of western Melanesian chert and obsidian sources, as well as Lapita sites on the Reefs/Santa Cruz Islands (taken from Sheppard 1993: Fig. 1).

Not all situations are as clear-cut as this. Let us consider the case of obsidian in archaeological assemblages from Oceania, where several distributional and sourcing studies have been conducted. Obsidian is essentially a point resource, occurring in specific lava flows. In Near Oceania obsidian sources exist on New Britain, Fergusson Island, and Lou/Pam Islands (White 1996:199; see Figure 6.12). The obsidian flakes and retouched tools that appear in archaeological assemblages away from these sources had to arrive there through some mechanism, one of which might have been trade.

The amount of obsidian in these assemblages is usually substantially less than the amount of chert or basalt (Sheppard 1996:101). In fact, the total weight of obsidian tools and debitage on most Oceanic islands is quite small. Figure 6.13 illustrates obsidian cores from three Lapita (early pottery) sites on the Reefs/Santa Cruz Islands, which are located not far from obsidian sources. These cores are variable in shape and technique and many are quite small—often a rough indicator of material scarcity. On these sites Sheppard (1993:127) estimated total obsidian weights of 245, 26.44, and 9.5 kg. On more remote islands total obsidian weights are frequently less than this, inducing some researchers to propose that the entire lot

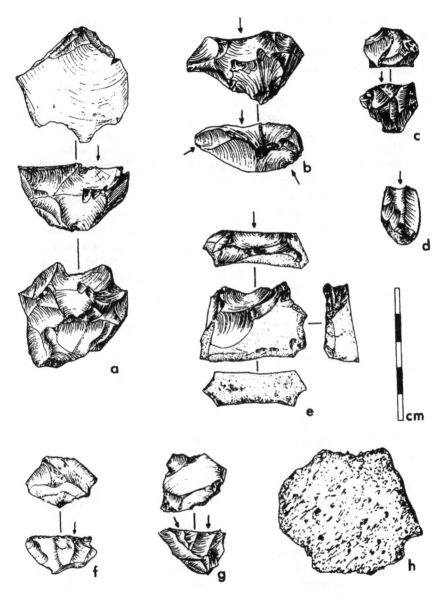

Figure 6.13. Obsidian cores from three Lapita sites on the Reefs/Santa Cruz Islands (taken from Sheppard 1993: Fig. 3).

on any particular island could have arrived not through trade, but in one colonizing canoe load.

This problem is resolvable, but not without more knowledge of archaeological obsidian distributions from well-dated sites, additional sourcing of artifacts from those sites, and an influx of information from the sources. Some studies of obsidian sources have been conducted (e.g., Specht et al. 1988), but it is usually impossible to attribute an accurate date to any quarrying activity, as the quarriers tended not to leave diagnostic trash or radiometrically datable material behind.

The exploitation of these sources was not static, but tended to change over time. We are only beginning to understand the operative forces involved, but at least one study has explored geological factors that would have affected the availability of obsidian. Working with the historically important West New Britain sources, Torrence et al. (1996) correlated changes in the archaeological distribution of obsidian artifacts with specific geological events. One of these was sea level change, accompanied by tectonic uplift, which might have inundated a particular locale at one time but have made it more accessible by canoe at another. Another event was the eruption of Mt. Witori at about 3500 BP, which would have radically transformed the coastline and cut off northern water access to the Mopir obsidian source on New Britain Island. This eruption caused a precipitous decline in the exploitation of Mopir obsidian during the Lapita period (ca. 3500-1500 BP).

Other research has involved the archaeological sites on which obsidian ended up. Sheppard's work on the Reefs/Santa Cruz Islands, for instance, has established that, in Lapita times, obsidian from the Talasea source dominated all other source areas. That Talasea dominated the nearby Mopir source on New Britain is explainable through landform transformations that would have resulted from the eruption of Mt. Witori, as discussed above. More enigmatic is why the source of these tools was 2000 km north in New Britain rather than the perfectly usable Vanua Lava source in the Banks Islands only 400 km to the south. Perhaps this obsidian did arrive during colonization, but Sheppard's (1993:129) calculations of obsidian quantities from Reefs/Santa Cruz sites are consistent with more than one colonizing boat load.

Just as puzzling is the use to which these obsidian objects were put. Despite the fact that obsidian makes a very useful tool for certain purposes and the material occurs in reduced frequencies on archaeological sites, one might expect to see economizing behavior in its employment. Yet use-wear analysis has not detected over-use of tools; indeed, many obsidian tools were not utilized at all (Sheppard 1993:135). Clearly, the value of obsidian was not particularly utilitarian in nature. But if it was social or ceremonial, in what capacity did it function? These and similar questions are waiting to be answered with the lithic dataset.

So after all this research on the occurrence of obsidian artifacts in Oceania, what have we learned about the role of trade in explaining the distribution of obsidian? According to several scholars, not very much of a specific nature. Sheppard's calculations suggest there was more obsidian on archaeological sites than could be explained by invoking one colonizing boatload, but he could not be more specific than that. And White (1996:204), considering the distribution of obsidian in Near Oceania, concluded, "With the possible exception of small quantities of obsidian moving east into Remote Oceania in the period 3300-2500 B.P. and the west into Indonesia somewhat later (and even this exception is not certain), *any* of the mechanisms comparable to those of the recent past in both organization and scale, or indeed, others not known recently, could have been utilized." Thus the mechanisms through which trade in Oceania was conducted were not always clear-cut, as they were in the Colha example. A lot more work with the lithic database is going to have to be accomplished before the nature of prehistoric Oceanic obsidian trade is understood.

Resource Control

Most models of lithic procurement and supply have assumed equal access to source areas for all prehistoric players. In most situations this is a necessary assumption, because the nature and extent of control over a resource at any point in time is usually unknowable. Occasionally, however, a region yields data that shed some light on the issue of prehistoric control, generating research questions such as the following:

Q32: How can an analyst determine the nature and extent of control exercised by a subset of a prehistoric population over a specific resource?

The Mayan settlement of Colha, described above, has provided information on the issue of resource control. Specializing in the production of specific chert tool types that were traded throughout the area of Mayan influence, Colha is one of our best examples of a prehistoric trading and production center. But what was the political dimension of this network? Did local Mayan elite authorities restrict access to the chert source or employ specialists full-time in the production of these goods? On the contrary, lensing of workshop midden deposits suggests that flintknapping was an intermittent activity at the site, i.e., that craft specialists were not working full-time at this occupation (Shafer 1985:309). This implies that neither the resource nor the tools produced from that resource were tightly controlled. Likewise, it is probable that no full-time shell bead specialists ever emerged at Cahokia or any of its outlier settlements, nor was any monopoly of this craft ever achieved by any Mississippian polity (Yerkes 1989:103). In fact, even in early states such as Sumeria in the Uruk period, chipped stone tool production tended to be decentralized in a large number of households, rather than controlled by a central authority (Pope 1994; Pope and Pollock 1995).

The proto-Chumash bead producers in the Channel Islands of California, described previously, contrast with this scenario in certain respects. Here two geographically separated groups—the islands and the mainland—have provided information that shed some light on the nature of political control of the bead resource (and of the lithic tools that were used to exploit this resource). Some mainland habitations of the Middle, Transitional and Late periods have yielded vast quantities of finished beads, suggesting that the people who lived there constituted a principal consumer market for the bead trade. The islands have yielded copious evidence of workshop debris—bead-making waste, rejects, spent microdrills—but very few complete beads in residential context. This evidence suggests that island people were the principal bead producers, but they did not consume many of the beads they produced.

Arnold and Munns (1994:487) believe that the island bead makers were peripherally attached specialists whose modes of production were probably not monitored, but whose patterns of product distribution were controlled by members of a high-ranking elite located on the mainland. This level of control, while far from absolute, may have been more tightly organized by a ruling class than most other late prehistoric specialists in North and Central America. The evidence on which this conclusion was based has been derived primarily from bead manufacture data, though evidence of lithic drill manufacture on the islands has been important in understanding the role of certain island locales in the overall bead production system. This and other studies related to complex societies have been encapsulated in Table 6.5.

Material Replacement

Almost nobody in the modern world uses stone for tools anymore. Technologies like chipped stone are replaced because another material or technique is better suited to the intended task, is more convenient, is more readily available, or costs less. Previously dominant lithic technologies have been replaced by 1) a different lithic technology, as chipped stone by ground stone axes in Europe and the Levant; 2) a different container type, as soapstone bowls by pottery in eastern North America; or 3) a wholesale replacement of tool types, as occurred throughout the world upon the development of metallurgy. Each of these issues is chronological in nature and requires data for which chronological and associational control is accurate and precise.

Table 6.5.   Issues involving the production and distribution of surplus goods.

Organ. response	Lithic elements	Types of analysis	References
Craft specialization	Lithic end products	Technology; reduction sequence; modeling	Shafer & Hester 1983; Hester 1985; Shafer 1985; Hester & Shafer 1991; McSwain 1991; Dockall & Shafer 1993; Dockall 1994
Craft specialization	Lithic industrial mfg. components	Technology; measurements; use-wear	Yerkes 1983, 1989; Arnold 1992; Arnold & Munns 1994; Rosen 1997b
Trade	All	Distributional	Yerkes 1989; Santone 1997
Trade	Obsidian	Technology; distributions; use-wear	Specht et al. 1988; Sheppard 1993; Torrence et al. 1996; White 1996
Sociopolitical control	Manufacturing tools (eg, drills); all	Distributional; technological	Shafer 1985; Yerkes 1989; Arnold & Munns 1994; Pope 1994; Pope & Pollock 1995

Interest in issues of replacement has increased in recent years as archaeologists have gradually come to realize that, in most cases, replacement was not a one-shot occurrence, but a multi-dimensional, processual phenomenon with some time depth. This interest has contributed to formulating general research questions like the following, from which more specific queries have been posed:

Q33: What is the nature and process of replacement of lithic tools either by other types of lithic tools or by tools of other materials?

The most comprehensive treatment of the replacement of stone by metal has been conducted by Steve Rosen (1996, 1997b) for the Levant. Recording lithic industries from the Neolithic through Iron Age, Rosen discovered that absolute quantities of retouched tools and debitage in lithic assemblages decreased through time. But equally important was the temporal decrease in typological diversity, as certain tool types dropped out of the cultural repertoire while others remained. Among the first to go were stone arrowheads and burins, but these declines were caused more by a decrease in hunting and activities in which burins were engaged than by a superior metal counterpart. The termination of stone axe and microdrill production by the Early Bronze Age was precipitated largely by superior copper equivalents, but even here the issue was not related solely to utilitarian efficiency, but also to the establishment of trade routes and dependable supplies of copper. The last stone objects to be replaced by metal in the Levant were sickle blades, which were present on Near Eastern sites until at least 800 BC (Rosen 1996:145). Flint blades were about equal to metal in efficiency and were cheaper, having been the product of specialized production and exchange for several centuries.

In many cultural groups, stone objects continued to be produced and traded long after their primary utilitarian function had been usurped by competing tools made from another material. As stone became associated more and more with pristine lifestyles and older traditions, it increasingly assumed a ritual or sacred character. In the Northern Territory of Australia, European contact with Aborigines resulted in rapid replacement of Native spear points, knives and chisels by metal ones. Yet large points and other objects of stone continued to be produced and valued as gifts and items for exchange with distant trading partners—clearly a useful adaptive strategy, reinforcing social bonds that could be of critical importance in times of stress (Paton 1994; Head and Fullagar 1997). In contact situations in North America, the stone tools of tribes such as the Pawnee also came under selective pressure from an incursion of more efficient metal implements. Some of the stone items were retained but only in a sacred context, such as shamans' knives used for inducing curative bleeding (Hudson 1993). Certain lithic objects, of course, served sacred functions long before the replacement of stone by metal; research into cases of more remote antiquity is discussed in greater detail in Box 6.2.

Box 6.2. Sacred Stones

The discussion in chapter 6 is not meant to suggest that the only occasion in the past for which objects of stone assumed a sacred dimension was when they were replaced or threatened by some other material. Stones of sacred character have probably existed throughout prehistory, but detecting a sacred or ritually charged stone object within a prehistoric assemblage is difficult and usually requires excellent contextual association. Indeed, archaeologists have recently been much more attentive to possible ritualized use of stone than ever before. In the Early Archaic of southeastern North America, for example, arguments have been preferred for the employment of certain distinctive objects, such as the Turkey-tail and Kirk corner-notched points and the well-made Dalton Sloan biface, as ceremonial items or trade regulators (Sassaman 1994; Krakker 1997; Walthall and Koldehoff 1998). A little later in time, bannerstones may have been made as special ceremonial items, manufactured by marginalized uplands peoples in exchange for pottery (Sassaman 1998).

The ritual use of stone is more apparent among the ancient Maya, because we can now read their glyphs and have a pretty good idea what they were up to. We know, for instance, that the hafted celt was iconographically associated with warfare, specifically with lightning-wars or axe-events that frequently coincided with the end of the rainy season and were timed with the appearance of Venus in the night sky (Thompson 1996).

Known sacred areas of Mayan sites are also mines of information about the sacred character of implements, and at least one study of lithic material from one of these has been published. This was April Sievert's (1992) analysis of items from the Sacred Cenote at Chichen Itza—the same cenote about which Bishop Diego de Landa wrote and that E. H. Thompson investigated by diving to the bottom and dredging up artifacts. Sievert's analysis was all about bloodletting, sacrifice and copal, and resulted in a panoply of traits that can be used to indicate the sacred nature of stone artifacts. These kinds of studies provide a titillating glimpse into the potentially vast arena of ritually charged lithic objects in the prehistoric record, only a few of which have been carefully analyzed.

For other objects, the ritual or symbolic nature of a specimen is apparent, but its specific meaning is unknown. Such is the situation surrounding chert *eccentrics*, which have been knapped to unique, often bizarre, shapes and are occasionally very large and patently non-functional in the traditional sense. Eccentrics in primary deposition have been discovered in ritual caches or burials at such Belizian Mayan settlements as Colha, Lamanai, and Altun Ha (Shafer 1991:38-40).

The replacement of stone tools in a cultural repertoire is not limited solely to the relationship of stone with metal. In some cases the term can refer to the replacement of one lithic technology by another, particularly in the context of massive changes in other elements of society. A case in point is Michael Stafford's (1999) analysis of stone tools from southern Scandinavia at the cusp of food production. Stafford found a smooth continuum of lithic technologies from the late Mesolithic through the early Neolithic, suggesting that the indigenous Mesolithic population developed a Neolithic economy in place—a scenario quite different from postulating that a migrating population brought food production and other Neolithic traits to this land. Evidence on which these conclusions were based was essentially technological in nature: the people may have accepted domestication and a horticultural way of life, but they retained traditional ways of making stone implements. A summary of some tool replacement studies has been compiled in Table 6.6.

CONCLUDING REMARKS

The foregoing discussion admittedly constitutes a meager sampling of the literature of lithic analysis; for a more comprehensive recent review, see Odell (2000, 2001). If this chapter has provided a few useful examples of archaeological issues for which lithic data have been informative and a few specific techniques

Table 6.6.   Issues involving the replacement of stone technologies.

Replacement type	Tool types	Types of analysis	References
Stone by metal	All	Typological	Rosen 1996, 1997b
Stone by metal; stone retains sacred character	All	Ethnographic	Hudson 1993; Paton 1994; Head & Fullagar 1997
One stone technology by another	All	Technological	Stafford 1999

that have proven appropriate for resolving these issues, it will have served its intended purpose. The lithic database will not provide relevant information for every question a researcher might entertain, but it can, with some creativity, be applied to an impressively wide range of problems.

Readers of this book today will presumably be the lithic analysts of tomorrow. Your job is to improve on our record, to employ these principles in building a better database and more accurate interpretations. This will entail solidifying our knowledge of fundamental relationships in fracture mechanics, technological modeling, use-wear, and a host of other issues. It will involve innovative techniques and new ways of perceiving archaeological situations. Most of all, it will necessitate tolerance and keeping an open mind. When one of you writes this manual in 2012, the year that Mayan reckoning of the future ceases, there ought to be plenty of new things to discuss.

References

Adams, Jenny L. 1993 Toward Understanding the Technological Development of Manos and Metates. *Kiva* 58: 331–355.

1997 *Manual for a Technological Approach to Ground Stone Analysis.* Center for Desert Archeology, Tucson.

1999 Refocusing the Role of Food-Grinding Tools as Correlates for Subsistence Strategies in the U.S. Southwest. *American Antiquity* 64: 475–498.

2002 *Ground Stone Analysis: a Technological Approach.* University of Utah Press, Salt Lake City.

Agenbroad, Larry D. 1978 *The Hudson-Meng Site: an Alberta Bison Kill in the Nebraska High Plains.* Caxton Printers, Ltd., Caldwell, Idaho.

Ahler, Stanley A. 1971 *Projectile Point Form and Function at Rodgers Shelter, Missouri.* Missouri Archaeological Society, Research Series 8.

1989a Experimental Knapping with KRF and Midcontinent Cherts: Overview and Applications. In *Experiments in Lithic Technology,* edited by D. Amick and R. Mauldin, pp. 199–234. BAR International Series 528, Oxford.

1989b Mass Analysis of Flaking Debris: Studying the Forest Rather Than the Tree. In *Alternative Approaches to Lithic Analysis,* edited by D. Henry and G. Odell, pp. 85–118. Archeological Papers of the American Anthropological Association, no. 1. Washington, D.C.

Ahler, Stanley A., and R. Bruce McMillan 1976 Material Culture at Rodgers Shelter: a Reflection of Past Human Activities. In *Prehistoric Man and His Environments: a Case Study in the Ozark Highland,* edited by W. R. Wood and R. B. McMillan, pp. 163–199. Academic Press, New York.

Amick, Daniel S. 1994 Technological Organization and the Structure of Inference in Lithic Analysis: an Examination of Folsom Hunting Behavior in the American Southwest. In *The Organization of North American Prehistoric Chipped Stone Technologies,* edited by P. Carr, pp. 9–34. International Monographs in Prehistory, Ann Arbor.

1999 Raw Material Variation in Folsom Stone Tool Assemblages and the Division of Labor in Hunter-Gatherer Societies. In *Folsom Lithic Technology,* edited by D. Amick, pp. 169–187.

Amick, Daniel S., and Philip J. Carr 1996 Changing Strategies of Lithic Technological Organization. In *Archaeology of the Mid-Holocene Southeast,* edited by K. Sassaman and D. Anderson, pp. 41–56. University Press of Florida, Gainesville.

Amick, Daniel S., and Raymond P. Mauldin 1989 (editors) *Experiments in Lithic Technology.* BAR International Series 528. Oxford.

1997 Effects of Raw Material on Flake Breakage Patterns. *Lithic Technology* 22: 18–32.

Amick, Daniel S., Raymond P. Mauldin, and Steven A. Tomka 1988 An Evaluation of Debitage Produced by Experimental Bifacial Core Reduction of a Georgetown Chert Nodule. *Lithic Technology* 17: 26–36.

Anderson, Patricia C. 1980 A Testimony of Prehistoric Tasks: Diagnostic Residues on Stone Tool Working Edges. *World Archaeology* 12: 181–193.

1992 Experimental Cultivation, Harvest and Threshing of Wild Cereals and Their Relevance for Interpreting the Use of Epipaleolithic and Neolithic Artefacts. In *Préhistoire de l'Agriculture*, edited by P. Anderson, pp. 179–209. Editions du CNRS. Monographie du CRA, no. 6, Paris.

Andree, I. 1922 *Bergbau in der Vorzeit 1. Bergbau auf Feuerstein, Kupfer Zinn und Salz in Europa.* Leipzig.

Andrefsky, William, Jr. 1994 The Geological Occurrence of Lithic Material and Stone Tool Production Strategies. *Geoarchaeology* 9: 345–362.

1998 *Lithics: Macroscopic Approaches to Analysis.* Cambridge University Press, Cambridge.

Annegarn, H. J., and S. Bauman 1990 Geological and Mineralogical Applications of PIXE: a Review. *Nuclear Instruments and Methods in Physics Research* B49: 264–270.

Arnold, Jeanne E. 1992 Complex Hunter-Gatherer-Fishers of Prehistoric California: Chiefs, Specialists, and Maritime Adaptations of the Channel Islands. *American Antiquity* 57: 60–84.

Arnold, Jeanne E., and Ann Munns 1994 Independent or Attached Specialization: the Origin of Shell Bead Production in California. *Journal of Field Archaeology* 21: 473–489.

Atchison, Jennifer, and Richard Fullagar 1998 Starch Residues on Pounding Implements from Jinmium Rock-Shelter. In *A Closer Look: Recent Australian Studies of Stone Tools*, edited by R. Fullagar, pp. 109–125. Sydney University, Archaeological Methods Series 6. Sydney.

Austin, Robert J. 1999 Technological Characterization of Lithic Waste-Flake Assemblages: Multivariate Analysis of Experimental and Archaeological Data. *Lithic Technology* 24: 53–68.

Baesemann, Renate 1986 Natural Alterations on Stone Artefact Materials. In *Technical Aspects of Microwear Studies on Stone Tools*, edited by L. Owen and G. Unrath. *Early Man News* 9/10/11: 97–102.

Baffier, Dominique, Sylvie Beyries, and Pierre Bodu 1991 Histoire d'ochre à Pincevent. La question des lames ocrées. In *25 ans d'études technologiques en préhistoire*, pp. 215–234. XIème Rencontres Internationales d'Archéologie et d'Histoire d'Antibes. Editions APDCA, Juan-les-Pins.

Bailey, Berkly 2000 *The Geoarchaeology of Day Creek Chert.* PhD dissertation, Department of Anthropology, University of Oklahoma.

Bakewell, Edward F. 1996 Petrographic and Geochemical Source-Modeling of Volcanic Lithics from Archaeological Contexts: a Case Study from British Camp, San Juan Island, Washington. *Geoarchaeology* 11: 119–140.

Balme, Jane, and Wendy E. Beck 2002 Starch and Charcoal: Useful Measures of Activity Areas in Archaeological Rockshelters. *Journal of Archaeological Science* 29: 157–166.

Bamforth, Douglas B. 1988 Investigating Microwear Polishes with Blind Tests: the Institute Results in Context. *Journal of Archaeological Science* 15: 11–23.

Bamforth, Douglas B., George R. Burns, and Craig Woodman 1990 Ambiguous Use Traces and Blind Test Results: New Data. *Journal of Archaeological Science* 17: 413–430.

Banks, William E., and Marvin Kay 2003 High-Resolution Casts for Lithic Use-Wear Analysis. *Lithic Technology* 28: 27–34.

Barnes, Alfred S. 1939 The Differences between Natural and Human Flaking on Prehistoric Flint Implements. *American Anthropologist* 41: 99–112.

Barton, Huw, Robin Torrence, and Richard Fullagar 1998 Clues to Stone Tool Function Re-Examined: Comparing Starch Grain Frequencies on Used and Unused Obsidian Artefacts. *Journal of Archaeological Science* 25: 1231–1238.

Bement, Leland C. 1999 *Bison Hunting at Cooper Site: Where Lightning Bolts Drew Thundering Herds.* University of Oklahoma Press, Norman.

Benito del Rey, Luis, and Jose-Manuel Benito Alvarez 1994 La taille actuelle de la pierre à la manière préhistorique: l'example des pierres pour *Tribula* à Cantalejo (Segovia-Espagne). *Bulletin de la Sociéte Préhistorique Française* 91: 214–222.

Bienenfeld, Paula 1995 Duplicating Archaeological Microwear Polishes with Epoxy Casts. *Lithic Technology* 20: 29–39.

Bierwirth, Susan L. 1996 *Lithic Analysis in Southwestern France: Middle Paleolithic Assemblages from the Site of La Quina*. BAR International Series 633, Oxford.

Binder, Didier 1984 Systèmes de débitage laminaire par pression: Exemples Chasséens provençaux. In *Préhistoire de la pierre taillée 2: Economie du débitage laminaire: technologie et expérimentation*, compiled by IIIème Table Rond de Technologie Lithique, pp. 71–84. Cercle de Recherches et d'Etudes Préhistorique, Meudon.

Binford, Lewis R. 1962 Archaeology as Anthropology. *American Antiquity* 28: 217–225.

  1964 A Consideration of Archaeological Research Design. *American Antiquity* 29: 425–441.

  1973 Interassemblage Variability—the Mousterian and the "Functional" Argument. In *The Explanation of Culture Change: Models in Prehistory*, edited by C. Renfrew, pp. 227–254. Duckworth, London.

  1977 Forty-Seven Trips. In *Stone Tools as Cultural Markers*, edited by R. S. V. Wright, pp. 24–36. Australian Institute of Aboriginal Studies, Canberra.

  1979 Organization and Formation Processes: Looking at Curated Technologies. *Journal of Anthropological Research* 35: 255–273.

  1980 Willow Smoke and Dogs' Tails: Hunter-Gatherer Settlement Systems and Archaeological Site Formation. *American Antiquity* 45: 4–20.

  2001 Where Do Research Problems Come from? *American Antiquity* 66: 669–678.

Binford, Lewis R., and Sally R. Binford 1966 A Preliminary Analysis of Functional Variability in the Mousterian of Levallois Facies. *American Anthropologist* 68: 238–295.

Binford, Sally R. 1968 Ethnographic Data and Understanding the Pleistocene. In *Man the Hunter*, edited by R. Lee and I. DeVore, pp. 274–275. Aldine/Atherton, Chicago.

Blades, Brooke S. 2001 *Aurignacian Lithic Economy: Ecological Perspectives from Southwestern France*. Kluwer Academic/Plenum, New York.

Blalock, Hubert M., Jr. 1972 *Social Statistics*. McGraw-Hill, New York.

Blatt, Harvey, Gerard Middleton, and Raymond Murray 1980 *Origin of Sedimentary Rocks*. Second edition. Prentice-Hall, Englewood Cliffs, NJ.

Bleed, Peter 1986 The Optimal Design of Hunting Weapons: Maintainability or Reliability. *American Antiquity* 51: 737–747.

Bobrowski, Peter T., and Bruce F. Ball 1989 The Theory and Mechanics of Ecological Diversity in Archaeology. In *Quantifying Diversity in Archaeology*, edited by R. Leonard and G. Jones, pp. 4–12. Cambridge University Press, Cambridge.

Bodu, Pierre 1991 Les magdaléniens de Pincevent: Chasseurs de rennes et...tailleurs de pierre. In *Actes des seminaires publics d'archéologie*, edited by A. Richard, pp. 20–27. Centre Regional de Documentation Archéologique, La Citadelle-Besancon, Region de Franche-Comte, France.

Boëda, Eric 1986 *Approche technologique du concept Levallois et évolution de son champ d'application*. PhD dissertation, Département de Préhistoire, Université de Paris X.

Boldurian, Anthony T., Phillip T. Fitzgibbons, and Phillip H. Shelley 1985 Fluting Devices in the Folsom Tradition: Patterning in Debitage Formation and Projectile Point Basal Configuration. *Plains Anthropologist* 30: 293–303.

Bonnichsen, Robson 1977 *Models for Deriving Cultural Information from Stone Tools*. National Museum of Man, Mercury Series, Archaeological Survey of Canada, Paper no. 60. Ottawa.

Bonnichsen, Robson, Larry Hodges, Walter Ream, Katherine G. Field, Donna L. Kirner, Karen Selsor, and R. E. Taylor 2001 Methods for the Study of Ancient Hair: Radiocarbon Dates and Gene Sequences from Individual Hairs. *Journal of Archaeological Science* 28: 775–785.

Bordaz, Jacques 1965 The Threshing Sledge. *Natural History* 74: 26–29.

  1970 *Tools of the Old and New Stone Age*. Natural History Press, Garden City, NY.

Bordes, Francois 1961 *Typologie du paléolithique ancien et moyen*. Publications de l'Institut de Préhistoire de l'Universit de Bordeaux, Memoire no. 1. Imprimeries Delmas, Bordeaux.

Bordes, Francois, and Denise de Sonneville-Bordes 1970 The Significance of Variability in Paleolithic Assemblages. *World Archaeology* 2: 61–73.

Bostyn, F., and Y. Lanchon (editors) 1992 *Jablines le Haut-Chateau (Seine-et-Marne): une minière du silex au Néolithique*. Document d'Archéologie Française, vol. 35. Paris.

Bousman, C. Britt 1993 Hunter-Gatherer Adaptations, Economic Risk and Tool Design. *Lithic Technology* 18: 59–86.

Bradbury, Andrew P. 1998 The Examination of Lithic Artifacts from an Early Archaic Assemblage: Strengthening Inferences through Multiple Lines of Evidence. *Midcontinental Journal of Archaeology* 23: 263–288.

Bradbury, Andrew P., and Philip J. Carr 1995 Flake Typologies and Alternative Approaches: an Experimental Assessment. *Lithic Technology* 20: 100–115.

  1999 Examining Stage and Continuum Models of Flake Debris Analysis: an Experimental Approach. *Journal of Anthropological Science* 26: 105–116.

Bradley, Bruce A. 1975 Lithic Reduction Sequences: a Glossary and Discussion. In *Lithic Technology: Making and Using Stone Tools*, edited by E. Swanson, pp. 5–13. Mouton, The Hague.

Brainerd, G. W. 1951 The Place of Chronological Ordering in Archaeological Analysis. *American Antiquity* 16: 301–313.

Brass, Leanne 1998 Modern Stone Tool Use as a Guide to Prehistory in the New Guinea Highlands. In *A Closer Look: Recent Australian Studies of Stone Tools*, edited by R. Fullagar, pp. 19–28. Sydney University, Archaeological Methods Series 6. Sydney.

Braswell, Geoffrey E., E. Wyllys Andrews V., and Michael D. Glascock 1994 The Obsidian Artifacts of Quelepa, El Salvador. *Ancient Mesoamerica* 5: 173–192.

Braswell, Geoffrey E., and Michael D. Glascock 1998 Interpreting Intrasource Variation in the Composition of Obsidian: the Geoarchaeology of San Martin Jilotepeque, Guatemala. *Latin American Antiquity* 9: 353–369.

Brew, J. O. 1946 The Use and Abuse of Taxonomy. In *The Archaeology of Alkali Ridge, Southern Utah*, edited by J. O. Brew, pp. 44–66. Peabody Museum Papers, vol. 21, Cambridge.

Brink, John W. 1978 *An Experimental Study of Microwear Formation on Endscrapers*. National Museum of Man, Mercury Series, National Museums of Canada, Paper no. 83. Ottawa.

Briuer, Frederick L. 1976 New Clues to Stone Tool Functions: Plant and Animal Residues. *American Antiquity* 41: 478–484.

Burton, John 1980 Making Sense of Waste Flakes: New Methods for Investigating the Technology and Economics behind Chipped Stone Assemblages. *Journal of Archaeological Science* 7: 131–148.

Butzer, Karl 1982 *Archaeology as Human Ecology*. Cambridge University Press, Cambridge.

Callahan, Errett 1979 The Basics of Biface Knapping in the Eastern Fluted Point Tradition: a Manual for Flintknappers and Lithic Analysts. *Archaeology of Eastern North America* 7: 1–180.

  1987 *An Evaluation of the Lithic Technology in Middle Sweden during the Mesolithic and Neolithic*. Societas Archaeologica Upsaliensis, Aun 8, Uppsala.

Carmichael, Ian S. E., Francis J. Turner, and John Verhoogen 1974 *Igneous Petrology*. McGraw-Hill, New York.

Carneiro, Robert L. 1974 On the Use of the Stone Axe by the Amahuaca Indians of Eastern Peru. *Ethnologische Zeitschrift Zurich* 1: 107–122.

  1979 Tree Felling with the Stone Ax: an Experiment Carried Out among the Yanomamo Indians of Southern Venezuela. In *Ethnoarchaeology*, edited by C. Kramer, pp. 21–58. Columbia University Press, New York.

Carr, Philip J., and Andrew P. Bradbury 2001 Flake Debris Analysis, Levels of Production, and the Organization of Technology. In *Lithic Debitage: Context, Form, Meaning*, edited by W. Andrefsky, Jr., pp. 126–146. University of Utah Press, Salt Lake City.

Cattaneo, C., K. Gelsthorpe, P. Phillipos, and R. J. Sokol 1993 Blood Residues on Stone Tools: Indoor and Outdoor Experiments. *World Archaeology* 25: 29–43.

Chatters, James C. 1987 Hunter-Gatherer Adaptations and Assemblage Structure. *Journal of Anthropological Archaeology* 6: 336–375.

Christenson, Andrew L. 1987 The Prehistoric Tool Kit. In *Prehistoric Stone Technology on Northern Black Mesa, Arizona*, edited by W. Parry and A. Christenson, pp. 43–93. Center for Archaeological Investigations, Southern Illinois University at Carbondale, Occasional Paper no. 12.

Church, Tim 1994 *Lithic Resource Studies: a Sourcebook for Archaeologists*. Lithic Technology, Special Publication no. 3. Tulsa.

Church, T., and C. Caraveo 1996 The Magnetic Susceptibility of Southwestern Obsidian: an Exploratory Study. *North American Archaeologist* 17: 271–285.

Clark, Geoffrey A. 1989 Romancing the Stones: Biases, Style and Lithics at La Riera. In *Alternative Approaches to Lithic Analysis*, edited by D. Henry and G. Odell, pp. 27–50. Archeological Papers of the American Anthropological Association, no. 1. Washington, D.C.

Clark, Grahame 1975 *The Earlier Stone Age Settlement of Scandinavia*. Cambridge University Press, Cambridge.

Clark, Grahame, and Stuart Piggott 1933 The Age of the British Flint Mines. *Antiquity* 7: 166–183.

Clark, John E. 1991a Flintknapping and Debitage Disposal among the Lacandon Maya of Chiapas, Mexico. In *The Ethnoarchaeology of Refuse Disposal*, edited by E. Staski and L. D. Sutro, pp. 63–78. Anthropological Research Papers, no. 42. Arizona State University, Tempe.

　　1991b Modern Lacandon Lithic Technology and Blade Workshops. In *Maya Stone Tools*, edited by T. R. Hester and H. J. Shafer, pp. 251–265.

Clemente, Ignacio, and Juan F. Gibaja 1998 Working Processes on Cereals: an Approach through Microwear Analysis. *Journal of Archaeological Science* 25: 457–464.

Cobb, Charles R. 2000 *From Quarry to Cornfield: the Political Economy of Mississippian Hoe Production*. University of Alabama Press, Tuscaloosa.

Codere, Helen 1990 Kwakiutl: Traditional Culture. *Handbook of North American Indians, vol. 7: Northwest Coast*, edited by W. Suttles, pp. 359–377. Smithsonian Institution Press, Washington, DC.

Conard, Nicholas J., and Daniel S. Adler 1997 Lithic Reduction and Hominid Behavior in the Middle Paleolithic of the Rhineland. *Journal of Anthropological Research* 53: 147–175.

Cooney, Gabriel, and Stephen Mandal 1995 Getting to the Core of the Problem: Petrological Results from the Irish Stone Axe Project. *Antiquity* 69: 969–980.

Cotterell, Brian, and Johan Kamminga 1986 Finials on Stone Flakes. *Journal of Archaeological Science* 13: 451–461.

　　1987 The Formation of Flakes. *American Antiquity* 52: 675–708.

　　1990 *Mechanics of Pre-Industrial Technology*. Cambridge University Press, Cambridge.

Cox, K. A., and H. A. Smith 1989 Perdiz Point Damage Analysis. *Bulletin of the Texas Archaeological Society* 60: 283–301.

Crabtree, Don E. 1966 A Stoneworker's Approach to Analyzing and Replicating the Lindenmeier Folsom. *Tebiwa* 9: 3–39.

　　1968 Mesoamerican Polyhedral Cores and Prismatic Blades. *American Antiquity* 33: 446–478.

　　1970 Flaking Stone with Wooden Implements. *Science* 169: 146–153.

　　1972 *An Introduction to Flintworking*. Occasional Papers of the Idaho University Museum, no. 28, Pocatello.

Craddock, P. T., M. R. Cowell, M. N. Leese, and M. J. Hughes 1983 The Trace Element Composition of Polished Flint Axes as an Indicator of Source. *Archaeometry* 26: 135–163.

Crawford, O. G. S. 1935 A Primitive Threshing Machine. *Antiquity* 9: 335–339.

Curwen, Cecil 1930 Prehistoric Flint Sickles. *Antiquity* 4: 179–186.

　　1935 Agriculture and the Flint Sickle in Palestine. *Antiquity* 9: 62–66.

Custer, Jay F., John Ilgenfritz, and Keith R. Doms 1988 A Cautionary Note on the Use of Chemstrips for Detection of Blood Residues on Prehistoric Stone Tools. *Journal of Archaeological Science* 15: 343–345.

Czeisla, E., S. Eickhoff, N. Arts, and D. Winter (editors) 1990 *The Big Puzzle: International Symposium on Refitting Stone Artefacts*. Studies in Modern Archaeology, vol. 1. Holos, Bonn, Germany.

Daniel, I. Randolph, Jr., and Robert Butler 1996 An Archaeological Survey and Petrographic Description of Rhyolite Sources in the Uwharrie Mountains, North Carolina. *Southern Indian Studies* 45: 1–37.

De Bie, Marc 1998 Late Paleolithic Tool Production Strategies: Technological Evidence from Rekem (Belgium). In *Lithic Technology: from Raw Material Procurement to Tool Production*, edited by S. Milliken and M. Peresani, pp. 91–95. Workshop no. 12 of the XIII International Congress of Prehistoric and Protohistoric Sciences, Forli, Italy, 1996.

Del Bene, Terry A. 1979 Once upon a Striation: Current Models of Striation and Polish Formation. In *Lithic Use-Wear Analysis*, edited by B. Hayden, pp. 167–177. Academic Press, New York.

d'Errico, Francesco, and Joelle Espinet-Moucadel 1986 L'emploi du microscope électronique à balayage pour l'étude expérimentale de traces d'usure: raclage sur bois de cervidé. *Bulletin de la Société Préhistorique Française* 83: 91–96.

Dibble, Harold L. 1995 Raw Material Availability, Intensity of Utilization, and Middle Paleolithic Assemblage Variability. In *The Middle Paleolithic Site of Combe-Capelle Bas (France)*, edited by H. Dibble and M. Lenoir, pp. 289–315. University Museum Monograph 91, University of Pennsylvania, Philadelphia.

Dibble, Harold L., and John C. Whittaker 1981 New Experimental Evidence on the Relation between Percussion Flaking and Flake Variation. *Journal of Archaeological Science* 6: 283–296.

Dickson, Don 1996 The Production of Modern Lithic Scatters and Related Problems. *Lithic Technology* 21: 155–156.

Dockall, John E. 1994 Oval Biface Celt Variability during the Maya Late Preclassic. *Lithic Technology* 19: 52–68.

    1997 Wear Traces and Projectile Impact: a Review of the Experimental and Archaeological Evidence. *Journal of Field Archaeology* 24: 321–331.

Dockall, John E., and Harry J. Shafer 1993 Testing the Producer-Consumer Model for Santa Maria Corozal, Belize. *Latin American Antiquity* 4: 158–179.

Downs, Elinor F., and Jerold M. Lowenstein 1995 Identification of Archaeological Blood Proteins: a Cautionary Note. *Journal of Archaeological Science* 22: 11–16.

Drennan, Robert D. 1996 *Statistics for Archaeologists: a Commonsense Approach*. Plenum Press, New York.

Dunnell, Robert C. 2000 Type-Variety System. In *Archaeological Method and Theory: an Encyclopedia*, edited by L. Ellis, pp. 638–640. Garland Publishing Co., New York.

Ehlers, Ernest G., and Harvey Blatt 1982 *Petrology: Igneous, Sedimentary, and Metamorphic*. W. H. Freeman and Co., San Francisco.

Eisele, J. A., D. D. Fowler, G. Haynes, and R. A. Lewis 1995 Survival and Detection of Blood Residues on Stone Tools. *Antiquity* 69: 36–46.

Erlandson, J. M., J. D. Robertson, and C. Descantes 1999 Geochemical Analysis of Eight Red Ochres from Western North America. *American Antiquity* 64: 517–526.

Evans, John 1897 *The Ancient Stone Implements, Weapons, and Ornaments of Great Britain*. London: Longmans, Green, Reader and Dyer.

Evans, J. Bryant, Madeleine G. Evans, and Edwin R. Hajic 1997 Paleoindian and Early Archaic Occupations at the CB-North Site, Madison County, Illinois. *Midcontinental Journal of Archaeology* 22: 159–196.

Evans, O. F. 1957 Probable Uses of Stone Projectile Points. *American Antiquity* 23: 83–84.

Fagan, Brian M. 1987 *The Great Journey: the Peopling of Ancient America*. Thames and Hudson, London.

Farnsworth, Kenneth B., and John B. Walthall 1983 In the Path of Progress: Development of Illinois Highway Archeology, and the FAP 408 Project. *American Archeology* 3: 169–181.

Faulkner, Alaric 1972 *Mechanical Principles of Flintworking*. PhD dissertation, Department of Anthropology, Washington State University, Pullman. University Microfilms, Ann Arbor.
    1974 Mechanics of Eraillure Formation. *Newsletter of Lithic Technology* 2: 4–12.
Faulkner, Charles H., and Major C. R. McCollough 1973 *Introductory Report of the Normandy Reservoir Salvage Project: Environmental Setting, Typology, and Survey*. Department of Anthropology, University of Tennessee, Report of Investigations 11.
Feder, Kenneth L. 1996 *The Past in Perspective*. Mayfield, Mountain View, CA.
Felder, P. J. 1981 Prehistoric Flint Mining at Ryckhold-St. Geertruid (The Netherlands) and Grimes Graves (England). *Staringia* 6: 57–62.
Ferguson, J. A., and R. E. Warren 1992 Chert Resources of Northern Illinois: Discriminant Analysis and an Identification Key. *Illinois Archaeology* 4: 1–37.
Fiedel, Stuart J. 1996 Blood from Stones? Some Methodological and Interpretive Problems in Blood Residue Analysis. *Journal of Archaeological Science* 23: 139–147.
Figgins, J. D. 1927 The Antiquity of Man in America. *Natural History* 27: 229–239.
Fischer, Anders, Peter Vemming Hansen, and Peter Rasmussen 1984 Macro and Micro Wear Traces on Lithic Projectile Points: Experimental Results and Prehistoric Examples. *Journal of Danish Archaeology* 3: 19–46.
Fish, Paul R. 1978 Consistency in Archaeological Measurement and Classification: a Pilot Study. *American Antiquity* 43: 86–89.
Flenniken, J. Jeffrey 1978 Reevaluation of the Lindenmeier Folsom: a Replication Experiment in Lithic Technology. *American Antiquity* 43:473–480.
Flenniken, J. Jeffrey, and J. Haggerty 1979 Trampling as an Agency in the Formation of Edge Damage: an Experiment in Lithic Technology. *Northwest Anthropological Research Notes* 13: 208–214.
Ford, James A. 1954a Comment on A. C. Spaulding, "Statistical Techniques for the Discovery of Artifact Types." *American Antiquity* 19: 390–391.
    1954b The Type Concept Revisited. *American Anthropologist* 56: 42–54.
Fowler, William S. 1966 The Horne Hill Soapstone Quarry. *Bulletin of the Massachusetts Archaeological Society* 27: 17–28.
    1967 Oaklawn Quarry: Stone Bowl and Pipe Making. *Bulletin of the Massachusetts Archaeological Society* 29: 1–15.
Fox, William A. 1984 Dhoukani Flake Blade Production in Cyprus. *Lithic Technology* 13: 62–68.
Fredericksen, Clayton 1985 The Detection of Blood on Prehistoric Flake Tools. *New Zealand Archaeological Association Newsletter* 28: 155–164.
Freeman, Leslie G. 1968 A Theoretical Framework for Interpreting Archaeological Materials. In *Man the Hunter*, edited by R. Lee and I. DeVore, pp. 262–267. Aldine/Atherton, Chicago.
Frison, George C. 1978 *Prehistoric Hunters of the High Plains*. Academic Press, New York.
    1979 Observations on the Use of Stone Tools: Dulling of Working Edges of Some Chipped Stone Tools in Bison Butchering. In *Lithic Use-Wear Analysis*, edited by B. Hayden, pp. 258–268. Academic Press, New York.
    1989 Experimental Use of Clovis Weaponry and Tools on African Elephants. *American Antiquity* 54: 766–784.
Frison, George C., and Bruce A. Bradley 1980 *Folsom Tools and Technology at the Hanson Site, Wyoming*. University of New Mexico Press, Albuquerque.
Fullagar, R., and J. Field 1997 Pleistocene Seed-Grinding Implements from the Australian Arid Zone. *Antiquity* 71: 300–307.
Fullagar, Richard, Tom Loy, and Stephen Cox 1998 Starch Grains, Sediments and Stone Tool Function: Evidence from Bitokara, Papua New Guinea. In *A Closer Look: Recent Australian Studies of Stone Tools*, edited by R. Fullagar, pp. 49–60. Sydney University, Archaeological Methods Series 6.

Fullagar, Richard, Betty Meehan, and Rhys Jones 1992 Residue Analysis of Ethnographic Plant-Working and Other Tools from Northern Australia. In *Préhistoire de l'agriculture: nouvelles approaches expérimentales et ethnographiques*, edited by P. Anderson, pp. 39–53. Centre de Recherches Archéologiques, CNRS, Monographie du CRA no. 6. Paris.

Gallagher, J. 1977 Contemporary Stone Tools in Ethiopia: Implications for Archaeology. *Journal of Field Archaeology* 4: 407–414.

Garling, Stephanie J. 1998 Megafauna on the Menu? Haemoglobin Crystallization of Blood Residues from Stone Artifacts at Cuddie Springs. In *A Closer Look: Recent Australian Studies of Stone Tools*, edited by R. Fullagar, pp. 29–48. Sydney University, Archaeological Methods Series 6.

Geneste, J.-M., and S. Maury 1997 Contributions of Multidisciplinary Experimentation to the Study of Upper Paleolithic Projectile Points. In *Projectile Technology*, edited by H. Knecht, pp. 165–189. Plenum, New York.

Gero, Joan 1978 Summary of Experiments to Duplicate Post-Excavational Damage to Tool Edges. *Lithic Technology* 7: 34.

Gifford, Charlette, and George H. Odell 1999 Digging in Museums: WPA Archaeology in the Grand River Valley as Seen from the Duck Creek Site. *Bulletin of the Oklahoma Anthropological Society* 48: 83–111.

Gifford-Gonzalez, D., D. Damrosch, J. Pryor, and R. Thunen 1985 The Third Dimension in Site Structure: an Experiment in Trampling and Vertical Dispersal. *American Antiquity* 50: 803–818.

Gillieson, D. S., and J. Hall 1982 Bevelling Bungwall Bashers: a Use-Wear Study from Southeast Queensland. *Australian Archaeology* 14: 43–61.

Goffer, Zvi 1980 *Archaeological Chemistry: a Sourcebook on the Applications of Chemistry to Archaeology*. John Wiley & Sons, New York.

Gordus, A. A., J. B. Griffin, and G. A. Wright 1971 Activation Analysis Identification of the Geologic Origins of Prehistoric Obsidian Artifacts. In *Science and Archaeology*, edited by R. Brill, pp. 222–234. MIT Press, Cambridge.

Gould, R. A., D. A. Koster, and A. H. L. Sontz 1971 The Lithic Assemblage of the Western Desert Aborigines of Australia. *American Antiquity* 36: 149–169.

Grace, Roger 1993a New Methods in Use-Wear Analysis. In *Traces et fonction: Les gestes retrouvés*, edited by P. Anderson, S. Beyries, M. Otte, and H. Plisson, pp. 385–387. ERAUL no. 50, Liège.

1993b The Use of Expert Systems in Lithic Analysis. In *Traces et fonction: Les gestes retrouvés*, edited by P. Anderson, S. Beyries, M. Otte, and H. Plisson, pp. 389–400. ERAUL no. 50, Liège.

1996 Use-Wear Analysis: the State of the Art. *Archaeometry* 38: 209–229.

Graves, Paul 1994 My Strange Quest for Leroi-Gourhan: Structuralism's Unwitting Hero. *Antiquity* 68: 457–460.

Greiser, Sally T. 1977 Micro-Analysis of Wear Patterns on Projectile Points and Knives from the Jurgens Site, Kersey, Colorado. *Plains Anthropologist* 22: 107–116.

Griffin, J. B. 1965 Hopewell and the Dark Black Glass. *Michigan Archaeologist* 11: 115–155.

Griffin, J. B., A. A. Gordus, and G. A. Wright 1969 Identification of the Sources of Hopewellian Obsidian in the Middle West. *American Antiquity* 34: 1–14.

Griffith, Alan Arnold 1920 The Phenomena of Rupture and Flow in Solids. *Philosophical Transactions of the Royal Society of London* A221: 163–198.

1921 The Theory of Rupture. *Proceedings of the 1st International Congress for Applied Mechanics*, p. 55. Delft.

Gryba, Eugene M. 1988 A Stone Age Pressure Method of Folsom Fluting. *Plains Anthropologist* 33: 53–66.

Gurfinkel, D. M., and U. M. Franklin 1988 A Study of the Feasibility of Detecting Blood Residue on Artifacts. *Journal of Archaeological Science* 15: 83–97.

Hall, Jay, Su Higgins, and Richard Fullagar 1989 Plant Residues on Stone Tools. In *Plants in Australian Archaeology*, edited by W. Beck, A. Clarke, and L. Head. *Tempus* 1: 136–160.

Hamon, Caroline 2003 De l'utilisation des outils de mouture, broyage et polissage au Néolithique en Bassin Parisien: Apports de la tracéologie. *Bulletin de la Société Préhistorique Française* 100: 101–116.

Hard, R. J., R. P. Mauldin, and G. R. Raymond 1996 Mano Size, Stable Carbon Isotope Ratios, and Macrobotanical Remains as Multiple Lines of Evidence of Maize Dependence in the American Southwest. *Journal of Archaeological Method and Theory* 3: 253–318.

Hardy, Bruce L., and Gary T. Garufi 1998 Identification of Woodworking on Stone Tools through Residue and Use-Wear Analyses: Experimental Results. *Journal of Archaeological Science* 25: 177–184.

Hartz, N., and H. Winge 1906 Om uroxen fra Vig. Saret og draebt med flintvaben. *Aarboger* 21: 225–236.

Harwood, Gill 1988 Microscopic Techniques: II. Principles of Sedimentary Petrography. In *Techniques in Sedimentology*, edited by M. Tucker, pp. 108–173. Blackwell Scientific Publications, Oxford.

Hatch, J. W., J. W. Michels, C. M. Stevenson, B. E. Scheetz, and R. A. Geidel 1990 Hopewell Obsidian Studies: Behavioral Implications of Recent Sourcing and Dating Research. *American Antiquity* 55: 461–479.

Hay, Conran A. 1977 Use-Scratch Morphology: a Functionally Significant Aspect of Edge Damage on Obsidian Tools. *Journal of Field Archaeology* 4: 491–494.

Hayden, Brian 1977 Stone Tool Functions in the Western Desert. In *Stone Tools as Cultural Markers: Change, Evolution and Complexity*, edited by R.V.S. Wright, pp. 178–188. Australian Institute of Aboriginal Studies, Canberra.

1979 (editor) *Lithic Use-Wear Analysis*. Academic Press, New York.

1990 The Right Rub: Hide Working in High Ranking Households. In *The Interpretive Possibilities of Microwear Studies*, edited by B. Graslund, H. Knutsson, K. Knutsson, and J. Taffinder, pp. 89–102. Societas Archaeologica Upsaliensis, AUN 14. Uppsala, Sweden.

Hayden, Brian, Nora Franco, and Jim Spafford 1996 Evaluating Lithic Strategies and Design Criteria. In *Stone Tools: Theoretical Insights into Human Prehistory*, edited by G. Odell, pp. 9–49. Plenum Press, New York.

Hayden, Brian, and W. Karl Hutchings 1989 Whither the Billet Flake? In *Experiments in Lithic Technology*, edited by D. Amick and R. Mauldin, pp. 235–257. BAR International Series 528, Oxford.

Head, Leslie, and Richard Fullagar 1997 Hunter-Gatherer Archaeology and Pastoral Contact: Perspectives from the Northwest Northern Territory. *World Archaeology* 28: 418–428.

Heider, Karl G. 1967 Archaeological Assumptions and Ethnographical Facts: a Cautionary Tale from New Guinea. *Southwestern Journal of Anthropology* 23: 52–64.

1970 *The Dugum Dani: a Papuan Culture in the Highlands of West New Guinea*. Aldine, Chicago.

Henry, Donald O. 1989 Correlations between Reduction Strategies and Settlement Patterns. In *Alternative Approaches to Lithic Analysis*, edited by D. Henry and G. Odell, pp. 139–155.

Henry, D. O., C. V. Haynes, and B. Bradley 1976 Quantitative Variations in Flaked Stone Debitage. *Plains Anthropologist* 21: 57–61.

Hester, Thomas R. 1985 The Maya Lithic Sequence in Northern Belize. In *Stone Tool Analysis: Essays in Honor of Don E. Crabtree*, edited by M. Plew, J. Woods, and M. Pavesic, pp. 187–210. University of New Mexico, Albuquerque.

Hester, Thomas R., Delbert Gilbow, and Alan D. Albee 1973 A Functional Analysis of "Clear Fork" Artifacts from the Rio Grande Plain, Texas. *American Antiquity* 38: 90–96.

Hester, Thomas R., and Robert F. Heizer 1972 Problems in Functional Interpretation: Scraper-Planes from the Valley of Oaxaca, Mexico. *Contributions of the University of California Research Facility*, Berkeley, no. 14: 107–123.

Hester, Thomas R., and Harry J. Shafer 1975 An Initial Study of Blade Technology on the Central and Southern Texas Coast. *Plains Anthropologist* 16: 175–185.

1991 (editors) *Maya Stone Tools*. Prehistory Press, Madison, WI.

Hibbard, M. J. 1995 *Petrography to Petrogenesis*. Prentice Hall, Englewood Cliffs, NJ.

Hofman, Jack L. 1981 The Refitting of Chipped-Stone Artifacts as an Analytical and Interpretive Tool. *Current Anthropology* 22: 35–50.

1992 Recognition and Interpretation of Folsom Technological Variability on the Southern Plains. In *Ice Age Hunters of the Rockies*, edited by D. Stanford and J. Day, pp. 193–224. Denver Museum of Natural History, Denver.

Hofman, Jack L., and James Enloe (editors) 1992 *Piecing Together the Past: Applications of Refitting Studies in Archaeology*. BAR International Series, Oxford.

Hofman, Jack L., Lawrence W. Todd, and Michael B. Collins 1991 Identification of Central Texas Edwards Chert at the Folsom and Lindenmeier Sites. *Plains Anthropologist* 36: 297–308.

Holliday, Vance T. 1991 (editor) *Soils in Archaeology: Landscape Evolution and Human Occupation*. Smithsonian Institution Press, Washington, D.C.

1992 (editor) *Soils in Archaeology: Landscape Evolution and Human Occupation*. Smithsonian Institution Press, Washington, D.C.

1996 *Paleoindian Geoarchaeology of the Southern High Plains*. University of Texas Press, Austin.

Holmes, William H. 1891 Manufacture of Stone Arrow-points. *American Anthropologist* 4: 49–58.

1894a An Ancient Quarry in Indian Territory. *Bureau of American Ethnology Bulletin*, no. 21.

1894b Natural History of Flaked Stone Implements. In *Memoirs of the International Congress of Anthropology*, edited by C. S. Wake, pp. 120–139. Schulte, Chicago.

1919 *Handbook of Aboriginal American Antiquities. Part I: Introduction and Lithic Industries*. Bureau of American Ethnology, Bulletin 60. Washington, D.C.

Hornell, J. 1930 The Cypriot Threshing Sledge. *Man* 30: 135–149.

Hudler, Dale 1997 *Determining Clear Fork Tool Function through Use-Wear Analysis: a Discussion of Use-Wear Methods and Clear Fork Tools*. University of Texas at Austin, Texas Archeological Research Laboratory, Studies in Archeology 25.

Hudson, L. 1993 Protohistoric Pawnee Lithic Economy. *Plains Anthropologist* 38: 265–277.

Hughes, Richard E. 1992 Another Look at Hopewell Obsidian Studies. *American Antiquity* 57: 515–523.

Hurcombe, Linda 1988 Some Criticisms and Suggestions in Response to Newcomer *et al.* (1986). *Journal of Archaeological Science* 15: 1–10.

Hyland, D. C., J. M. Tersak, J. M. Adovasio, and M. I. Siegel 1990 Identification of the Species of Origin of Residue Blood on Lithic Material. *American Antiquity* 55: 104–112.

Ingbar, Eric E. 1994 Lithic Material Selection and Technological Organization. In *The Organization of North American Prehistoric Chipped Stone Tool Technologies*, edited by P. Carr, pp. 45–56. International Monographs in Prehistory, Ann Arbor.

Ingbar, Eric E., Mary Lou Larson, and Bruce Bradley 1989 A Non-Typological Approach to Debitage Analysis. In *Experiments in Lithic Technology*, edited by D. S. Amick and R. P. Mauldin, pp. 117–136. BAI International Series, no. 528. Oxford.

Inizan, Marie-Louise, Hélène Roche, and Jacques Tixier 1992 *Technology of Knapped Stone*. Préhistoire de la Pierre Taillée, tome 3, CREP, Meudon.

Irwin, Henry T., and H. M. Wormington 1970 Paleo-Indian Tool Types in the Great Plains. *American Antiquity* 35: 24–34.

Ives, D. J. 1984 The Crescent Hills Prehistoric Quarrying Area: More Than Just Rocks. In *Prehistoric Chert Exploitation: Studies from the Midcontinent*, edited by B. M. Butler and E. E. May, pp. 187–196. Center for Archaeological Investigations, Southern Illinois University, Occasional Paper no. 2, Carbondale.

Jackson, Thomas L., and Michael W. Love 1991 "Blade Running:" Middle Preclassic Obsidian Exchange and the Introduction of Prismatic Blades at La Blanca, Guatemala. *Ancient Mesoamerica* 2: 47–59.

Jelinek, Arthur J. 1965 Lithic Technology Conference, Les Eyzies, France. *American Antiquity* 31: 277–278.

Jeske, Robert J., and Rochelle Lurie 1993 The Archaeological Visibility of Bipolar Technology: an Example from the Koster Site. *Midcontinental Journal of Archaeology* 18: 131–160.

Johnson, Jay K. 1989 The Utility of Production Trajectory Modeling as a Framework for Regional Analysis. In *Alternative Approaches to Lithic Analysis*, edited by D. Henry and G. Odell, pp. 119–138. Archaeological Papers of the American Anthropological Association, no. 1. Washington, D.C.

1996 Lithic Analysis and Questions of Cultural Complexity: the Maya. In *Stone Tools: Theoretical Insights into Human Prehistory*, edited by G. Odell, pp. 159–179. Plenum Press, New York.

2001 Some Reflections on Debitage Analysis. In *Lithic Debitage: Context, Form, Meaning*, edited by W. Andrefsky, Jr., pp. 15–20. University of Utah Press, Salt Lake City.

Johnson, Lucy Lewis 1978 A History of Flint-Knapping Experimentation, 1838–1976. *Current Anthropology* 19: 337–359.

Jones, George T., Donald K. Grayson, and Charlotte Beck 1983 Artifact Class Richness and Sample Size in Archaeological Surface Assemblages. In *Lulu Linear Punctated: Essays in Honor of George Irving Quimby*, edited by R. Dunnell and D. Grayson, pp. 55–73. University of Michigan, Museum of Anthropology, Anthropological Papers, no. 72.

Judge, W. James 1973 *Paleoindian Occupation of the Central Rio Grande Valley in New Mexico*. University of New Mexico Press, Albuquerque.

Julien, Michele, Claudine Carlin, and Boris Valentin 1991 Dechets de silex, dechets de pierres chauffées de l'interêt des remontages à Pincevent (France). In *Piecing Together the Past: Applications of Refitting Studies in Archaeology*, edited by J. Hofman and J. Enloe, pp. 287–295. BAR International Series, Oxford.

Kaminska, Jolanta, Elzbieta Mycielska-Dowgiallo, and Karol Szymczak 1993 Postdepositional Changes on Surfaces of Flint Artifacts as Observed under a Scanning Electron Microscope. In *Traces et foncion: Les gestes retrouvés*, edited by P. Anderson, S. Beyries, M. Otte, and H. Plisson, pp. 467–476. ERAUL, no. 50, Liège.

Kamminga, Johan 1981 The Bevelled Pounder: an Aboriginal Stone Tool Type from Southeast Queensland. *Proceedings of the Royal Society of Queensland* 92: 31–35.

1982 *Over the Edge: Functional Analysis of Australian Stone Tools*. Anthropology Museum, University of Queensland, Occasional Papers in Anthropology, no. 12.

Kamp, Katherine A. 1995 A Use-Wear Analysis of the Function of Basalt Cylinders. *Kiva* 61: 109–119.

Katz, Paul R. 1976 *A Technological Analysis of the Kansas City Hopewell Chipped Stone Industry*. PhD dissertation, Department of Anthropology, University of Kansas. University Microfilms, Ann Arbor.

Kay, Marvin 1996 Microwear Analysis of Some Clovis and Experimental Chipped Stone Tools. In *Stone Tools: Theoretical Insights into Human Prehistory*, edited by G. Odell, pp. 315–344. Plenum, New York.

Kazaryan, H. 1993 Butchery Knives in the Mousterian Sites of Armenia. In *Traces et fonction: les gestes retrouvés*, edited by P. Anderson, S. Beyries, M. Otte, and H. Plisson, pp. 79–85. ERAUL, no. 50, Liège.

Kealhofer, Lisa, Robin Torrence, and Richard Fullagar 1999 Integrating Phytoliths within Use-Wear/ Residue Studies of Stone Tools. *Journal of Archaeological Science* 26: 527–546.

Keeley, Lawrence H. 1980 *Experimental Determination of Stone Tool Uses: a Microwear Analysis*. University of Chicago Press, Chicago.

1982 Hafting and Retooling: Effects on the Archaeological Record. *American Antiquity* 47: 798–809.

Keeley, Lawrence H., and Mark H. Newcomer 1977 Microwear Analysis of Experimental Flint Tools: a Test Case. *Journal of Archaeological Science* 4: 29–62.

Kehoe, Alice Beck 1992 *North American Indians: a Comprehensive Account*. Prentice Hall, Englewood Cliffs, NJ.

Keller, Charles M. 1966 The Development of Edge Damage Patterns on Stone Tools. *Man* 1: 501–511.

Kelly, Isabel T., and Catherine S. Fowler 1986 Southern Paiute. *Handbook of North American Indians*, vol. 11: *Great Basin*, edited by W. d'Azevedo, pp. 368–397. Smithsonian Institution Press, Washington, DC.

Kelly, John E. 1991 The Evidence for Prehistoric Exchange and Its Implications for the Development of Cahokia. In *New Perspectives on Cahokia: Views from the Periphery*, edited by J. Stoltman, pp. 65–92. Prehistory Press, Madison.

Kelly, Robert L. 1983 Hunter-gatherer Mobility Strategies. *Journal of Anthropological Research* 39: 277–306.

1985 *Hunter-Gatherer Mobility and Sedentism: a Great Basin Survey*. PhD dissertation, Department of Anthropology, University of Michigan. University Microfilms, Ann Arbor.

1988 The Three Sides of a Biface. *American Antiquity* 53: 717–734.

Kerrich, J. E., and D. L. Clarke 1967 Notes on the Possible Misuse and Errors of Cumulative Percentage Frequency Graphs for the Comparison of Prehistoric Artefact Assemblages. *Proceedings of the Prehistoric Society* n.s. 33: 57–69.

Kintigh, Keith W. 1984 Measuring Archaeological Diversity by Comparison with Simulated Assemblages. *American Antiquity* 49: 44–54.

1989 Sample Size, Significance, and Measures of Diversity. In *Quantifying Diversity in Archaeology*, edited by R. Leonard and G. Jones, pp. 25–36. Cambridge University Press, Cambridge.

Knudson, Ruthann 1979 Inference and Imposition in Lithic Analysis. In *Lithic Use-Wear Analysis*, edited by B. Hayden, pp. 269–281. Academic Press, New York.

Knutsson, Kjel 1988 *Patterns of Tool Use: Scanning Electron Microscopy of Experimental Quartz Tools*. Societas Archaeologica Upsaliensis, AUN 10. Uppsala, Sweden.

Knutsson, K., and R. Hope 1984 The Application of Acetate Peels in Lithic Usewear Analysis. *Archaeometry* 26: 1.

Kobayashi, Hiroaki 1975 The Experimental Study of Bipolar Flakes. In *Lithic Technology: Making and Using Stone Tools*, edited by E. Swanson, pp. 115–127. Mouton, The Hague.

Kobayashi, Tatsuo 1970 Microblade Industries in the Japanese Archipelago. *Arctic Anthropology* 7: 38–58.

Koldehoff, Brad 1987 The Cahokia Flake Tool Industry: Socioeconomic Implications for Late Prehistory in the Central Mississippi Valley. In *The Organization of Core Technology*, edited by J. Johnson and C. Morrow, pp. 151–185. Westview Press, Boulder.

Kooyman, Brian P. 2000 *Understanding Stone Tools and Archaeological Sites*. University of Calgary Press, Calgary.

Kooyman, B., M. E. Newman, and H. Ceri 1992 Verifying the Reliability of Blood Residue Analysis on Archaeological Tools. *Journal of Archaeological Science* 19: 265–269.

Kozák, Vladimír 1972 Stone Age Revisited. *Natural History* 81: 14–24.

Krakker, J. J. 1997 Biface Caches, Exchange, and Regulatory Systems in the Prehistoric Great Lakes Region. *Midcontinental Journal of Archaeology* 22: 1–41.

Kroeber, Theodora 1961 *Ishi in Two Worlds*. University of California Press, Berkeley.

Kuhn, Steven L. 1991 "Unpacking" Reduction: Lithic Raw Material Economy in the Mousterian of West-central Italy. *Journal of Anthropological Archaeology* 10: 76–106.

1993 Mousterian Technology as Adaptive Response: a Case Study. In *Hunting and Animal Exploitation in the Later Paleolithic and Mesolithic of Eurasia*, edited by G. Peterkin, H. Bricker, and P. Mellars, pp. 25–31. Archeological Papers of the American Anthropological Association. Washington, D.C.

1994 A Formal Approach to the Design and Assembly of Mobile Toolkits. *American Antiquity* 59: 426–442.

1995 *Mousterian Lithic Technology: an Ecological Perspective.* Princeton University Press, Princeton.

Laplace, Georges 1964 Essai de typologie systematique. *Annals of the University of Ferrara,* n.s., 15, vol. 1.

1974 La typologie analytique: base rationale d'étude des industries lithiques et osseuses. Editions CNRS, *Banque de données archéologiques.* Congrès de Marseille, 1972.

Larson, Mary Lou 1994 Toward a Holistic Analysis of Chipped Stone Assemblages. In *The Organization of North American Prehistoric Chipped Stone Tool Technologies,* edited by P. Carr, pp. 57–69. International Monographs in Prehistory, Ann Arbor.

Larson, Mary Lou, and Eric E. Ingbar 1992 Perspectives on Refitting: Critique and a Complementary Approach. In *Piecing Together the Past,* edited by J. L. Hofman and J. Enloe, pp. 151–162. BAR International Series 578. Oxford.

Larson, Mary Lou, and Marcel Kornfeld 1997 Chipped Stone Nodules: Theory, Method, and Examples. *Lithic Technology* 22: 4–18.

Latham, Thomas S., Paula A. Sutton, and Kenneth L. Verosub 1992 Non-Destructive XRF Characterization of Basaltic Artifacts from Truckie, California. *Geoarchaeology* 7: 81–101.

Lavin, L., and D. R. Prothero 1992 Prehistoric Procurement of Secondary Sources: the Case for Characterization. *North American Archaeologist* 13: 97–113.

Lawn, B. R., and D. B. Marshall 1979 Mechanisms of Microcontact Fracture in Brittle Solids. In *Lithic Use-Wear Analysis,* edited by B. Hayden, pp. 63–82. Academic Press, New York.

Lawn, B. R., and T. R. Wilshaw 1975 *Fracture of Brittle Solids.* Cambridge University Press, Cambridge.

Lawrence, Robert A. 1979 Experimental Evidence for the Significance of Attributes Used in Edge-Damage Analysis. In *Lithic Use-Wear Analysis,* edited by B. Hayden, pp. 113–121. Academic Press, New York.

Leach, Jeff D., and Raymond P. Mauldin 1995 Additional Comments on Blood Residue Analysis in Archaeology. *Antiquity* 69: 1020–1022.

Leakey, Louis S. B. 1934 *Adam's Ancestors.* Methuen and Co., London.

LeMoine, Genviève M. 1997 *Use-Wear Analysis on Bone and Antler Tools of the Mackenzie Inuit.* BAR International Series 679, Oxford.

Levi-Sala, Irene 1986 Experimental Replication of Post-Depositional Surface Modifications on Flint. In *Technical Aspects of Microwear Studies on Stone Tools,* edited by L. Owen and G. Unrath. *Early Man News* 9/10/11: 103–109.

1993 Use-Wear Traces: Processes of Development and Post-Depositional Alterations. In *Traces et foncion: Les gestes retrouvés,* edited by P. Anderson, S. Beyries, M. Otte, and H. Plisson, pp. 401–416. ERAUL, no. 50, Liège.

1996 *A Study of Microscopic Polish on Flint Implements.* BAR International Series 629. Oxford.

Lewenstein, Suzanne M. 1987 *Stone Tool Use at Cerros: the Ethnoarchaeological and Use-Wear Evidence.* University of Texas Press, Austin.

Lewis, Douglas W., and David McConchie 1994 *Analytical Sedimentology.* Chapman and Hall, New York.

Loy, Thomas H. 1983 Prehistoric Blood Residues: Detection on Tool Surfaces and Identification of Species of Origin. *Science* 220: 1269–1271.

1993 The Artifact as Site: an Example of the Biomolecular Analysis of Organic Residues on Prehistoric Tools. *World Archaeology* 25: 44–63.

1994 Methods in the Analysis of Starch Residues on Prehistoric Stone Tools. In *Tropical Archaeobotany: Applications and New Developments*, edited by J. Hather, pp. 86–114. Routledge, London.

Loy, Thomas H., and E. James Dixon 1998 Blood Residues on Fluted Points from Eastern Beringia. *American Antiquity* 63: 21–46.

Loy, Thomas H., and Andrée R. Wood 1989 Blood Residue Analysis at Çayonu Tepesi, Turkey. *Journal of Field Archaeology* 16: 451–460.

Luedtke, Barbara E. 1976 *Lithic Material Distributions and Interaction Patterns during the Late Woodland Period in Michigan*. PhD dissertation, Department of Anthropology, University of Michigan.

1992 *An Archaeologist's Guide to Chert and Flint*. Institute of Archaeology, University of California, Los Angeles, Archaeological Research Tools 7.

Luedtke, Barbara E., and J. T. Meyers 1984 Trace Element Variation in Burlington Chert: a Case Study. In *Prehistoric Chert Exploitation: Studies from the Midcontinent*, edited by B. M. Butler and E. E. May, pp. 287–298. Center for Archaeological Investigations, Southern Illinois University, Occasional Paper no. 2, Carbondale.

Lurie, Rochelle 1989 Lithic Technology and Mobility Strategies: the Koster Site Middle Archaic. In *Time, Energy and Stone Tools*, edited by R. Torrence, pp. 46–56. Cambridge University Press, Cambridge.

MacDonald, D. H. 1995 Mobility and Raw Material Use at the Hunting Camp Spring Site (35WA96), Blue Mountains, Oregon. *North American Archaeologist* 16: 343–361.

Magne, Martin P. R. 1985 *Lithics and Livelihood: Stone Tool Technologies of Central and Southern Interior British Columbia*. Archaeological Survey of Canada, Mercury Series, Paper no. 133. National Museum of Man, Ottawa.

2001 Debitage Analysis as a Scientific Tool for Archaeological Knowledge. In *Lithic Debitage*, edited by W. Andrefsky, Jr., pp. 21–30.

Magne, Martin P. R., and David Pokotylo 1981 A Pilot Study in Bifacial Lithic Reduction Sequences. *Lithic Technology* 10: 34–47.

Mallouf, Robert J. 1981 *A Case Study of Plow Damage to Chert Artifacts: the Brookeen Creek Cache, Hill County, Texas*. Texas Historical Commission, Office of the State Archeologist, Report 33, Austin.

Mansur, Maria Estela 1982 Microwear Analysis of Natural and Use Striations: New Clues to the Mechanisms of Striation Formation. In *Tailler! Pour quoi faire: Recent Progress in Microwear Studies*, edited by D. Cahen, pp. 213–233. Studia Praehistorica Belgica 2. Tervuren.

Mansur-Franchomme, Maria Estela 1983 *Traces d'utilisation et technologie lithique: Exemples de la Patagonie*. PhD dissertation, Université de Bordeaux I.

1986 *Microscopie du matériel lithique préhistorique: traces d'utilisation, altérations naturelles, accidentelles et technologiques*. Cahiers du Quaternaire no. 9, CNRS, Bordeaux.

Mauldin, Raymond P., and Daniel S. Amick 1989 Investigating Patterning in Debitage from Experimental Bifacial Core Reduction. In *Experiments in Lithic Technology*, edited by D. Amick and R. Mauldin, pp. 67–88. BAR International Series, Oxford.

Mauldin, Raymond P., Jeff D. Leach, and Daniel S. Amick 1995 On the Identification of Blood Residues on Paleoindian Artifacts. *Current Research in the Pleistocene* 12: 85–87.

McBirney, Alexander R. 1993 *Igneous Petrology*. Second edition. Jones and Bartlett, Boston.

McBrearty, Sally, Laura Bishop, Thomas Plummer, Robert Dewar, and Nicholas Conard 1998 Tools Underfoot: Human Trampling as an Agent of Lithic Artifact Edge Modification. *American Antiquity* 63: 108–129.

McDonald, M. M. A. 1991 Technological Organization and Sedentism in the Epipaleolithic of Dakhleh Oasis, Egypt. *African Archaeological Review* 9: 81–109.

McDonnell, Robert D., Henk Kars, and J. Ben H. Jansen 1997 Petrography and Geochemistry of Flint from Six Neolithic Sources in Southern Limburg (The Netherlands) and Northern Belgium. In *Siliceous Rocks and Culture*, edited by A. Ramos-Millan and M. A. Bustillo, pp. 371–384. Universidad de Granada, Monográfica Arte y Arqueología.

McDougall, J. M., D. H. Tarling, and S. E. Warren 1983 Magnetic Sourcing of Obsidian Samples from Mediterranean and Near Eastern Sources. *Journal of Archaeological Science* 10: 441–452.

McSwain, R. 1991 A Comparative Evaluation of the Producer-Consumer Model for Lithic Exchange in Northern Belize. *Latin American Antiquity* 2: 337–351.

Meeks, Scott C. 2000 *The Use and Function of Late Middle Archaic Projectile Points in the Midsouth*. Office of Archaeological Services, University of Alabama Museums, Report of Investigations 77. Moundsville.

Mellars, Paul A. 1970 Some Comments on the Notion of 'Functional Variability' in Stone-Tool Assemblages. *World Archaeology* 2: 74–89.

　1989 Chronologie du moustérien du sud-ouest de la France: actualisation du débat. *l'Anthropologie* 93: 53–72.

Meurers-Balke, J., and J. Luning 1992 Some Aspects and Experiments Concerning the Processing of Glume Wheats. In *Préhistoire de l'Agriculture*, edited by P. Anderson, pp. 341–362. Editions du CNRS, Monographie du CRA, no. 6, Paris.

Mewhinney, H. 1964 A Skeptic Views the Billet Flake. *American Antiquity* 30: 203–204.

Meyers, J. T. 1970 *Chert Resources of the Lower Illinois Valley*. Illinois State Museum, Reports of Investigations, no. 18. Springfield.

Migal, Witold 1997 Reconstruction of the Flint Extraction System in Krzemionki. In *Siliceous Rocks and Culture*, edited by A. Ramos-Millan and M. Bustillo, pp. 315–325. Editorial Universidad de Granada, Granada.

Miller, John 1988 Cathodoluminescence Microscopy. In *Techniques in Sedimentology*, edited by M. Tucker, pp. 174–190. Blackwell Scientific Publications, Oxford.

Mitchum, Beverly 1991 Lithic Artifacts from Cerros, Belize: Production, Consumption, and Trade. In *Maya Stone Tools*, edited by T. Hester and H. Shafer, pp. 45–53. Prehistory Press, Madison, WI.

Moholy-Nagy, Hattula, and Fred W. Nelson 1990 New Data on Sources of Obsidian Artifacts from Tikal, Guatemala. *Ancient Mesoamerica* 1: 71–80.

Moir, J. Reid 1912 The Natural Fracture of Flint and Its Bearing upon Rudimentary Flint Implements. *Proceedings of the Prehistoric Society of East Anglia* 1: 171–184.

　1920 *Pre-Paleolithic Man*. W. E. Harrison, The Ancient House, Ipswich.

Morris, D. H. 1990 Changes in Groundstone Following the Introduction of Maize into the American Southwest. *Journal of Anthropological Research* 46: 177–194.

Morrow, Carol A. 1984 A Biface Production Model for Gravel-Based Chipped Stone Industries. *Lithic Technology* 13: 20–28.

Morrow, Toby A. 1996a Bigger Is Better: Comments on Kuhn's Formal Approach to Mobile Tool Kits. *American Antiquity* 61: 581–590.

　1996b Lithic Refitting and Archaeological Site Formation Processes: a Case Study from the Twin Ditch Site, Greene County, Illinois. In *Stone Tools: Theoretical Insights into Human Prehistory*, edited by G. H. Odell, pp. 345–373. Plenum, New York.

　1997 A Chip Off the Old Block: Alternative Approaches to Debitage Analysis. *Lithic Technology* 22: 51–69.

Moss, Emily H. 1983 *The Functional Analysis of Flint Implements: Pincevent and Pont d'Ambon*. BAR International Series 177. Oxford.

　1986 What Microwear Analysts Look At. In *Technical Aspects of Microwear Studies on Stone Tools*, edited by L. Owen and G. Unrath. *Early Man News* 9/10/11: 91–96.

1987 A Review of "Investigating Microwear Polishes with Blind Tests." *Journal of Archaeological Science* 14: 473–481.

Movius, Hallam L., Jr., Nicholas C. David, Harvey M. Bricker, and R. Berle Clay 1968 *The Analysis of Certain Major Classes of Upper Paleolithic Tools.* American School of Prehistoric Research, Peabody Museum, Harvard University, Bulletin no. 26.

Mueller, James W. 1974 *The Use of Sampling in Archaeological Survey.* American Antiquity, Memoirs no. 28. Washington, D.C.

1975 (editor) *Sampling in Archaeology.* University of Arizona Press, Tucson.

Nance, Jack D. 1981 Statistical Fact and Archaeological Faith: Two Models in Small-Sites Sampling. *Journal of Field Archaeology* 8: 151–165.

Nance, Jack D., and Bruce F. Ball 1981 The Influence of Sampling Unit Size on Statistical Estimates in Archeological Site Sampling. In *Plowzone Archaeology*, edited by M. O'Brien and D. Lewarch, pp. 51–70. Vanderbilt Publications in Anthropology no. 27, Nashville.

Nash, D. T. 1993 Distinguishing Stone Artifacts from Naturefacts Created by Rockfall Processes. In *Formation Processes in Archaeological Context*, edited by P. Goldberg, D. Nash, and M. Petraglia, pp. 125–138. Prehistory Press, Madison, WI.

Nations, James D. 1989 The Lacandon Maya Bow and Arrow: an Ethnoarchaeological Example of Postclassic Lowland Maya Weapon Manufacture. In *La Obsidiana en Mesoamerica*, edited by M. Gaxiola and J. E. Clark, pp. 449–457. Instituto Nacional de Antropologia e Historia, Mexico City.

Nations, James D., and John E. Clark 1983 The Bows and Arrows of the Lacandon Maya. *Archaeology* 36: 36–43.

Neff, Hector, and Michael D. Glascock 1995 The State of Nuclear Archaeology in North America. *Journal of Radioanalytical and Nuclear Chemistry* 196: 275–286.

Nelson, D. E., T. H. Loy, J. S. Vogel, and J. R. Southon 1986 Radiocarbon Dating Blood Residues on Prehistoric Stone Tools. *Radiocarbon* 28: 170–174.

Nelson, Margaret C. 1991 The Study of Technological Organization. In *Archaeological Method and Theory*, vol. 3, edited by M. Schiffer, pp. 57–100. University of Arizona Press, Tucson.

Nelson, M. C., and H. Lippmeier 1993 Grinding-Tool Design as Conditioned by Land-Use Pattern. *American Antiquity* 58: 286–305.

Nelson, Nels C. 1916 Flint Working by Ishi. In *William Henry Holmes Anniversary Volume*, edited by F. W. Hodge, pp. 397–402. Washington, D.C.

Nelson, Richard K. 1973 *Hunters of the Northern Forest.* University of Chicago Press, Chicago.

Neshko, John, Jr. 1969–70 Bakerville Stone Bowl Quarry. *Bulletin of the Massachusetts Archaeological Society* 31: 1–10.

Newcomer, Mark 1970 Some Quantitative Experiments in Handaxe Manufacture. *World Archaeology* 3: 85–93.

Newcomer, Mark, Roger Grace, and Romana Unger-Hamilton 1986 Investigating Microwear Polishes with Blind Tests. *Journal of Archaeological Science* 13: 203–217.

Newman, Margaret E., Howard Ceri, and Brian Kooyman 1996 The Use of Immunological Techniques in the Analysis of Archaeological Materials—a Response to Eisele; with Report of Studies at Head-Smashed-In Buffalo Jump. *Antiquity* 70: 677–682.

Newman, M., and P. Julig 1989 The Identification of Protein Residues on Lithic Artifacts from a Stratified Boreal Forest Site. *Canadian Journal of Archaeology* 13: 119–132.

Nielsen, Axel E. 1991 Trampling the Archaeological Record: an Experimental Study. *American Antiquity* 56: 483–503.

Nissen, Karen, and Margaret Dittemore 1974 Ethnographic Data and Wear Pattern Analysis: a Study of Socketed Eskimo Scrapers. *Tebiwa* 17: 67–88.

Noe-Nygaard, Nanna 1973 The Vig Bull: New Information on the Final Hunt. Museum of Mineralogy and Geology of the University of Copenhagen, Paleontological Papers no. 196. Copenhagen.

Norman, M. D., W. P. Leeman, D. P. Blanchard, J. G. Fitton, and D. James 1989 Comparison of Major and Trace Element Analyses by ICP, XRF, INAA and ID Methods. *Geostandards Newsletter* 13: 283–290.

Odell, George H. 1977 *The Application of Micro-wear Analysis to the Lithic Component of an Entire Prehistoric Settlement: Methods, Problems and Functional Reconstructions.* PhD dissertation, Department of Anthropology, Harvard University.

1978 Préliminaires d'une analyse fonctionnelle des pointes microlithiques de Bergumermeer, Pays-Bas. *Bulletin de la Société Préhistorique Française* 75: 37–49.

1980a Butchering with Stone Tools: Some Experimental Results. *Lithic Technology* 9: 39–48.

1980b Toward a More Behavioral Approach to Archaeological Lithic Concentrations. *American Antiquity* 45: 404–431.

1981a The Mechanics of Use-Breakage of Stone Tools: Some Testable Hypotheses. *Journal of Field Archaeology* 8: 197–209.

1981b The Morphological Express at Function Junction: Searching for Meaning in Lithic Tool Types. *Journal of Anthropological Research* 37: 319–342.

1984 Chert Resource Availability in the Lower Illinois Valley: a Transect Sample. In *Prehistoric Chert Exploitation: Studies from the Midcontinent*, edited by B. M. Butler and E. E. May, pp. 45–67. Southern Illinois University at Carbondale, Center for Archaeological Investigations, Occasional paper no. 2.

1985 Hill Creek Site Lithic Analysis. In *The Hill Creek Homestead and the Late Mississippian Settlement in the Lower Illinois Valley*, edited by M. Conner, pp. 55–144. Center for American Archeology, Research Series, vol. 1.

1986 Review of *Use-Wear Analysis of Flaked Stone Tools*, by Patrick C. Vaughan. *Lithic Technology* 15: 115–120.

1987 Analyse fonctionnelle des traces d'usure effectuée à une échelle régionale (l'Illinois). *l'Anthropologie* 91: 381–398.

1988 Addressing Prehistoric Hunting Practices through Stone Tool Analysis. *American Anthropologist* 90: 335–356.

1989a Experiments in Lithic Reduction. In *Experiments in Lithic Technology*, edited by D. Amick and R. Mauldin, pp. 163–198. BAR International Series 528, Oxford.

1989b Fitting Analytical Techniques to Prehistoric Problems with Lithic Data. In *Alternative Approaches to Lithic Analysis*, edited by D. Henry and G. Odell, pp. 159–182. Archeological Papers of the American Anthropological Association. Washington, D.C.

1994a Assessing Hunter-Gatherer Mobility in the Illinois Valley: Exploring Ambiguous Results. In *The Organization of North American Prehistoric Chipped Stone Tool Technologies*, edited by P. Carr, pp. 70–86. International Monographs in Prehistory, Ann Arbor.

1994b Prehistoric Hafting and Mobility in the North American Midcontinent: Examples from Illinois. *Journal of Anthropological Archaeology* 13: 51–73.

1994c The Role of Stone Bladelets in Middle Woodland Society. *American Antiquity* 59: 102–120.

1996 *Stone Tools and Mobility in the Illinois Valley: from Hunter-Gatherer Camps to Agricultural Villages.* International Monographs in Prehistory, Ann Arbor.

1998a Hoe. In *Archaeology of Prehistoric Native America: an Encyclopedia*, edited by G. Gibbon, pp. 364–365. Garland, New York.

1998b Investigating Correlates of Sedentism and Domestication in Prehistoric North America. *American Antiquity* 63: 553–571.

1999 The Organization of Labor at a Protohistoric Settlement in Oklahoma. *Journal of Field Archaeology* 26: 407–421.

2000 Stone Tool Research at the End of the Millennium: Procurement and Technology. *Journal of Archaeological Research* 8: 269–331.

2001 Stone Tool Research at the End of the Millennium: Classification, Function, and Behavior. *Journal of Archaeological Research* 9: 45–100.

2002 *La Harpe's Post: a Tale of French-Wichita Contact on the Eastern Plains.* University of Alabama Press, Tuscaloosa.

Odell, George H., and Frank Cowan 1986 Experimentation with Spears and Arrows Using Animal Targets. *Journal of Field Archaeology* 13: 195–212.

1987 Estimating Tillage Effects on Artifact Distributions. *American Antiquity* 52: 456–484.

Odell, George H., and Frieda Odell-Vereecken 1980 Verifying the Reliability of Lithic Use-Wear Assessments by "Blind Tests:" the Low-Power Approach. *Journal of Field Archaeology* 7: 87–120.

1989 First Impressions and Ultimate Reality: Excavation of the Day Site in Wagoner County, Oklahoma. *Bulletin of the Oklahoma Anthropological Society* 38: 19–48.

Odell-Vereecken, Frieda, and George H. Odell 1988 The Relationship between Collections and Archaeology as Tested at the Wilmoth Sites, Adair County, Oklahoma. *Bulletin of the Oklahoma Anthropological Society* 37: 191–218.

Osborne, Richard H. 1998 The Experimental Replication of a Stone Mortar. *Lithic Technology* 23: 116–123.

Oswalt, Wendell H. 1976 *An Anthropological Analysis of Food-Getting Technology.* John Wiley and Sons, New York.

Owen, Linda R., and Guenther Unrath 1989 Microtraces d'usure dues à la préhension. *l'Anthropologie* 93: 673–688.

Parkes, P. A. 1986 *Current Scientific Techniques in Archaeology.* St. Martin's Press, New York.

Parkington, John E. 1967 Some Comments on the Comparison and Classification of Archaeological Specimens. *South African Archaeological Bulletin* 22: 73–79.

Parry, William J. 1994 Prismatic Blade Technologies in North America. In *The Organization of North American Chipped Stone Technologies*, edited by P. Carr, pp. 87–98. International Monographs in Prehistory, Ann Arbor.

Parry, William J., and Robert L. Kelly 1987 Expedient Core Technology and Sedentism. In *The Organization of Core Technology*, edited by J. Johnson and C. Morrow, pp. 285–304. Westview Press, Boulder.

Pasty, Jean-François 2001 Le gisement paléolithiqe moyen de Nassigny (Allier). *Bulletin de la Société Préhistorique* 98: 5–20.

Paton, Robert 1994 Speaking through Stones: a Study from Northern Australia. *World Archaeology* 26: 172–184.

Patten, Bob 1999 *Old Tools—New Eyes: a Primal Primer of Flintknapping.* Stone Dagger Publications, Denver.

Patterson, Leland W. 1983 Criteria for Determining the Attributes of Man-Made Lithics. *Journal of Field Archaeology* 10: 297–307.

Pawlik, Alfred 1983 Horn Experimentation in Use-Wear Analysis. In *Traces et fonction: Les gestes retrouvés*, edited by P. Anderson, S. Beyries, M. Otte, and H. Plisson, pp. 211–224. ERAUL no. 50, Liège.

1995 *Die mikroskopische Analyse von Steingeraten: Experimente—Auswertungsmethoden—Artefaktanalysen.* Urgeschichtliche Materialhefte 10. Verlag Archaeologica Venatoria, Tubingen.

Peacock, Evan 1991 Distinguishing between Artifacts and Geofacts: a Test Case from Eastern England. *Journal of Field Archaeology* 18: 345–361.

Pearsall, Deborah M. 1978 Phytolith Analysis of Archaeological Soils: Evidence for Maize Cultivation in Formative Ecuador. *Science* 199: 177–178.

1982 Phytolith Analysis: Applications of a New Paleoethnobotanical Technique in Archaeology. *American Anthropologist* 84: 862–871.

2000 *Paleoethnobotany: a Handbook of Procedures.* Second edition. Academic Press, San Diego.

Pearsall, Deborah M., and Dolores R. Piperno 1990 Antiquity of Maize Cultivation in Ecuador: Summary and Reevaluation of the Evidence. *American Antiquity* 55: 324–337.

Peet, Robert K. 1974 The Measurement of Species Diversity. *Annual Review of Ecology and Systematics* 5: 285–307.

Pelegrin, Jacques 1984 Débitage par pression sur silex: Nouvelles expérimentations. In *Préhistoire de la pierre taillée 2: Economie du débitage laminaire: technologie et expérimentation,* compiled by IIIème Table Rond de Technologie Lithique, pp. 117–127. Cercle de Recherches et d'Etudes Préhistorique, Meudon.

Penman, John T., and J. N. Gunderson 1999 Pipestone Artifacts from Upper Mississippi Valley Sites. *Plains Anthropologist* 44: 47–57.

Petraglia, M., D. Knepper, P. Glumac, M. Newman, and C. Sussman 1996 Immunological and Microwear Analysis of Chipped-Stone Artifacts from Piedmont Contexts. *American Antiquity* 61: 127–135.

Peyrony, D., H. Kidder, and H. Noone 1949 Outils en silex émoussées du Paléolithic supérieur. *Bulletin de la Société Préhistorique Française* 46: 298–301.

Phagan, Carl J. 1976 *A Method for the Analysis of Flakes in Archaeological Assemblages: a Peruvian Example.* PhD dissertation, Department of Anthropology, Ohio State University. University Microfilms, Ann Arbor.

Phillips, Philip 1959 Application of the Wheat-Gifford-Wasley Taxonomy to Eastern Ceramics. *American Antiquity* 24: 117–125.

Pielou, E. C. 1966 The Measurement of Diversity in Different Types of Biological Collections. *Journal of Theoretical Biology* 13: 131–144.

Piperno, Dolores R. 1984 A Comparison and Differentiation of Phytoliths from Maize and Wild Grasses: Use of Morphological Criteria. *American Antiquity* 49: 361–383.

1988 *Phytolith Analysis: an Archaeological and Geological Perspective.* Academic Press, San Diego.

Piperno, Dolores R., Karen H. Clary, Richard G. Cooke, Anthony J. Ranere, and Doris Weiland 1985 Preceramic Maize in Central Panama: Phytolith and Pollen Evidence. *American Anthropologist* 87: 871–878.

Piperno, Dolores R., and Irene Holst 1998 The Presence of Starch Grains on Prehistoric Stone Tools from the Humid Neotropics: Indications of Early Tuber Use and Agriculture in Panama. *Journal of Archaeological Science* 25: 765–776.

Pitts, Michael W. 1978 On the Shape of Waste Flakes as an Index of Technological Change in Lithic Industries. *Journal of Archaeological Science* 5: 17–37.

Pitts, Michael W., and Roger M. Jacobi 1979 Some Aspects of Change in Flaked Stone Industries of the Mesolithic and Neolithic in Southern Britain. *Journal of Archaeological Science* 6: 163–177.

Plisson, Hugues 1983 An Application of Casting Techniques for Observing and Recording Microwear. *Lithic Technology* 12: 17–21.

1985 *Etude fonctionnelle des outillages lithiques préhistoriques par l'analyse des micro-usures, recherche méthodologique et archéologique.* PdD dissertation, Université de Paris I.

1986 Altération des micropolis d'usage: quelques expériences complémentaires. In *Technical Aspects of Microwear Studies on Stone Tools,* edited by L. Owen and G. Unrath. *Early Man News* 9/10/11: 111–116.

Plisson, H., and M. Mauger 1988 Chemical and Mechanical Alteration of Microwear Polishes: an Experimental Approach. *Helinium* 27: 3–16.

Plisson, H., and B. Schmider 1990 Etude préliminaire d'une série de pointes de Chatelperron de la Grotte du Renne à Arcy-sur-Cure: Approche morphométrique, technologique et tracéologique.

In *Paléolithique moyen récent et paléolithique supérieur ancien en Europe*, edited by C. Farizy, pp. 313–318. Mémoires du Musée de Préhistoire de l'Ile de France, Nemours.

Pope, Melody K. 1994 Mississippian Microtools and Uruk Blades: a Comparative Study of Chipped Stone Production, Use, and Economic Organization. *Lithic Technology* 19: 128–145.

Pope, Melody K., and Susan Pollock 1995 Trade, Tools, and Tasks: a Study of Uruk Chipped Stone Industries. *Research in Economic Anthropology* 16: 227–265.

Pope, Saxton T. 1917 Yahi Archery. *University of California Publications in American Archaeology and Ethnology* 13: 103–152.

Prentiss, William C. 1998 The Reliability and Validity of a Lithic Debitage Typology: Implications for Archaeological Interpretation. *American Antiquity* 63: 635–650.

2001 Reliability and Validity of a "Distinctive Assemblage" Typology: Integrating Flake Size and Completeness. In *Lithic Debitage*, edited by W. Andrefsky, Jr., pp. 147–172. University of Utah Press, Salt Lake City.

Prentiss, William C., and Eugene J. Romanski 1989 Experimental Evaluation of Sullivan and Rozen's Debitage Typology. In *Experiments in Lithic Technology*, edited by D. Amick and R. Mauldin, pp. 89–99. BAR International Series528, Oxford.

Preston, D. 1999 Woody's Dream. *The New Yorker*, November, 1999, pp. 80–87.

Pritchard-Parker, Mari A., and John A. Torres 1998 Analysis of Experimental Debitage from Hammerstone Use and Production: Implications for Ground Stone Use. *Lithic Technology* 23: 139–146.

Prost, Dominique C. 1988 Essai d'étude sur les mécanismes d'enlèvement produits par les façons agricoles et le piètinement humain sur les silex expérimentaux. In *Industries lithiques: Tracéologie et technologie*, edited by S. Beyries, pp. 49–63. BAR International Series 411, Oxford.

Pryor, John H. 1988 The Effects of Human Trample Damage on Lithics: a Consideration of Crucial Variables. *Lithic Technology* 17: 45–50.

Purdy, Barbara A. 1981 *Florida's Prehistoric Stone Technology*. University Presses of Florida, Gainesville.

Raab, L. M., R. F. Cande, and D. W. Stahle 1979 Debitage Graphs and Archaic Settlement Patterns in the Arkansas Ozarks. *Midcontinental Journal of Archaeology* 4: 167–182.

Ray, C. 1937 Probable Uses of Flint End-Scrapers. *American Antiquity* 37: 303–306.

Read, D. W. 1974 Some Comments on Typologies in Archaeology and an Outline of Methodology. *American Antiquity* 39: 216–242.

Read, D. W., and G. Russell 1996 A Method for Taxonomic Typology Construction and an Example: Utilized Flakes. *American Antiquity* 61: 663–684.

Ricklis, Robert A., and Kim A. Cox 1993 Examining Lithic Technological Organization as a Dynamic Cultural Subsystem: the Advantages of an Explicitly Spatial Approach. *American Antiquity* 58: 444–461.

Roberts, Frank H. H., Jr. 1936 Additional Information on the Folsom Complex: Report on the Second Season's Investigations at the Lindenmeier Site in Northern Colorado. *Smithsonian Miscellaneous Collections* 95(10).

Robinson, W. S. 1951 A Method for Chronologically Ordering Archaeological Deposits. *American Antiquity* 16: 293–301.

Rodon Borras, Teresa 1990 Chemical Process of Cleaning in Microwear Studies: Conditions and Limits of Attack. Application to Archaeological Sites. In *The Interpretive Possibilities of Microwear Studies*, edited by B. Graslund, H. Knuttson, K. Knutsson, and J. Taffinder, pp. 179–184. Societas Archaeologica Upsaliensis, AUN 14. Uppsala, Sweden.

Roe, Derek 1964 The British Lower and Middle Paleolithic: Some Problems, Methods of Study and Preliminary Results. *Proceedings of the Prehistoric Society* 30: 245–267.

1970 *Prehistory: an Introduction*. MacMillan and Co., London.

Root, Matthew J. 1997 Production for Exchange at the Knife River Flint Quarries, North Dakota. *Lithic Technology* 22: 33–50.

Root, Matthew J., Jerry D. William, Marvin Kay, and Lisa K. Shifrin 1999 Folsom Ultrathin Biface and Radial Break Tools in the Knife River Flint Quarry Area. In *Folsom Lithic Technology: Explorations in Structure and Variation*, edited by D. Amick, pp. 144–168. International Monographs in Prehistory, Ann Arbor.

Rosen, Arlene Miller 1992 Phytoliths as Indicators of Ancient Irrigation Farming. In *Préhistoire de l'Agriculture*, edited by P. Anderson, pp. 281–287. Editions du CNRS, Monographie du CRA, no. 6, Paris.

1993 Phytolith Evidence for Early Cereal Exploitation in the Levant. In *Current Research in Phytolith Analysis: Applications in Archaeology and Paleoecology*, edited by D. Pearsall and D. Piperno, vol. 10, pp. 160–171.

Rosen, Arlene Miller, and Steven Weiner 1994 Identifying Ancient Irrigation: a New Method Using Opaline Phytoliths from Emmer Wheat. *Journal of Archaeological Science* 21: 125–132.

Rosen, Steven A. 1996 The Decline and Fall of Flint. In *Stone Tools: Theoretical Insights into Human Prehistory*, edited by G. Odell, pp. 129–158. Plenum, New York.

1997a Beyond Milk and Meat: Lithic Evidence for Economic Specialization in the Early Bronze Age Pastoral Periphery in the Levant. *Lithic Technology* 22: 99–109.

1997b *Lithics after the Stone Age: a Handbook of Stone Tools from the Levant*. AltaMira Press, Walnut Creek, California.

Rosenfeld, Andrée 1970 The Examination of the Use Marks on Some Magdalenian End Scrapers. *British Museum Quarterly* 35: 176–182.

Rots, Veerle 2002 *Hafting Traces on Flint Tools: Possibilities and Limitations of Macro- and Microscopic Approaches*. PhD dissertation, Departement Archeologie, Kunstwetenschappen en Musicologie, Katholieke Universiteit Leuven.

Rouse, Irving 1939 *Prehistory in Haiti, a Study in Method*. Yale University Publications in Anthropology, no. 21, New Haven.

1960 The Classification of Artifacts in Archaeology. *American Antiquity* 25: 313–323.

Rovner, Irwin 1971 Potential of Opal Phytoliths for Use in Paleoecological Reconstruction. *Quaternary Research* 1: 343–359.

Rovner, Irwin, and George Agogino 1967 An Analysis of Fluted and Unfluted Folsom Points from Blackwater Draw. *The Masterkey* 41: 131–137.

Santone, L. 1997 Transport Costs, Consumer Demand, and Patterns of Intraregional Exchange: a Perspective on Commodity Production and Distribution from Northern Belize. *Latin American Antiquity* 8: 71–88.

Sassaman, Kenneth E. 1994 Changing Strategies of Biface Production in the South Carolina Coastal Plain. In *The Organization of North American Prehistoric Chipped Stone Tool Technologies*, edited by P. Carr, pp. 99–117. International Monographs in Prehistory, Ann Arbor.

1998 Crafting Cultural Identity in Hunter-Gatherer Economies. In *Craft and Social Identity*, edited by C. Costin, pp. 93–107. Archaeological Papers of the American Anthropological Association, no. 8, Washington, DC.

Schiffer, Michael Brian 1976 *Behavioral Archeology*. Academic Press, New York.

Schiffer, Michael Brian, and James M. Skibo 1997 The Explanation of Artifact Variability. *American Antiquity* 62: 27–50.

Schneider, Joan S. 1996 Analysis of Ground Stone Artifacts. In *Archaeological Laboratory Methods: an Introduction*, by M. Q. Sutton and B. S. Arkush, pp. 69–99. Kendall/Hunt Publishing Co., Dubuque, Iowa.

Schnurrenberger, Douglas, and Alan L. Bryan 1985 A Contribution to the Study of the Naturefact/Artifact Controversy. In *Stone Tool Analysis: Essays in Honor of Don E. Crabtree*, edited by M. Plew, J. Woods, and M. Pavesic, pp. 133–159. University of New Mexico Press, Albuquerque.

Schousboe, Ragnar 1977 Microscopic Edge Structures and Micro-Fractures on Obsidian. *Lithic Technology* 6: 14–21.

Schultz, Jack M. 1992 The Use-Wear Generated by Processing Bison Hides. *Plains Anthropologist* 37: 333–351.

Schwantes, G. 1923 *Das Beil als Scheide zwischen Palaolithikum und Neolithikum*. Archiv fur Anthropologie, N. F., Band 20.

Seelenfreund, Andrea, Charles Rees, Roger Bird, Graham Bailey, Robert Bárcena, and Victor Durán 1996 Trace-Element Analysis of Obsidian Sources and Artifacts of Central Chile (Maule River Basin) and Western Argentina (Colorado River). *Latin American Antiquity* 7: 7–20.

Sellet, Frederic 1993 Chaine Operatoire: the Concept and Its Applications. *Lithic Technology* 18: 106–112.

Selley, Richard C. 1988 *Applied Sedimentology*. Academic Press, London.

Semenov, Sergei A. 1964 *Prehistoric Technology*. Translated by M. W. Thompson. Adams and Dart, Bath.

    1970 The Forms and Funktions of the Oldest Tools. *Quartar* 21: 1–20.

Serizawa, C., H. Kajiwara, and K. Akoshima 1982 Experimental Study of Microwear Traces and Its Potentiality (in Japanese). *Archaeology and Natural Science* 14: 67–87.

Shackley, M. Steven 1992 The Upper Gila River Gravels as an Archaeological Obsidian Source Region: Implications for Models of Exchange and Interaction. *Geoarchaeology* 7: 315–326.

    1998 Gamma Rays, X-Rays and Stone Tools: Some Recent Advances in Archaeological Geochemistry. *Journal of Archaeological Science* 25: 259–270.

Shafer, Harry J. 1983 Ancient Maya Chert Workshops in Northern Belize, Central America. *American Antiquity* 48: 519–543.

    1985 A Technological Study of Two Maya Workshops at Colha, Belize. In *Stone Tool Analysis: Essays in Honor of Don E. Crabtree*, edited by M. Plew, J. Woods, and M. Pavesic, pp. 277–315. University of New Mexico, Albuquerque.

    1991 Late Preclassic Formal Stone Tool Production at Colha, Belize. In *Maya Stone Tools*, edited by T. Hester and H. Shafer, pp. 31–44. Prehistory Press, Madison, WI.

Shafer, Harry J., and Thomas R. Hester 1983 Ancient Maya Chert Workshops in Northern Belize, Central America. *American Antiquity* 48: 519–543.

Shafer, Harry J., and Richard G. Holloway 1979 Organic Residue Analysis in Determining Stone Tool Function. In *Lithic Use-Wear Analysis*, edited by B. Hayden, pp. 385–299. Academic Press, New York.

Shanks, Orin C., Marcel Kornfeld, and Dee Dee Hawk 1999 Protein Analysis of Bugas-Holding Tools: New Trends in Immunological Studies. *Journal of Archaeological Science* 26: 1183–1191.

Shea, John J. 1987 On Accuracy and Relevance in Lithic Use-Wear Studies. *Lithic Technology* 16: 44–50.

    1988a Methodological Considerations Affecting the Choice of Analytical Techniques in Lithic Use-Wear Analysis: Tests, Results, and Application. In *Industries lithiques: Traceologie et technologie*, vol. II, edited by S. Beyries, pp. 65–81. BAR International Series 411(ii), Oxford.

    1988b Spear Points from the Middle Paleolithic of the Levant. *Journal of Field Archaeology* 15: 441–450.

Shea, J. J., and J. D. Klenck 1993 An Experimental Investigation of the Effects of Trampling on the Results of Lithic Microwear Analysis. *Journal of Archaeological Science* 20: 175–194.

Shelley, Philip H. 1990 Variation in Lithic Assemblages: *Journal of Field Archaeology* 17: 187–193.

Shen, Chen 1999 Were "Utilized Flakes" Utilized? An Issue of Lithic Classification in Ontario Archaeology. *Ontario Archaeology* 68: 63–73.

Shen, Chen, and Shejiang Wang 2000 A Preliminary Study of the Anvil-Chipping Technique: Experiments and Evaluations. *Lithic Technology* 25: 81–100.

Shepherd, R. 1980 *Prehistoric Mining and Allied Industries*. Academic Press, New York.

Sheppard, Peter J. 1993 Lapita Lithics: Trade/Exchange and Technology. A View from the Reefs/Santa Cruz. *Archaeology in Oceania* 28: 121–137.

1996 Hard Rock: Archaeological Implications of Chert Sourcing in Near and Remote Oceania. In *Oceanic Culture History: Essays in Honour of Roger Green*, edited by J. Davidson, G. Irwin, B. Leach, A. Pawley, and D. Brown, pp. 99–115. New Zealand Journal of Archaeology Special Publication, Aukland.

Shingleton, Kenneth L., Jr., George H. Odell, and Thomas M. Harris 1994 Atomic Absorption Spectrophotometry Analysis of Ceramic Artefacts from a Protohistoric Site in Oklahoma. *Journal of Archaeological Science* 21: 343–358.

Shockey, Don 1994 Fluorescence and Heat Treatment of Three Lithic Materials Found in Oklahoma. *Bulletin of the Oklahoma Anthropological Society* 43: 86–100.

1995 Some Observations of Polarization and Fluorescence in Primary and Secondary Source Lithic Materials. *Bulletin of the Oklahoma Anthropological Society* 44: 91–115.

Shott, Michael 1986 Technological Organization and Settlement Mobility: an Ethnographic Examination. *Journal of Anthropological Research* 42: 15–51.

1994 Size and Form in the Analysis of Flake Debris: Review and Recent Approaches. *Journal of Archaeological Method and Theory* 1: 69–110.

2003 Chaine Opératoire and Reduction Sequence. *Lithic Technology* 28: 95–105.

Sieveking, G. de G., P. Bush, J. Ferguson, P. T. Craddock, M. J. Hughes, and M. R. Cowell 1972 Prehistoric Flint Mines and their Identification as Sources of Raw Material. *Archaeometry* 14: 151–176.

Sievert, April K. 1992 *Maya Ceremonial Specialization: Lithic Tools from the Sacred Cenote at Chichen Itza, Yucatan*. Prehistory Press, Madison.

1994 The Detection of Ritual Tool Use through Functional Analysis: Comparative Examples from the Spiro and Angel Sites. *Lithic Technology* 19: 146–156.

Sillitoe, Paul 1979 Stone Versus Steel. *Mankind* 12: 151–161.

1998 *An Introduction to the Anthropology of Melanesia: Culture and Tradition*. Cambridge University Press, Cambridge.

2000 *Social Change in Melanesia: Development and History*. Cambridge University Press, Cambridge.

Skertchly, Sydney B. J. 1879 *On the Manufacture of Gun-Flints, the Methods of Excavating for Flint, the Age of Palaeolithic Man, and the Connection between Neolithic Art and Gun-Flint Trade*. Memoirs of the Geological Survey of England and Wales, London.

Skibo, James M., William H. Walker, and Axel E. Nielsen (editors) 1995 *Expanding Archaeology*. University of Utah Press, Salt Lake City.

Smith, P. R., and M. T. Wilson 1992 Blood Residues on Ancient Tool Surfaces: a Cautionary Note. *Journal of Archaeological Science* 19: 237–241.

Smolla, G. 1987 Prehistoric Flint Mining: the History of Research—a Review. In *The Human Uses of Flint and Chert*, edited by G. de G. Sieveking and M. Newcomer, pp. 127–129. Cambridge University Press, Cambridge.

Sobolik, Kristin D. 1996 Lithic Organic Residue Analysis: an Example from the Southwestern Archaic. *Journal of Field Archaeology* 23: 461–469.

Sollberger, J. B. 1985 A Technique for Folsom Fluting. *Lithic Technology* 14: 41–50.

Sonnenfeld, J. 1962 Interpreting the Function of Primitive Implements. *American Antiquity* 28: 56–65.

Sonneville-Bordes, Denise de, and Jean Perrot 1954–56 Lexique typologique du Paléolithique supérieur. Outillage lithique. *Bulletin de la Société Préhistorique Française* 51: 327–335; 52: 76–79; 53: 408–412; 53: 547–549.

Spaulding, Albert C. 1953 Statistical Techniques for the Discovery of Artifact Types. *American Antiquity* 18: 305–318.

1954 Reply to Ford. *American Antiquity* 19: 391–393.

Specht, J. R., R. Fullagar, R. Torrence, and N. Baker 1988 Prehistoric Obsidian Exchange in Melanesia: a Perspective from the Talasea Sources. *Australian Archaeology* 27: 3–16.

Stafford, Barbara D. 1977 Burin Manufacture and Utilization: an Experimental Study. *Journal of Field Archaeology* 4: 235–246.

Stafford, C. Russell (editor) 1985 *The Campbell Hollow Archaic Occupations: a Study in Spatial Structure and Site Function in the Lower Illinois Valley.* Center for American Archeology, Research Series, vol. 4.

     1991 Archaic Period Logistical Foraging Strategies in West-Central Illinois. *Midcontinental Journal of Archaeology* 16: 212–246.

Stafford, Michael 1999 *From Forager to Farmer in Flint: a Lithic Analysis of the Prehistoric Transition to Agriculture in Southern Scandinavia.* Aarhus University Press, Aarhus.

Stahle, David W., and James E. Dunn 1984 *An Experimental Analysis of the Size Distribution of Waste Flakes from Biface Reduction.* Arkansas Archeological Survey, Technical Paper no. 2. Fayetteville.

Stein, Julie K., and William R. Ferrand (editors) 2001 *Sediments in Archaeological Context.* University of Utah Press, Salt Lake City.

Sterud, Eugene L. 1978 Changing Aims of Americanist Archaeology: a Citations Analysis of American Antiquity—1946–1975. *American Antiquity* 43: 294–302.

Stevenson, Christopher M., and Michael O. McCurry 1990 Chemical Characterization and Hydration Rate Development for New Mexican Obsidian Sources. *Geoarchaeology* 5: 149–170.

Stevenson, Christopher M., Barry Scheetz, and James W. Hatch 1992 Reply to Hughes. *American Antiquity* 57: 524–525.

Stewart, Frank Henderson 2001 Hidatsa. *Handbook of North American Indians, vol. 13: Plains*, edited by R. DeMallie, pp. 329–348. Smithsonian Institution Press, Washington, DC.

Stiner, Mary C., and Steven L. Kuhn 1992 Subsistence, Technology, and Adaptive Variation in Middle Paleolithic Italy. *American Anthropologist* 94: 306–339.

Stone, T. 1994 The Impact of Raw-Material Scarcity on Ground-Stone Manufacture and Use: an Example from the Phoenix Basin Hohokam. *American Antiquity* 59: 680–694.

Stordeur, Daniele (editor) 1987 *Le main et l'outil.* Travaux de la Maison de l'Orient 15, Lyon.

Sudbury, Byron 1975 Ka-3, the Deer Creek Site: an Eighteenth Century French Contact Site. *Bulletin of the Oklahoma Anthropological Society* 24: 1–135.

Sullivan, Alan P. III 1987 Probing the Sources of Variability: a Regional Case Study near Homolovi Ruins, Arizonza. *North American Archaeologist* 8: 41–71.

Sullivan, Alan P. III, and Kenneth C. Rozen 1985 Debitage Analysis and Archaeological Interpretation. *American Antiquity* 50: 755–779.

Texier, Pierrre-Jean 1984 Le debitage par pression et la mécanique de la rupture fragile: initiation et propagation des fractures. In *Préhistoire de la pierre taillée 2: Economie du débitage laminaire*, collected by Unité de Recherches Archéologiques, CNRS, pp. 139–147.

Therin, Michael 1998 The Movement of Starch Grains in Sediments. In *A Closer Look: Recent Australian Studies of Stone Tools*, edited by R. Fullagar, pp. 61–72. Sydney University, Archaeological Methods Series 6.

Thomas, David Hurst 1970 Archaeology's Operational Imperative: Great Basin Projectile Points as a Test Case. *Annual Report, UCLA Archaeological Survey*, edited by N. N. Leonard III, J. A. Rasson, and D. A. Decker. Department of Anthropology, UCLA, volume 12, pp. 31–60.

Thomas, David Hurst, Lorann S. A. Pendleton, and Stephen C. Cappannari 1986 Western Shoshone. *Handbook of North American Indians, vol. 11: Great Basin*, edited by W. d'Azevedo, pp. 262–283. Smithsonian Institution Press, Washington, DC.

Thompson, Marc 1996 Correlation of Maya Lithic and Glyphic Data. *Lithic Technology* 21: 120–133.

Timmins, Peter A. 1994 Alder Creek: a Paleo-Indian Crowfield Phase Manifestation in the Region of Waterloo, Ontario. *Midcontinental Journal of Archaeology* 19: 170–197.

Tixier, Jacques 1974 *Glossary for the Description of Stone Tools with Special Reference to the Epipaleolithic of the Maghreb*. Translation by M. Newcomer. Newsletter of Lithic Technology, Special Publication no. 1.

1984 Le débitage par pression. In *Préhistoire de la pierre taillée 2: Economie du débitage laminaire: technologie et expérimentation*, compiled by IIIème Table Rond de Technologie Lithique, pp. 57–70. Cercle de Recherches et d'Etudes Préhistorique, Meudon.

Tomenchuk, John 1985 *The Development of a Wholly Parametric Use-Wear Methodology and Its Application to Two Selected Samples of Epipaleolithic Chipped Stone Tools from Hayonim Cave, Israel*. PhD dissertation, University of Toronto.

Tomka, Steven A. 1989 Differentiating Lithic Reduction Techniques: an Experimental Approach. In *Experiments in Lithic Technology*, edited by D. Amick and R. Mauldin, pp. 137–161. BAR International Series 528, Oxford.

2001 The Effect of Processing Requirements on Reduction Strategies and Tool Form: a New Perspective. In *Lithic Debitage: Context, Form, Meaning*, edited by W. Andrefsky, Jr., pp. 207–223. University of Utah Press, Salt Lake City.

Torrence, R., J. Specht, R. Fullagar, and G. R. Summerhayes 1996 Which Obsidian Is Worth It? A View from the West New Britain Sources. In *Oceanic Culture History: Essays in Honour of Roger Green*, edited by J. M. Davidson, G. Irwin, B. F. Leach, A. Pawley, and D. Brown, pp. 211–224. New Zealand Journal of Archaeology, Special Publication.

Tringham, R., G. Cooper, G. Odell, B. Voytek, and A. Whitman 1974 Experimentation in the Formation of Edge Damage: a New Approach to Lithic Analysis. *Journal of Field Archaeology* 1: 171–196.

Tsirk, Are 1979 Regarding Fracture Initiations. In *Lithic Use-Wear Analysis*, edited by B. Hayden, pp. 83–96. Academic Press, New York.

Tucker, Maurice E. 1991 *Sedimentary Petrology: an Introduction to the Origin of Sedimentary Rocks*. Second edition. Blackwell Scientific Publications, Oxford.

Tuross, Noreen, Ian Barnes, and Richard Potts 1996 Protein Identification of Blood Residues on Experimental Stone Tools. *Journal of Archaeological Science* 23: 289–296.

Tykot, Robert H., and Albert J. Ammerman 1997 New Directions in Central Mediterranean Obsidian Studies. *Antiquity* 71: 1000–1006.

Unger-Hamilton, Romana 1984 The Formation of Use-Wear Polish on Flint: Beyond the "Deposit versus Abrasion" Controversy. *Journal of Archaeological Science* 11: 91–98.

1989 Analyse expérimentale des microtraces d'usure: quelques controverses actuelles. *l'Anthropologie* 93: 659–672.

1992 Experiments in Harvesting Wild Cereals and Other Plants. In *Préhistoire de l'Agriculture*, edited by P. Anderson, pp. 211–224. Editions du CNRS, Monographie du CRA, no. 6, Paris.

Unrath, G., and W. Lindemann 1984 Reproduktionsstoffe in der Micro-Gebrauchsspurenforschung. *Early Man News* 7/8: 61–80. Tubingen.

Unrath, Guenther, Linda Owen, Annelou van Gijn, Emily H. Moss, Hugues Plisson, and Patrick Vaughan 1986 An Evaluation of Microwear Studies: a Multi-Analyst Approach. In *Technical Aspects of Microwear Studies on Stone Tools*, edited by L. Owen and G. Unrath. *Early Man News* 9/10/11: 117–176. Tubingen.

van Gijn, Annelou 1986 Fish Polish, Fact and Fiction. In *Technical Aspects of Microwear Studies on Stone Tools*, edited by L. Owen and G. Unrath. *Early Man News* 9/10/11: 13–27.

1998 A Closer Look: a Realistic Attempt to "Squeeze Blood from Stones." In *A Closer Look: Recent Australian Studies of Stone Tools*, edited by R. Fullagar, pp. 189–194. Sydney University, Archaeological Methods Series 6.

van Peer, P. 1992 *The Levallois Reduction Strategy*. Prehistory Press, Madison, WI.

Vaughan, Patrick C. 1985 *Use-Wear Analysis of Flaked Stone Tools*. University of Arizona Press, Tucson.

Wallis, Lynley, and Sue O'Connor 1998 Residues on a Sample of Stone Points from the West Kimberley. In *A Closer Look: Recent Australian Studies of Stone Tools*, edited by R. Fullagar, pp. 149–178. Sydney University, Archaeological Methods Series 6.

Walthall, John A., and Brad Koldehoff 1998 Hunter-Gatherer Interaction and Alliance Formation: Dalton and the Cult of the Long Blade. *Plains Anthropologist* 43: 257–273.

Warren, S. Hazzledine 1914 The Experimental Investigation of Flint Fracture and Its Application to the Problems of Human Implements. *Journal of the Royal Anthropological Institute* 44: 412–450.

1923 Sub-Soil Pressure Flaking. *Proceedings of the Geologists' Association* 34: 153–175.

Waters, Michael R. 1992 *Principles of Geoarchaeology: a North American Perspective*. University of Arizona Press, Tucson.

Wedel, Mildred Mott 1981 *The Deer Creek Site, Oklahoma: a Wichita Village Sometimes Called Ferdinandina, an Ethnohistorian's View*. Oklahoma Historical Society, Series in Anthropology, no. 5. Oklahoma City.

Weinstein-Evron, M., B. Lang, S. Ilani, G. Steinitz, and D. Kaufman 1995 K/Ar Dating as a Means of Sourcing Levantine Epipaleolithic Basalt Implements. *Archaeometry* 37: 37–40.

Whallon, Robert 1978 Threshing Sledge Flints: a Distinctive Pattern of Wear. *Paleorient* 4: 319–324.

White, J. Peter 1967 Ethno-archaeology in New Guinea: Two Examples. *Mankind* 6: 409–414.

1968 Ston Naip Bilong Tumbuna: the Living Stone Age in New Guinea. In *La préhistoire: Problèmes et tendences*, edited by D. de Sonneville-Bordes, pp. 511–516. Editions du CNRS, Paris.

1969 Typologies for Some Prehistoric Flaked Stone Artifacts of the Australian New Guinea High-lands. *Archaeology and Physical Anthropology in Oceania* 4: 18–46.

1996 Rocks in the Head: Thinking about the Distribution of Obsidian in Near Oceania. In *Oceanic Culture History: Essays in Honour of Roger Green*, edited by J. Davidson, G. Irwin, B. Leach, A. Pawley, and D. Brown, pp. 199–209. New Zealand Journal of Archaeology Special Publication, Auckland.

White, J. Peter, and David H. Thomas 1972 What Mean These Stones? Ethnotaxonomic Models and Archaeological Interpretations in the New Guinea Highlands. In *Models in Archaeology*, edited by D. L. Clarke, pp. 275–308. Methuen, London.

Whittaker, John C. 1994 *Flintknapping: Making and Understanding Stone Tools*. University of Texas Press, Austin.

1996 Athkiajas: a Cypriot Flintknapper and the Threshing Sledge Industry. *Lithic Technology* 21: 108–120.

Whittaker, John C., and Michael Stafford 1999 Replicas, Fakes and Art: the Twentieth-Century Stone Age and Its Effects on Archaeology. *American Antiquity* 64: 203–214.

Wilke, Philip J., and Leslie A. Quintero 1996 Near Eastern Neolithic Millstone Production: Insights from Research in the Arid Southwestern United States. In *Neolithic Chipped Stone Industries of the Fertile Crescent, and Their Contemporaries in Adjacent Regions*, edited by S. Kozlowski and H. Gebel, pp. 243–260. Studies in Near Eastern Production, Subsistence, and Environment 3, Berlin, ex oriente.

Williams, Howel, Francis J. Turner, and Charles M. Gilbert 1982 *Petrography: an Introduction to the Study of Rocks in Thin Sections*. W. H. Freeman and Company, San Francisco.

Williams-Thorpe, Olwen, Don Aldriss, Ian J. Rigby, and Richard S. Thorpe 1999 Geochemical Prove-nancing of Igneous Glacial Erratics from Southern Britain, and Implications for Prehistoric Stone Implement Distributions. *Geoarchaeology* 14: 209–246.

Williams-Thorpe, Philip J. Potts, and Peter C. Webb 1999 Field-Portable Non-Destructive Analysis of Lithic Archaeological Samples by X-Ray Fluorescence Instrumentation Using a Mercury Iodide Detector: Comparison with Wavelength-Dispersive XRF and a Case Study in British Stone Axe Provenancing. *Journal of Archaeological Science* 26: 215–237.

Wilmsen, Edwin N., and Frank H. H. Roberts, Jr. 1984 *Lindenmeier, 1934–1974: Concluding Report on Investigations*. Smithsonian Contributions to Anthropology, no. 24. Washington, D.C.

Wilson, Marjorie 1989 *Igneous Petrogenesis.* Unwin Hyman, London.

Winters, Howard D. 1969 *The Riverton Culture, a Second Millennium Occupation in the Central Wabash Valley.* Illinois State Museum, Reports of Investigations, no. 13.

Witthoft, John 1967 Glazed Polish on Flint Tools. *American Antiquity* 32: 383–388.

Wobst, H. Martin 1978 The Archaeo-ethnology of Hunter-Gatherers or the Tyranny of the Ethnographic Record in Archaeology. *American Antiquity* 43: 303–309.

Wood, W. Raymond, and Lee Irwin 2001 Mandan. In *Handbook of North American Indians, vol. 13: Plains,* edited by R. DeMallie, pp. 349–364. Smithsonian Institution Press, Washington, DC.

Woods, John C. 1988 Projectile Point Fracture Patterns and Inferences about Tool Function. *Idaho Archaeologist* 11: 3–7.

Wright, K. I. 1994 Ground-Stone Tools and Hunter-Gatherer Subsistence in Southwest Asia: Implications for the Transition to Farming. *American Antiquity* 59: 238–263.

Wright, M. K. 1993 Simulated Use of Experimental Maize Grinding Tools from Southwestern Colorado. *Kiva* 58: 345–355.

Wylie, Henry G. 1975 Tool Microwear and Functional Types from Hogup Cave, Utah. *Tebiwa* 17: 1–31.

Yamada, Shoh 1993 The Formation Process of "Use-Wear Polishes." In *Traces et fonction: les gestes retrouvés,* edited by P. Anderson, S. Beyries, M. Otte, and H. Plisson, pp. 433–446. Centre de Recherches Archéologiques du CNRS, no. 50. Liège.

Yerkes, Richard W. 1983 Microwear, Microdrills, and Mississippian Craft Specialization. *American Antiquity* 48: 499–518.

— 1987 *Prehistoric Life on the Mississippi Floodplain: Stone Tool Use, Settlement Organization, and Subsistence Practices at the Labras Lake Site, Illinois.* University of Chicago Press, Chicago.

— 1989 Mississippian Craft Specialization on the American Bottom. *Southeastern Archaeology* 8: 93–106.

— 1990 Using Microwear Analysis to Investigate Domestic Activities and Craft Specialization at the Murphy Site, a Small Hopewell Settlement in Licking County, Ohio. In *The Interpretive Possibilities of Microwear Studies,* edited by B. Graslund, H. Knutsson, K. Knutsson, and J. Taffinder, pp. 167–176. Societas Archaeologica Upsaliensis. Uppsala, Sweden.

Yohe, Robert M. II, Margaret E. Newman, and Joan S. Schneider 1991 Immunological Identification of Small-Mammal Proteins on Aboriginal Milling Equipment. *American Antiquity* 56: 659–666.

Young, D., and D. B. Bamforth 1990 On the Macroscopic Identification of Used Flakes. *American Antiquity* 55: 403–440.

Young, L. C. 1994 Lithics and Adaptive Diversity: an Examination of Limited-Activity Sites in Northeast Arizona. *Journal of Anthropological Research* 50: 141–154.

Index

Aborigines, stone tool use, 157, 216
Abrader
  function of, 45
  Illinois system, 82
Abrasive modifications
  ground stone tools, 74–85
  meaning of, 64
Adzes
  as bifacial tool, 65
  tranchet adze, 206
Afton points, mass analysis, 131
Agate, for sharp-edge tools, 19
Agricultural equipment
  damage/modification from, 69–74
  plow damage experiments, 71–73
Agricultural tools, types of, 176
Aguadulce (Panama), starch grain analysis, 161
Ahler, Stan, 131
Alder Creek (Ontario) site, stage of tool manufacture, 122
Alibates, visual sourcing of, 28, 30
Altun Ha (Belize), ritual stone objects, 217
American Antiquity effect, 124
Ames Hemastix test, 166
Amorphous cores, 63
Amphibole, chemical composition, 17
Anderson, Patricia, 164
Andesite
  crystal structure, 16
  for ground stone tools, 83
  and sharp-edge tools, 17, 21
  texture, 17
Animal blood. See Blood residues
Animal hide. See Hide
Animal processing, 185–187
  bison example, 186–187
  butchering tools, 186

Animal procurement, 177–181
  projectile points, 177–180
  scavenging, 180
Anisotropic, definition of, 31
Antler
  and percussion flaking, 59, 61
  for percussive tools, 44
  for pressure flaking, 61–62
Anvil technique, 60–61
Aphanitic crystal structure, stone containing, 16
Argillite, for sharp-edge tools, 21
Arrowroot starch, analysis of, 161
Artifact, definition of, 4
Assemblage
  of complex societies, 10
  definition of, 4, 6
  type collection concept, 90–91
Assemblage comparisons, 110–118
  Brainerd-Robinson coefficients, 116–118
  cumulative graph in, 113–114
  by evenness, 112–113
  evenness measure, 112–113
  by richness, 111–112
  snowflake diagrams, 115–116
Assemblage variability, 6–7
  analysis of. See Lithic analysis
  Mousterian tools, 7
  primary agency issue, 62–63
  theories of, 6–7
  types issue, 7
Atomic absorption spectroscopy (AAS), 3, 38–39
  obsidian sourcing study, 36
  pros/cons of, 38–39
Attribute
  definition of, 87
  discrete attribute, 125